NEW DIRECTIO[NS]
WOMEN, PEAC[E]
SECURITY

Edited by
Soumita Basu, Paul Kirby and
Laura J. Shepherd

BRISTOL
UNIVERSITY
PRESS

First published in Great Britain in 2020 by

Bristol University Press
1–9 Old Park Hill
Bristol
BS2 8BB
UK
t: +44 (0)117 954 5940
www.bristoluniversitypress.co.uk

British Library Cataloguing in Publication Data
A catalogue record for this book is available from the British Library

ISBN 978-1-5292-0774-3 hardcover
ISBN 978-1-5292-0775-0 paperback
ISBN 978-1-5292-0778-1 ePub
ISBN 978-1-5292-0777-4 ePdf

Cover design by Blu Inc
Front cover: Getty / oxygen

This book is dedicated to all those who work towards feminist peace, in its intersectional, anti–militarist, anti–imperialist and sustainable iterations, often in hostile environments and with limited resources.
Thank you for all that you do.

Contents

Acknowledgements

We are grateful to have learned so much from all our contributors, as well as colleagues who have participated in panels and workshops organized in the lead up to this book. These include two workshops convened by Paul Kirby and Laura J. Shepherd: 'Women, Peace and Security post-2015: Concepts, Criticisms, and Challenges' (London, 2016) and 'The Futures of Women, Peace, and Security: New Directions in Research on the Women, Peace and Security Agenda' (Baltimore, 2017), organized with support from the British International Studies Association and the International Studies Association respectively. Thanks are also due to Caitlin Hamilton for her assistance, to an anonymous reviewer who provided helpful comments on the whole draft manuscript, and to Stephen Wenham and Caroline Astley at Bristol University Press for helping us make this volume so accessible, engaging and timely.

In addition:

For a tremendous intellectual journey and for ensuring that this book was feminist in its making as well, thank you, Laura and Paul. Much of my work on this book involved balancing editorial commitments with the preoccupations of a new parent. Many thanks to my family, especially Amitabh, fellow editors and friends for helping me along with patience and good humour.

Soumita Basu, New Delhi

The work of editing this volume and contributing to its first chapter was enabled by my participation in the Gender, Justice and Security Hub, funded by UK Research and Innovation through the Global Challenges Research Fund. I am grateful for the environment provided by the LSE Centre for Women, Peace and Security, where much of the thinking for this volume happened, and especially to Professor Christine Chinkin for her leadership there. My peerless co-editors made the process more enjoyable than I had any reason to expect, and I hope for many more collaborations with them in the third decade of WPS.

Paul Kirby, London

My work on this project was enabled by a grant from the Australian Research Council for a project titled 'Women, Peace and Security: Rethinking Policy, Advocacy and Implementation' (DP160100212). I am extremely grateful for this support, and the opportunities it afforded me. I want to acknowledge Caitlin Hamilton's work on this project more broadly, as well as on this manuscript in particular, as already mentioned. I also want to express my deepest appreciation for, and admiration of, my brilliant co-editors, for their wisdom, wit and insight.

Laura J. Shepherd, Sydney

Notes on Contributors

Louise Allen is a global gender, peace and security consultant and an experienced women peace and security advocate. She has been commissioned both by NATO and the UN to undertake independent assessments of their work on women, peace and security, how they mainstream gender and engage with women's civil society organizations. She has worked alongside women, indigenous and refugee human rights defenders and civil society in Australia, in the Pacific and at the UN both in Geneva and New York. From 2014 to September 2018, she was the Executive Director of the New York-based NGO Working Group on Women, Peace and Security. This is a civil society coalition of 18 NGOs which conducts analysis, advocacy and monitoring, and calls for the full implementation of the Women, Peace and Security agenda by the UN Security Council, UN Leadership and by member states. Prior to that she led the advocacy team at Amnesty International Australia for six years, was the second-in-charge of a corporate government relations practice and started her career as a police media liaison officer. Louise has her Masters in International Relations from the University of Sydney.

Anna Applebaum researches access to civil and human rights and gender in peace and security processes. She is concurrently a J.D. candidate at New York University School of Law. She has published numerous reports and articles on the gendered dynamics of peace and conflict, with recent publications focusing on disaster recovery, transitional justice and gang violence. She served as a 2015–2017 Hillary Rodham Clinton Research Fellow at the Georgetown Institute for Women, Peace and Security. She has worked and consulted for various non-profit organizations, and she served as a McLarty Scholar at Vital Voices Global Partnership. She received her Master of Public Service from the Clinton School of Public Service and was awarded a George E. Mylonas Scholarship in Humanities at her alma mater, Washington University in St Louis.

Marta Bautista Forcada is currently working with the Pathfinders Initiative for Peaceful and Just Societies at the NYU Center on International Cooperation. As a member of the Women's International League for Peace and Freedom's (WILPF) Working Group on Women, Peace and Security (WPS) in Spain, she supported the consultations with civil society organizations convened by the Spanish government to draft the second Spanish National Action Plan for the Implementation of the WPS agenda. She has worked with various NGOs including Geneva for Human Rights, Amnesty International, WILPF, NYU Peace Research and Education Program, the Institute for Economics and Peace and the International Peace Institute. She has conducted field research in Colombia, focusing on FARC-EP ex-combatants' perceptions of the 2016 Peace Agreement implementation process and the reparation's system. She earned an MS in Global Affairs from New York University as a La Caixa Fellow (2016), and she holds a Bachelor's degree in Political Science from Universitat Pompeu Fabra in Barcelona, Spain.

Soumita Basu is an assistant professor in International Relations at the South Asian University, New Delhi. She has held the Hayward R. Alker and Mellon postdoctoral fellowships at the University of Southern California and Kenyon College respectively, and also worked with Women in Security, Conflict Management and Peace (WISCOMP) in New Delhi and Kashmir. Soumita has published on gender, security and the UN in edited volumes as well as journals, including *International Affairs*, *International Political Science Review*, *International Studies Perspectives*, *Politics & Gender* and *Security Dialogue*.

Louise Chappell is Scientia Professor and Director of the Australian Human Rights Institute, based in the Law Faculty, University of New South Wales, Sydney and prior to this she held an Australian Research Council Future Fellowship. Louise has published widely in the areas of gender politics, women's rights and feminist institutionalism. Her first book, *Gendering Government* (University of British Columbia Press, 2002) won the American Political Science Association's Victoria Schuck Prize, and her most recent monograph *The Politics of Gender Justice at the International Criminal Court* (Oxford University Press, 2015) was awarded the Carole Pateman Prize for the best book in gender and politics by the Australian Political Science Association. Louise's current research focuses on reparations and the ICC, and the backlash to women's rights in international human rights venues.

Christine Chinkin, FBA, CMG, is the founding Director of the Centre for Women, Peace and Security at the London School of Economics, a Professorial Research Fellow at the Centre, a William W. Cook Global Law Professor at the University of Michigan and a member of the Bar of England and Wales and Matrix Chambers. She was previously Professor of International Law at the LSE. She is the author of many articles on international law and human rights law, in particular on the human rights of women. She is co-author of *The Boundaries of International Law: A Feminist Analysis* (Manchester University Press, 2000, with Hilary Charlesworth), *The Making of International Law* (Oxford University Press, 2007, with Alan Boyle) and of *International Law and New Wars* (Cambridge University Press, 2017, with Mary Kaldor).

Catia Cecilia Confortini served as WILPF's International Vice President from 2015 to 2018. She is Associate Professor in the Peace and Justice Studies Program at Wellesley College, Massachusetts. Confortini holds a PhD from the University of Southern California's School of International Relations as well as a Master's Degree in International Peace Studies from the Joan B. Kroc Institute at the University of Notre Dame. She is the author of *Intelligent Compassion: Feminist Critical Methodology in the Women's International League for Peace and Freedom* (Oxford University Press, 2012). Her research and publications explore the contributions of women's peace activism to peace studies as an academic field and as a practice, as well as feminist theorizing of peace and violence. She is co-editor (with Tiina Vaittinen) of *Gender, Global Health, and Violence* (Rowman & Littlefield International, 2019) and with Tarja Väyrynen, Élise Féron, Peace Medie and Swati Parashar of *Handbook of Feminist Peace Research* (Routledge, forthcoming). She was a Fulbright Finland Foundation Scholar at the Tampere Peace Research Institute, Finland, in the autumn of 2019.

sam cook is an independent feminist scholar, activist and artist from South Africa. Her PhD in international politics from the University of California, Santa Cruz – entitled 'Encountering Metis: Feminist Articulations of Security Council Practice' – is a creative exploration of the quotidian practices of policymaking and of feminist interventions in women, peace and security (WPS) policy. From 2005 to 2010 she was Director of the PeaceWomen Project at the Women's International League of Peace and Freedom, United Nations Office and from 2010 to 2011 was the Research and Communications Director for the LGBT organization IGLHRC (now OutRight International). Her work has been published in *International Affairs*, the LSE WPS Working Paper

Series, the *Emory International Law Review* and the *South African Law Journal*, and she has contributed to several NGO publications.

Gema Fernández Rodríguez de Liévana is a practising lawyer and a researcher in the areas of human rights, women's rights and women, peace and security. She engages in litigation before national and regional courts (ECtHR, Inter-American system) and UN Treaty Bodies in cases concerning gender-based violence against women, discrimination, human trafficking and sexual and reproductive rights. She is currently a Managing Attorney at the NGO Women's Link Worldwide. She is a fellow and a current lecturer of the International Women's Human Rights Protection Program of the Women's Human Rights Training Institute (Bulgaria) and has been a visiting fellow at the Centre for Women, Peace and Security at the London School of Economics. She also conducts fact-finding research into human rights violations in the context of migration and occasionally publishes on these topics.

Nicole George is an associate professor in Peace and Conflict Studies in the school of Political Science and International Studies at the University of Queensland. She has a strong interest in the way gender and politics are configured in Pacific Island contexts, with a particular recent focus on the gendered impacts of conflict in the region and the roles played by women in peacebuilding and conflict transition. Recent publications on these themes appear in *International Affairs*, *International Feminist Journal of Politics*, *International Political Science Review* and the *Australian Journal of International Affairs*.

Anne Marie Goetz is Clinical Professor at the Centre for Global Affairs at New York University. She served at the United Nations between 2005 and 2014 as a Policy Director of Governance, Peace and Security, at UNIFEM and UN Women. From 1991 to 2005 she was a professorial fellow in Political Science at the Institute of Development Studies, University of Sussex. She also served the United Nations Development Program in Chad and Guinea in the mid-1980s. While at the UN, she spearheaded initiatives to build women's participation in representative politics, to promote women's empowerment in the UN's peacebuilding work in post-conflict situations, and to support the participation of women leaders and rights organizations in peace talks and post-conflict decision making. She worked with the UN Security Council to improve responses to sexual violence in conflict, and to build peacekeepers' capacities to prevent these abuses. She is the author of seven books on the subjects of gender, politics and policy in developing countries, and on accountability reforms – including the 2009 volume *Governing Women: Women in Politics and Governance in Developing Countries* (UNRISD/Routledge), and the UNIFEM flagship report *Who Answers to Women? Gender and Accountability* (2009).

Toni Haastrup is a senior lecturer in International Politics at University of Stirling, Scotland. She received her PhD in Politics from the University of Edinburgh. Her work at the intersection of feminist international politics, security studies and regionalism studies has appeared in a number of peer-reviewed journals including *JCMS: Journal of Common Market Studies*, *European Journal of Integration*, *International Negotiation*, the *South African Journal of International Affairs* and *Foreign Policy Analysis* among others. She has also published numerous book chapters. In early 2019, she was a visiting researcher at the Centre of Women, Peace and Security, London School of Economics and Lund University. Haastrup is currently the joint editor in chief of *JCMS: Journal of Common Market Studies*, a trustee of the African Studies Association, UK and a member of the International Studies Association's Committee on the Status of Women. Alongside her research, Haastrup teaches on themes in international politics and is an occasional media commentator.

Jamie J. Hagen is a lecturer in International Relations at Queen's University Belfast. She received her PhD in Global Governance and Human Security from the University of Massachusetts, Boston in 2018. Her work at the intersection of gender analysis, security studies and LGBTQ communities has appeared in a number of peer-reviewed journals including *International Affairs* (2016) and *Critical Studies on Security* (2017). In 2016 she wrote the working paper 'Sexual orientation and gender identity as part of the Women, Peace and Security Project' for the Centre for Women, Peace and Security at the London School of Economics and Political Science where she served as Visiting Fellow in 2019. Hagen has also written a number of book chapters including 'Extending acts of motherhood: Storytelling as resistance to stigma' for the forthcoming edited collection *Troubling Motherhood* (Oxford University Press, 2020). Hagen is currently the Associate Editor of Digital Media for the *International Feminist Journal of Politics* and is a member-at-large for the LGBTQA Caucus for the International Studies Association.

Lucy Hall is a lecturer at the University of Amsterdam and received her doctorate from UNSW Sydney, Australia. Her doctoral research explored the discursive construction of humanitarian protection norms to investigate the ways in which they are underpinned by logics of gender. Lucy has published several co-authored book chapters, in books such as *Gender Matters in Global Politics* (Routledge, 2015) and *Responsibility to Protect and Women, Peace and Security: Aligning the Protection Agendas* (Brill, 2013).

Cristina Hernández Lázaro holds an MA in Conflict Studies and Human Rights at Utrecht University, where she specialized in qualitative research, and a Bachelor's degree in Political Science from Universitat Pompeu Fabra in Barcelona, Spain. She has conducted field-work research on militarism in Israel, and she collaborated with the International Institute for Nonviolent Action in Barcelona through researching the current privatization and militarization of the Southern Spanish border. She has also conducted research on Private Military and Security Companies (PMSCs), gender and humanitarian action in order to contribute to the Shock Monitor platform, a PMSCs and Human Rights Observatory based in Barcelona. She has been involved in a variety of grassroots international cooperation initiatives and local social projects in countries such as Spain, Jordan, Perú, Costa Rica, Greece and Chile, mostly related to migration, social inclusion and human rights. She currently works as a coordinator in a reception centre for migrants who are minors in Catalonia.

Marjaana Jauhola is an Academy of Finland Research Fellow and Senior University Lecturer in Development Studies at the University of Helsinki, Finland. She holds a PhD in International Politics (2010) from Aberystwyth University. Her research focuses on populism and gendered politics of post-disaster and conflict reconstruction, and she conducts urban ethnography and life history documentaries (for details see www.scrapsofhope.fi). She has been an intimate part of the localization of WPS/UNSCR1325 in the Finnish context since 2001 when she translated the first resolution into the Finnish language. Her publications include *Post-Tsunami Reconstruction: Negotiating Normativity through Gender Mainstreaming Initiatives in Aceh, Indonesia* (Routledge, 2013) and 'Decolonizing branded peacebuilding: Abjected women talk back to the Finnish Women, Peace and Security agenda' in *International Affairs* (2016).

Paul Kirby is a research fellow at the London School of Economics and Political Science's Centre for Women, Peace and Security, and a Co-Director of the UKRI GCRF Gender, Justice and Security Hub. His research has focused primarily on feminist theories of conflict-related sexual violence and on the politics of the Women, Peace and

Security agenda in its diverse manifestations, including through several ongoing collaborations with Laura J. Shepherd. This work has been published in *Security Dialogue, International Affairs, European Journal of International Relations, Men and Masculinities* and *International Feminist Journal of Politics*. Paul has also contributed chapters to edited works on sexual violence against men, masculinities, wartime sexual violence, gender as an international political issue and narrative in International Relations. He has been a co-editor of both the *European Journal of International Relations* and *Millennium: Journal of International Studies*; co-editor of special issues of *International Affairs* and *International Feminist Journal of Politics*; and with Laura Shepherd currently co-edits the LSE Centre for Women, Peace and Security Working Paper Series.

Rita M. Lopidia is the Executive Director and co-founder of EVE Organization for Women Development, South Sudan and Uganda. She has more than ten years' experience in gender, women, peace and security in Sudan and South Sudan. A vocal human rights and peace activist, she has continuously confronted issues of sexual and gender based violence, space creation for South Sudanese women, and advocated for the development of the South Sudan UNSCR 1325 National Action Plan and the ratification of CEDAW. Rita organized women activists to demand for women and civil society participation in the IGAD led South Sudan Peace talks in Addis Ababa 2014–2015 as well as the High Level Revitalization Process 2017–2018. She was a delegate in both processes and a signatory to the Revitalized Agreement on the Resolution for the conflict in South Sudan – R-ARCSS (2018). Rita has worked extensively with internally displaced persons, documenting cases of sexual and gender-based violence in 2014. Rita has addressed the UNSC on several occasions on the situation of Women, Peace and Security in South Sudan. She was nominated for the Post of the Special Rapporteur on the Rights to Freedom of Peaceful Assembly and of Association in 2018. A Rotary Peace Fellow, she holds an Honors Degree in Applied and Industrial Science from the University of Juba, and two Masters Degrees in Human Resources Management and in International Politics and Security Studies from the University of Bradford.

Minna Lyytikäinen is a PhD candidate in Political Science at the University of Helsinki. Her research focus is on the evolution and implementation of international statebuilding policy, particularly the politics of inclusive statebuilding and feminist interventions in peace and conflict research. In her research, she has been documenting statebuilding policy processes (including the Women, Peace and

Security (WPS) agenda) in Nepal and in Finland. Previously, Minna worked as an independent policy consultant specializing in gender, peacebuilding and security, working, for example, with NGOs to develop guidelines for the integration of gender perspectives into conflict analysis frameworks. Minna has also worked as Senior Programme Officer at International Alert, a peacebuilding NGO, where she led the organization's thematic programme on gender and peacebuilding. In this role, Minna contributed to various WPS-related policy processes across organizations (the UN and the EU) and countries (particularly the UK, Liberia, Burundi and Nepal). Among her policy publications is the co-authored UN report *Planning for Action on Women, Peace and Security: National-level Implementation of Resolution 1325* (2010). Minna has a Master's degree in Development Studies from the London School of Economics and Political Science.

Rita Manchanda is a scholar-author and human rights advocate specializing on conflicts and peacebuilding in South Asia with particular attention to vulnerable and marginalized groups, that is, women, minorities, indigenous peoples and forcibly displaced persons. Her particular expertise is the intersection of gender studies with peace and security issues within the context of South Asia. She has been influential in shaping the regional women, peace and security scholarly and policy discourse. Also, as evident in the compilation of India CSO Report on Beijing Platform for Action +20 Review (UN Women 2014), she has a holistic understanding of the complex social dynamics that produce women's status vulnerability and resistance in India. Among her many publications is the multi-country five volume *SAGE Series in Human Rights Audits of Peace Processes* (SAGE, 2015) which she edited, as well as co-authoring two of the volumes. The edited volume *Women and the Politics of Peace: Narratives of Militarisation, Power and Justice* (SAGE, 2017) is a follow-up to her benchmark publication *Women, War and Peace in South Asia: Beyond Victimhood to Agency* (SAGE, 2001). Notable additional publications include the *No Nonsense Guide to Minority Rights in South Asia* (SAGE, 2009) and the edited volume *States in Conflict with their Minorities* (SAGE, 2010).

Briana Mawby is a researcher whose work focuses on gender, migration, environmental and conflict issues. She has published reports and articles on women's roles in peace and security issues, the nexus of peacebuilding and disaster response, security sector reform, inclusive disaster risk reduction, migration governance, human trafficking, gender-based violence, women's participation in the renewable energy sector and the integration of environmental and gender issues. Her work has focused on conflict- and crisis-affected communities in Africa, Asia, the Caribbean, Europe and Latin America. Briana has served as a researcher and analyst for the International Organization for Migration, the International Union for Conservation of Nature, the Overseas Development Institute, the World Bank and the Institute for the Study of International Migration. She also served as a 2015–2017 Hillary Rodham Clinton Research Fellow at the Georgetown Institute for Women, Peace and Security. Briana earned a Master of Arts in conflict resolution, including a Certificate in Refugees and Humanitarian Emergencies from Georgetown University and a Bachelor of Arts in international affairs from George Washington University.

Joy Onyesoh is the Women's International League for Peace and Freedom (WILPF) International President and past President of WILPF Nigeria. She is currently researching for her Doctoral Degree in Transformative Studies and studying for a Bachelor of Law degree. Joy has over 15 years of experience working with women from diverse cultural and philosophical backgrounds and is committed to the substantive participation of women in peace processes in Nigeria. In 2015, she worked with UN Women as the national coordinator of the first ever Women's Situation Room Nigeria (WSR). In recognition of her work mobilizing women's engagement in the general elections, the National Orientation Agency of Nigeria (NOA) granted her a National Citizen's Responsibility Award in May 2015. Joy is particularly invested in the full implementation of UNSCR 1325 and has facilitated its translation into four Nigerian indigenous languages.

Elizabeth Pearson is a lecturer in the Hillary Rodham Clinton School of Law and Criminology at Swansea University. She studied for her PhD in War Studies at King's College London, where she explored gender in both Islamist and radical right movements in the UK. Elizabeth is also an Associate Fellow at the London defence think tank RUSI and has worked with them on a five-country research project on gender and extremism, as well as on countering violent extremism (CVE) delivery in Nigeria. Elizabeth writes on gender and Boko Haram and in 2015 conducted a project with the European Union Technical Assistance to Nigeria's Evolving Security Challenges (EUTANS). Elizabeth holds a Master's degree in War Studies from King's College London, where she was a Simon O'Dwyer Russell prize-winner (2013). She also has a BA degree in German and Philosophy from Wadham College, University of Oxford and before academia spent more than 15 years with BBC radio, mainly in factual programmes for Radio Four.

Madeleine Rees has been the Secretary General of the Women's International League for Peace and Freedom since 2010. She has practised human rights law in the UK and Europe, bringing cases to the European Court of Human Rights and the European Court in Luxembourg. Between 1998 and 2010, she served the United Nations, first as Head of the Office of the High Commissioner for Human Rights and their gender expert in Bosnia and Herzegovina, then as the Head of the Women's Rights and Gender Unit for the Office of the High Commissioner for Human Rights. In Bosnia and Herzegovina she worked on counter trafficking, the rule of law, gender and post-conflict, transitional justice, and the protection of social and economic rights. She was made an OBE in 2014, awarded an honorary doctorate from Edinburgh University in 2015 and is now a Visiting Professor in Practice at the London School of Economics and Political Science.

Patricia Viseur Sellers is an international criminal lawyer. She is the Special Adviser on Gender in the Office of the Prosecutor at the International Criminal Court; a Visiting Fellow at the Kellogg College of the University of Oxford, in which capacity she teaches international criminal law and international human rights law; a Visiting Professor in Practice at the London School of Economics; and a Senior Research Fellow at the Human Rights Center of the University of California, Berkeley. She was the Legal Adviser for Gender and the Acting Head of the Legal Advisory Section at the Yugoslavia Tribunal (ICTY) from 1994 to 2007 and the Legal Adviser for Gender at the Rwanda Tribunal (ICTR) from 1995 to 1999. She was a member of, and developed the legal strategies for, the Office of the Prosecutor's trial teams in the *Akayesu*, *Furundžija* and *Kunarac et al* cases. The decisions in these landmark ICTY and ICTR cases remain the pre-eminent legal standards for the interpretation of sexual violence as war crimes, crimes against humanity, genocide, torture and enslavement.

Laura J. Shepherd is Professor of International Relations at the University of Sydney. Her primary research focuses on the UN's Women, Peace and Security agenda. She has written extensively on the formulation of UN Security Council Resolution 1325 and subsequent Women, Peace and Security resolutions. She has recently concluded a project examining the formation and implementation of the Women, Peace and Security agenda at national and international levels, funded by the Australian Research Council, and she also holds an ARC Future Fellowship to study the relationship between the Women, Peace and Security agenda and counter-terrorism/countering violent extremism initiatives in Australia, the UK and Sweden. Laura has strong interests in methodology, pedagogy and popular culture. Laura is author or editor of several books, including, most recently *Gender, UN Peacebuilding and the Politics of Space* (Oxford University Press, 2017) and *Routledge Handbook of Gender & Security* (Routledge, 2019, edited with Caron Gentry and Laura Sjoberg). Her work has appeared in journals such as *International Political Science Review, International Affairs,* and *International Feminist Journal of Politics.* She tweets from @drljshepherd, and blogs semi-regularly for *The Disorder of Things.*

Anna Stavrianakis is Professor of International Relations at the University of Sussex, UK, where she has taught since 2006. Her research and teaching interests are in the areas of war, militarism, security and academic activism. Her work has a particular focus on UK arms export policy, the international arms trade and international arms transfer control. She is the author of *Taking Aim at the Arms Trade: NGOs, Global Civil Society and the World Military Order* (Zed Books, 2010), and the co-editor of *Militarism and International Relations: Political Economy, Security, Theory* (Routledge, 2012, with Jan Selby) and of the Special Issue on 'Militarism and Security: Dialogue, Possibilities and Limits,' in *Security Dialogue* (2018, with Maria Stern). Her most recent articles include 'Controlling weapons circulation in a post-colonial militarised world', in *Review of International Studies* (2018) and 'Requiem for risk: Non-knowledge and domination in the govern-ance of weapons circulation', in *International Political Sociology* (2019).

United Nations Security Council Resolutions on Women, Peace and Security

At the time of writing, there are ten United Nations Security Council resolutions under the title of 'Women and peace and security'. In this edited collection, the resolutions are referenced by number and section, for example 'UNSCR 2242, paras. 11–13'. The ten resolutions are:

UNSCR 1325 (2000), S/RES/1325
UNSCR 1820 (2008), S/RES/1820
UNSCR 1888 (2009), S/RES/1888
UNSCR 1889 (2009), S/RES/1889
UNSCR 1960 (2010), S/RES/1960
UNSCR 2106 (2013), S/RES/2103
UNSCR 2122 (2013), S/RES/2122
UNSCR 2242 (2015), S/RES/2242
UNSCR 2467 (2019), S/RES/2467
UNSCR 2493 (2019), S/RES/2493

Foreword: Toward Strategic Instrumentalism

Anne Marie Goetz

This collection of essays explores the consequences of hitching a transformative feminist project to the vehicle of transnational security and international legal institutions. Chapters exposing neo-imperialist elements of implementation, as well as the consequences of retributive and carceral reactions to injustice, show that fitting the Women Peace and Security (WPS) agenda to the norms and practices of security and prosecutorial institutions can fail to transform structural inequalities and their cultural foundations. It doesn't help that the gender essentialism informing some aspects of the WPS agenda has made it vulnerable to a specific pattern of implementation that confirms patriarchal expectations about women's roles, encourages a focus on sexual victimhood, and supports apolitical approaches to, ironically, the most political aspect of the agenda, which is the call for women's leadership and participation in conflict prevention and resolution.

This cutting-edge volume addresses these pressing concerns. Produced by an impressively diverse set of writers, this wide-ranging set of contributions also explores some of the thematic issues that have been sidelined by the pursuit of the WPS agenda in international security frameworks, such as trafficking, climate, migration, economic inequality and the role of private security companies. Of particular value are the chapters with transcripts of conversations between some of the most important WPS policymakers and critics. These show feminist activists' and femocrats' (feminist bureaucrats) awareness of the painful tradeoffs between rights-based and instrumental policy justifications, between idealism and pragmatism, and a commitment to critical and strategic engagement with mainstream institutions.

Of most concern to a number of feminist peace activists is what is perceived to be an exaggerated (if, truth be told, historically belated) focus on conflict-related sexual violence instead of women's peace leadership. Starting with UN Security Council resolution 1820 in 2008, efforts to prevent and address conflict-related sexual violence have seen increasingly detailed Security Council instructions, such as including sexual violence in the designation criteria of sanctions committees, and institutional provisions, including training for peacekeepers, a dedicated Special Representative of the Secretary-General to monitor and lead responses on the issue, an increase in indictments and convictions for these crimes, and some new, if still inadequate, funding to support survivors. Although these actions include attention to conflict-related sexual violence against men and boys, critics worry that the focus on sexual injury confirms sexist framings of women's place as victims in peace and security analysis. In addition, a fixation on harms to women in the absence of support for women's leadership may produce responses ranging from paternalistic to coercive, involving the securitization of public space and restrictions on women's freedoms and mobility (Engle et al, 2020). It should be no surprise that the Security Council finds it easier to focus on a clear violation of international law than on the positive actions – frankly, the social engineering – needed to advance the 'soft law' concerns found in its resolutions on women's participation, leadership, gender analysis and peacebuilding (resolutions 1889, 2122, 2242, and 2493). The challenge governing the WPS field is how to hold the Security Council and individual states to account for their responsibilities in these areas.

In the struggle to translate a feminist political project into policy imperatives, femocrats and activists have inevitably reached for instrumental justifications. Research shows that women's participation in conflict resolution produces a more inclusive and longer lasting peace (see, for example, Krause et al, 2018), providing what might seem a highly persuasive reason to spend political capital on requiring mediators and parties to conflict to include women when populating delegations to negotiations. But the potential savings in lives and economic development available if women participate in conflict resolution have evidently not been sufficient to sway parties to peace talks to include them.

Twenty years on from the adoption of UNSCR 1325, women are still systematically excluded from peace talks. At the time of writing, these issues continue to dominate debates about WPS. A particularly bad year for this was 2018, with few to no women involved in peace or ceasefire talks (for Libya, Yemen and Central African Republic). In early 2019, it was clear that women were not to be included in the US's talks with the Taliban in Doha (regarding the conditions for a

US military drawdown in Afghanistan), nor was it clear whether there was scope for their inclusion in planned intra-Afghan talks that were to follow. Early in the process, the US negotiator, Zalmay Khalilizad, signalled that gender equality issues were to be treated as a domestic matter. Members of the Afghan Women's Network in Kabul indicated that they had been told by the US that they could not participate in the Doha talks because of the Taliban's implacable objections. Yet, on questioning Taliban leaders, they discovered that the Taliban had never been asked about this by the US, and did not in fact object to women's presence in the talks, provided they were modestly dressed.[1] This seemingly unilateral up-front exclusion suggests a posture of anticipatory surrender, a pre-emptive concession or perhaps a strategic signalling of a willingness to give way on women's rights. Surrender of international standards on women's rights had become a bargaining chip – possibly even a type of confidence-building measure, to encourage participation from a strongly misogynist negotiating party.

The promotion of women as leaders in conflict resolution is not impossible, but it is inconvenient. Significant political pressure from gender equality advocates is needed to move national and international actors to go to the mat for women's participation. But expectations that international actors should defend women's rights are apparently resented. This was confirmed by an unexpected source in the case of the US–Taliban talks. Cheryl Benard, the wife of the US negotiator, chastised Afghan feminists for expecting that their interests could be defended in international negotiations: 'It's time for Afghan feminists to put their shoulders to the wheel and start doing what women everywhere have had to do when they wanted their rights: fight for them', said Benard in a February 2019 article in *The National Interest*. Detailing US-funded women's empowerment efforts since the invasion of 2001, she suggested that the US had enabled 'a group of trained and educated and articulate potential leaders' and suggested that these women should not expect external help but should: 'face the fact that their platform of action is their own country, and that this is where they must show courage and strategic intelligence. Shaming their Western benefactors into doing it for them will not pave the road for their country's social change' (Benard, 2019). In an admirably restrained response, Palwasha Hassan, executive director of the Afghan Women's Educational Center, explained that Afghan women have been fighting for their rights for decades, have, for the 18 years since the international intervention, counselled peace talks rather than clearly unwinnable military confrontations, and do not expect rescue. Rather, they simply ask that their rights not be traded away in the interest of a short-term truce: 'We are not begging for our seat at the table. We are fighting for it. All we are asking is for those who call themselves our allies not to actively work against us' (Hassan, 2019).

Women's rights activism, whether in conflict-affected countries or not, is not recognized for its significance in building coalitions for deepening democracy or peace, and shaping potential political leaders. As a result, when the rare opportunities come for peace talks, women leaders are not identified as valuable participants. It is possible that the sexism embedded in male-dominated international institutions amplifies domestic patriarchies and cements women's exclusion from peace processes.

Feminists in international institutions are painfully aware of this possibility but are often stuck working a rearguard action against international–domestic patriarchal collusion. The secrecy of processes for identifying participants in the organization of peace talks, and even donor conferences for post-conflict states, and the fact that these processes are male-dominated, means that local female leaders may not be aware of negotiating opportunities, may not get a chance to bargain for inclusion. Even femocrats in international institutions supporting these processes may not be aware of such opportunities until too late. UN Women, for instance, often does not have a field office in the conflict countries in which steps are taken to begin talks, and even if it does, it is not informed. This can encourage a resort by femocrats to relatively apolitical, delayed and sideshow mechanisms to ensure some measure of women's inclusion, through the formation of women's consultative bodies that cross the lines of conflict, such as the Women's Advisory Board for the Syria talks, set up by UN Women in 2016 to support the work of the UN mediator.

The foundational assumption that women can find common cause merely on the basis of shared gender is untenable, however, particularly in a conflict situation. In the Syria case, women opposition activists and women apologists for Assad's regime have found little shared ground. On the opposition side, a number of women set up the Syrian Women's Political Movement (SWPM) in 2017 to demand inclusion in conflict resolution efforts. In contrast to the Women's Advisory Board, the SWPM cannot tolerate neutrality in the face of atrocities; it insists on a regime change project. The SWPM will not accept peace at any cost, but seeks to ensure that any post-conflict settlement (such as a new constitution) is grounded in a commitment to gender equality and builds governance structures capable of preventing the atrocities that are commonplace under Assad's regime. The SWPM insists on recognition and inclusion in peace talks and constitutional reform debates as a political collectivity with a vote, not as an advisory body.[2]

Femocrats within peace and security institutions are acutely aware of the risks of instrumentalism. As someone who has been on both sides of this discussion, as a UN policymaker, and as an academic who has dealt out her share of criticism of policy sell-outs, my sympathies are now with the femocrats. Instrumentalism is unavoidable in deeply gendered institutions that are hostile to or just unfamiliar with women's inclusion. What pains femocrats is how rarely academic analysts can see how carefully femocrats deploy instrumental arguments, how strategically they pick their fights and select opportunities to make advances.

The chapters in this book provide useful – even vivid – illustrations of some of the trade-offs and tensions involved in the global project of feminist engagement with peace and security institutions. As the book's editors show in the introductory chapter, WPS has grown into a substantial academic field. There is a growing policy community too: most of the 80-plus states that have formulated WPS National Action Plans have implementation arrangements; some countries claim to practise feminist foreign policy, no country in the rotating group of ten elected members on the Security Council can do without in-house gender expertise, a growing number of non-governmental organizations active in conflict resolution, mitigation and humanitarian work are addressing WPS issues, and there is increasing demand for gender experts in multilateral peacekeeping and political missions. These developments are also facing profound challenges, as are gender equality policy initiatives in other fields, from conservative populist governments and authoritarian governments that have exploited the mobilizing potential of misogyny and have boosted military spending and militant rhetoric in what Deniz Kandiyoti calls a project of 'masculine restoration' (Kandiyoti, 2019). Faced with resistance from unanticipated sources such as the US and Brazil, WPS advocates in multilateral policy spaces must now coordinate to take strategic and even evasive action to preserve gains and prevent co-optation of the agenda for reactionary purposes (Goetz and Jenkins, 2019). In the context of backlash, and under the pressures created by a crisis-driven field, practitioners more than ever need critical analysis, such as is found in this volume, as a compass to return them consistently to the feminist anti-imperial and anti-militaristic objectives at the origins of the WPS agenda.

Notes

[1] This observation was shared by Madeleine Rees, Secretary-General of the Women's International League for Peace and Freedom during a round-table discussion at the International Peace Institute in New York, USA, in late 2019.

[2] Syrian Women's Political Movement website: http://syrianwomenpm.org/en.

References

Benard, C. (2019) 'Afghan women are in charge of their own fate', *The National Interest*, 27 February, Available from: https://nationalinterest.org/feature/afghan-women-are-charge-their-own-fate-45777.

Engle, K., Nesiah, V. and Otto, D. (2020) 'Feminist approaches to international law', in J. Dunoff and M. Pollack (eds) *International Legal Theory: Foundations and Frontiers*, Cambridge: Cambridge University Press.

Goetz, A.M. and Jenkins, R. (2019) 'The WPS agenda 25 years after Beijing: perennial and emerging obstacles in multilateral responses and in the global peacebuilding landscape', Expert Paper for the UN Women Expert Group Meeting 'Beijing +25: Current context, emerging issues and prospects for gender equality and women's rights', New York, 25–26 September, Available from: www.unwomen.org/-/media/headquarters/attachments/sections/csw/64/egm/goetzjenkinsexpert%20paperdraftegmb25ep4.pdf?la=en&vs=844.

Hassan, P. (2019) 'Afghan women want a responsible U.S. withdrawal', *The National Interest*, 18 March, Available from: https://nationalinterest.org/blog/skeptics/afghan-women-want-responsible-us-withdrawal-47967.

Kandiyoti, D. (2019) 'Against all odds: the resilience and fragility of women's gender activism in Turkey', in D. Kandiyoti, N. Al-Ali and K. Spellman-Poots (eds) *Gender, Governance and Islam*, Edinburgh: Edinburgh University Press.

Krause, J., Krause, W. and Bränfors, P. (2018) 'Women's participation in peace negotiations and the durability of peace', *International Interactions*, 44(6): 985–1016.

Syria Justice and Accountability Center (2016) 'The controversy over the Syrian Women's Advisory Board', 7 April, Available from: https://syriaaccountability.org/updates/2016/04/07/the-controversy-over-the-syrian-womens-advisory-board/.

Women, Peace and Security: A Critical Cartography

Soumita Basu, Paul Kirby and Laura J. Shepherd

The Women, Peace and Security (WPS) agenda, associated with the United Nations Security Council resolutions of a similar name, is widely recognized as the most significant and wide-reaching global framework for advancing gender equality in military affairs, conflict resolution and security governance. The first of these resolutions, UN Security Council Resolution (UNSCR) 1325, bound the international community to ensure, among other provisions, greater participation of women in decision making in national, regional and international institutions; their further involvement in peacekeeping, field operations, mission consultation and peace negotiations; increased funds and other support to the gender work of UN entities; enhanced state commitments to the human rights of women and girls and the protection of those rights under international law; the introduction of special measures against sexual violence in armed conflict; and due consideration to the experiences and needs of women and girls in humanitarian, refugee, disarmament and post-conflict settings. As such, it was a ground-breaking commitment by the Security Council, the intergovernmental body charged with maintenance of international peace and security and widely regarded as a bastion of masculinized power and privilege (see Cohn, 2008), to acknowledge the significance of gender dynamics in active conflict situations and in peace and security governance. Nine subsequent resolutions, focused on varying themes and mechanisms, have been added to the agenda since then (the resolutions are summarized on p. xx of this volume).

In the 20 years since the passage of the foundational resolution, academics, advocates and independent analysts have produced a

significant volume of scholarship on the WPS agenda. This literature has sought to justify the aims of the agenda through research
on various aspects of women's vulnerability and women's agency;
innovated metrics of progress on the agenda's multiple goals; assessed
the nature of its implementation in diverse parts of the world; proposed
modifications to policy; and occasionally sounded a dissonant note in
critiquing the international politics of WPS. More recently, attention
has been drawn to new themes, such as the intersections between
countering violent extremism and WPS, the invisibility of race and
sexuality in WPS discourse and practice, and the engagement of men
within and alongside WPS. This literature has also considered the pro-
liferation of actors who are taking on, extending and transforming WPS
principles; the deepening and broadening of WPS can be detected in
new attitudes towards the agenda in foreign policy platforms and in
those organizations that have engaged with WPS principles beyond
the umbrella of the United Nations, such as the North Atlantic Treaty
Organization (NATO) and the African Union (AU).

The contributors to this edited volume reflect diversity in thinking
and methodological plurality, both of which are characteristic of
contemporary WPS scholarship. This introductory chapter sets out a
roadmap for readers, drawing attention to the landmarks that signify
the field of WPS research and practice, and offering critical orientation towards the field. The map unfolds in three sections. The first
section explores the emergence of 'WPS' as a discrete object of analysis,
showing how WPS has gone from peace activism at the margins of
world politics to a more significant landmark in the peace and security
environment than perhaps anyone could have envisaged. Part II draws
attention to the new themes and new actors that have gained visibility
in recent years. Further, it highlights the 'encounters' between the
various aspects of WPS, as well as the emerging 'horizons' that have
become perceptible in the contemporary field of study, thereby also
introducing contributions specific to the two parts of this volume.
The third and concluding section outlines some new contestations,
tensions and constellations of power, re-situating the new politics of
WPS – the focus of this volume – in relation to geographical, temporal
and institutional scales.

Map and territory

Twenty years after its inception, the reach of 'Women, Peace and
Security' is extensive, contested and uncertain. Ten Security Council
resolutions, over a hundred National Action Plans (including revised

iterations), and dozens of regional organizational policies now constitute a vast normative infrastructure of significant ambition but questionable impact. This textual layer of WPS is only the most legible,
and arguably the least informative, map of practice available. Beyond it
lies a universe of struggles, documented and undocumented, to incu-
bate and sustain feminist peace, waged by social movements, NGOs,
progressive political blocs, historians, artists, and citizens, in locations
from parliaments to households, all of which could reasonably be
seen as motivated by the same desires that instigated the agenda at
the turn of the 21st century. Concurrently, feminist scholarship on
peace and security has traced, and in important respects pre-empted,
developments in WPS policy and practice.

From the end of the First World War onwards, an interdisciplinary
body of literature – spanning the social sciences, humanities and
beyond – has made the case for recognizing women as subjects in the
analyses of armed conflicts and peacebuilding. Within the discipline of
International Relations, feminist and critical scholars have presented
richly detailed empirical research and theoretical innovation on this,
as well as peace and security more broadly; these have been valuable
resources for WPS scholars and practitioners, including for the authors
and editors of this volume. Furthermore, there was an active participation of scholar-practitioners such as Betty Reardon and Carol Cohn
in the 'complex network' of actors advocating for UNSCR 1325
(Cockburn, 2007, pp 145–146), a tradition that has continued as part
of WPS policy evolution.

As WPS gained traction *as* an agenda, a generation of scholars and
activists worked to advance, refine and challenge its constitutive parts.
Some operated as advocates, and later found the agenda wanting in
basic respects. Others took the agenda as one case study in gender-
mainstreaming and sought to uncover the sources of its diffusion. Still
others have seen in WPS another chapter in the co-optation of radical
politics to shore up the legitimacy of the usual suspects. To trace the
development of the field, we conducted a review of 240 articles and
book chapters focused on WPS, yielding several insights of note.[1]

A first finding relates to the *timing* of scholarly interest. Only one
WPS-related paper was published each year from 2003 to 2006, rising
to two or three in the lead-up to the 10th anniversary of UNSCR
1325. Thereafter, the pace accelerates. Thirty pieces were published
in 2011, dipping to between 20 and 25 a year until 2015, and then
rising again to totals in the mid-30s and mid-40s each year following
the 15th anniversary. The upward tick in interest is consistent with
academic production closely tracking policy landmarks, especially in

convening special issues and edited volumes timed to coincide with, or reflect on, anniversaries (see, for example, Olonisakin et al, 2011; special issues in *International Peacekeeping*, 2010; *International Feminist Journal of Politics*, 2011; *Australian Journal of International Affairs*, 2014; *International Affairs*, 2016; and *International Political Science Review*, 2016). The pattern is starkly at odds with the prevailing image of the academy as detached from public life. Instead, the pace of knowledge production has to a significant extent been set by opportunities to reflect on, and shape, real world politics.[2]

Judging by the documentary trail, it has only just become possible to speak of a WPS research *community* as such. Half of all WPS publications date from the latest three-year period examined (2016–2018), with the most influential material of the first decade generated by a small number of academics. The impression is somewhat misleading, as some 'canonical' early work on WPS does not register in bibliographic searches due to the way in which the agenda was originally formulated and understood. For example, Dianne Otto's hugely influential insights into feminist organizing – 'power and danger', 'the exile of inclusion', 'the Security Council's alliance of gender legitimacy' – were not framed with 'WPS' as the singular focus and so tend to fall outside of bibliographic records of the core archive (see Otto, 2009; 2010a; 2010b).[3]

The ambiguity in delimitations of the field in the decade following the passage of UNSCR 1325 points to a second insight: that the *coherence* of WPS as a research object is more recent than may be supposed. The *agenda* as such only comes into being in the late 2000s with the second and subsequent Security Council resolutions. But even before that point, criticism of UNSCR 1325 and its effects was frequently expressed not in terms of an internal logic specific to a policy or organizational form but as one site in a variegated and dynamic field of feminist activism. The contemporary hierarchical or sequential linkage of elements – the acronym 'WPS', the Security Council, the text of the resolutions, their key 'pillars', the mechanics of implementation, and national and regional variations on a theme – simply did not exist in the early years of UNSCR 1325. Efforts at the United Nations were theorized as one tactic in a broad and deep effort at transnational feminist organizing and mobilization, most obviously building on the World Conferences on Women, but extending far beyond UN-sponsored fora. The attempt to transform practices of 'international security' was conscious, and animated by the conviction that the power of the Security Council *could* be leveraged for feminist ends, but even here the vision was encompassing: to '[build] a social movement reaching out to those working on issues of human rights, international law, the environment, globalization and terrorism–related issues', in the words of two key advocates (Felicity Hill and Maha Muna in Cohn et al, 2004, p 132).

The closing of feminist space *through* the WPS agenda – and especially the fixation on wartime rape – has been much commented on (see, for example, Aroussi, 2011). To some extent, academics contributed to the narrowing of the agenda, underscoring a tension over the implementation of WPS that continues in the present (and which we examine in more detail later). Though the shift to a discrete WPS agenda is recent, we are able to make out other patterns in scholarly interest over time. A number of early interventions foregrounded peace politics, women's human rights, or otherwise recognized an implicit tension between feminist aims and Security Council practices (Kandiyoti, 2004; El-Bushra, 2007; Binder et al, 2008; Hudson, 2009; Tryggestad, 2010). We interpret this wariness against the backdrop of feminist peace scholarship, in which several early scholars of WPS were steeped. Emerging from the late 1980s' renaissance of feminist IR, figures like Carol Cohn, Cynthia Enloe and Cynthia Cockburn understood 'international peace and security' as a profoundly mas-culinist endeavour, and Resolution 1325 as a partial, pragmatic and limited impingement upon that domain.

As attention to the agenda grew, so scholarship concentrated on a select number of key issues and sites in which WPS was understood to happen. Of the ten most-cited pieces on WPS in our survey, it is not surprising that most focus primarily on the politics of the United Nations Security Council (Shepherd, 2008; Tryggestad, 2009; Bell and O'Rourke, 2010; Puechguirbal, 2010; Willett, 2010; Gibbings, 2011; Pratt and Richter-Devroe, 2011; Shepherd, 2011) with only two emphasizing the circulation of UNSCR 1325 beyond the UN (El-Bushra, 2007; McLeod, 2011). Significant fractions of the literature address issues of wartime sexual violence (for example, Simic, 2010; Aroussi, 2017; Reilly, 2018); women's inclusion in peacekeeping (for example, Henry, 2012; Karim, 2017; Deiana and McDonagh, 2018) or WPS as grounds for humanitarian intervention (for example, Dharmapuri, 2013; Davies et al, 2015), with contestations within the UN system fundamental in each instance. Following the growth in national strategies, scholars put questions of implementation – and suggestions for improvements – to the fore (for example, Diop, 2011; Lee-Koo, 2014; True, 2016; Swaine, 2017). The result was a pano-rama of case studies and detailed policy analysis as research programmes shifted away from the UN system towards patterns of diffusion, local-ization and failure.

The recognition of WPS as a policy field enabled doctoral students to take it as their focus, consolidating the 'generational' shift in a fairly direct sense: whereas early scholarship apprehended WPS through the prism of prior feminist struggles, more recent projects have undertaken closer readings in which the existence of a continuous, if evolving, agenda is taken as given. This work is developing as we write, and in directions that are not yet settled (as several of the contributors to this volume make clear). Thus a third insight from our survey – on which we expand later – is that WPS scholarship has become plural in parallel with the expansion and growing complexity of the agenda.

Charting the (ongoing) journey

From the very outset, the fanfare around the WPS agenda was tempered by the pragmatism of its advocates. Jennifer Klot, the Senior Governance Advisor at UNIFEM at the time, noted that the resolution's provisions are 'as specific and narrow as is the Security Council's mandate' (Klot, 2002, p 18). There have been many ebbs and flows in the formal WPS agenda since then. These have been widely discussed, both in scholarly and policy literatures, and it is apparent that this evolution does not allow for easy judgment. For instance, the disproportionate focus on conflict-related sexual violence, which has drawn much criticism, is also the issue area that has seen the most concrete developments: sanctions as a response to sexual violence were first mentioned in UNSCR 1820; the Office of the Special Representative of the Secretary-General on Sexual Violence in Conflict was established following the passage of UNSCR 1888, as was the requirement for yearly reports to the Security Council on sexual violence in conflict; sexual violence against men and boys was explicitly recognized in UNSCR 2106; and monitoring on sexual violence crimes was expanded in UNSCR 2467. And yet, backtracking on issues like sexual and reproductive rights is already in evidence with the 9th and 10th resolutions (the most recent at the time of writing) (Allen and Shepherd, 2019; Hossain et al, 2019; Ní Aoláin, 2019). More broadly, in the last 20 years, the agenda has expanded from its initial three 'P's – participation, protection and prevention – vis-à-vis armed conflicts, to the addition of the pillars of relief and recovery and normative framework; more recently, we see the inclusion of transitional justice and countering violent extremism (see Coomaraswamy et al, 2015). While such expansion has created new constituencies, the absence of strong implementation and accountability mechanisms to undergird this growth has compounded the precarity of the contemporary global WPS agenda.

The global framework of policy mechanisms and transnational advocacy efforts has provided the political rationale for the development of National Action Plans (NAPs) by governments for the implementation of WPS resolutions. Some of these NAPs have taken the agenda forward by identifying issue areas that are specific to their context. Carrie Reiling points to the use of development as a key concern in the NAPs of some African countries (Reiling, 2017 cited in True, 2019, p 141). The NAP adopted by the government of Nepal, with considerable inputs from local civil society actors and international agencies, includes provisions for widows, whose needs are otherwise not addressed in the WPS resolutions (Owen, 2011, p 617). The most enterprising use of the WPS resolutions, however, has been on the part of civil society organizations (CSOs), who have employed it to demand action from their governments and intergovernmental organizations such as the UN. Early on, women peace activists in Liberia brandished copies of the UNSCR 1325 during the peace negotiations to claim their places at the peace table. In certain cases, the distinction between the state's and the civil society's visions of the WPS agenda has been very apparent; Laura McLeod's research in Serbia, for example, highlights this tension (McLeod, 2011). In yet another case, that of India, both the state and civil society have had limited engagement with the formal WPS agenda, in large part due to reservations regarding the Security Council, the institutional home of the WPS resolutions (Basu, 2016).

Certainly, the multiple iterations of the WPS agenda are not independent either of the relevant actors that give meaning to it and are responsible for its implementation, nor the material and discursive contexts within which it is understood and operationalized. The three key sets of actors that have been associated with the agenda are intergovernmental organizations, especially the UN and its agencies; national governments; and local and transnational civil society actors. Over the years, there have been important developments that mark this engagement. The UN has seen a growing institutionalization of the WPS agenda, in the form of subsequent WPS resolutions, policy frameworks for implementation, new offices and usually more than one annual debate at the Security Council. Each of these have required intense efforts on the part of advocates, even as it has been difficult to ensure that the policy mechanisms are effectively implemented. Regional entities such as the North Atlantic Treaty Organization (Wright, 2016) and the African Union (Hendricks, 2017), which do not have a tradition of addressing the gender dimension in military affairs, have also taken the WPS agenda on board. In addition to the challenges relating to implementation, analysts have drawn attention to the negative ramifications of the increasing institutionalization of the WPS agenda. These include, among others, the assimilation of the more 'radical' aspects of gender politics into the 'business-as-usual' organizational culture at these organizations; and, related to this, the instrumentalization of women's inclusion in the arena of international peace and security, wherein the argument for increasing their participation is made on the basis of operational effectiveness and not gender equality.

The threat of co-option lends itself more easily to growing involvement of states with the WPS agenda. As of November 2019, 82 UN member states have adopted NAPs for the implementation of the WPS resolutions, with some states having moved on to the third or fourth iteration of their NAP.[4] While the significance of states in realizing the WPS agenda cannot be overstated, the nature of their engagement so far lends credence to feminist apprehensions regarding the state as an agent for positive transformations in gender politics. For instance, NAPs of countries in the global North tend to be 'outward-oriented', focusing on their mandate as donors or troop contributors, and do not reflect on WPS issues relating to their respective domestic context (see also Haastrup and Hagen, this volume). This speaks also to the observation that NAPs of countries in the global South may not have organic roots, and are usually developed with support from donor agencies and intergovernmental organizations; gender would not be a policy priority if not for the funding received, and 'expertise' imposed, from the international sphere. As such, both sets of NAPs do not only appear to 'gender-wash' states' security policies, but WPS becomes yet another pretext to perpetuate the dominance of the global North over the global South. A recent development, the emergence of 'feminist foreign policy', has added further complexity to governmental engagement with the WPS agenda, especially in relation to countries of the global North. Associated most famously with Sweden, but invoked in relation to other countries, including the United States, Canada, Norway and Australia, these have been discussed in relation to UNSCR 1325, in terms of both their concurrent development as well as such foreign policies providing a more favourable context within which to advance the WPS agenda (see Aggestam et al, 2018). Promising as this may seem, the extent to which a feminist foreign policy may reconfigure the agenda (or indeed, vice versa) is yet to be seen.

The third set of actors that have been integral to the evolution of WPS belong to civil society. The significance of transnational non-governmental organizations in the passage of UNSCR 1325 is widely recognized and much celebrated. As highlighted in the previous section, the origins of the resolution lie in feminist peace activism that precede the formal WPS agenda by several decades. Civil society groups have been involved in the drafting, monitoring and advocacy for the implementation of the resolutions. Conversely, the resolutions recognize and seek to support the role that women's organizations and civil society, more broadly, play in facilitating the implementation of provisions laid down in the WPS resolutions. This institutionalization, however, has come at a cost. In order to make sense to the decision makers, groups that seek to engage are bound by the formal policy language and mechanisms that inevitably restrict the scope of the agenda. There are tensions between those who speak this language, and others who remain distant (by choice or otherwise) from the corridors of power. Funding imperatives are also a concern. As in the case of other issue areas, individuals and organizations that are well-networked and professionalized are better positioned to accesses resources set aside by donors for civil society engagement compared to those who may have a deeper understanding of the specific contexts. Further, it is notable that in many parts of the world, local organizations whose work predates the formal agenda remain unaware of the mechanisms and their potential use in mobilizing resources and policy responses. As such, on the one hand, it should be acknowledged that the status gained by civil society is not only long overdue but needs further recognition and support. On the other hand, it is important for WPS advocates to remain vigilant of the perils of hyper-professionalization of civil society participation.

By necessity, an outline of the kind we present here – on the themes and actors that animate the contemporary WPS agenda – can only be painted in broad strokes. The complexities to which we draw attention in this introductory discussion are explored in greater detail in the subsequent chapters. These balance analytical imperatives common to WPS and other areas of feminist research (including security studies, peace studies, foreign policy analysis, diplomacy, and law and justice) alongside specially commissioned personal narratives and accounts from experts, policymakers and advocates working in the space of WPS policy and practice. Indeed, many of the contributors locate themselves at the intersections of scholarship and practice, and have engaged in feminist work in the peace and security arena from before the emergence of the formal WPS agenda.

Part I of the volume, entitled 'Encounters', assesses efforts to realize the WPS agenda in specific contexts, geographical and institutional, and political fallouts of the same. These include four chapters presented as conversations between academics, practitioners and indeed those whose work spans both worlds. In the opening conversation, Lucy

Hall interviews Rita Martin Lopidia about her organization's efforts to engender peace processes in South Sudan, particularly in relation to the WPS agenda and the country's NAP. Lopidia highlights the many challenges that impede the effective implementation of the resolutions. Continuing with the theme of local implications, Nicole George and Rita Manchanda in turn examine the limitations of the WPS agenda in securing peace and gender equality, in relation to the Pacific Islands and South Asia respectively. While George brings forth the negative ramifications of imposing the 'economic peace' paradigm on a region that has traditionally followed a different economic logic, Manchanda focuses on issues of militarization, transitional justice and women's involvement in peacebuilding efforts. It is evident from their analysis that universal frames of the WPS agenda are not equipped to speak to the lived experiences of women and men in these regions.

Next, Minna Lyytikäinen and Marjaana Jauhola reflect on their experience as civil society participants in the consultations organized by the Finnish Ministry of Foreign Affairs towards the development of the country's third WPS NAP. They employ auto-ethnography to critique the growing bureaucratization of such deliberations and bring to light the ways in which dissent was 'managed' during the series of consultations, as well as the resistance mounted by civil society actors. In the following chapter, Elizabeth Pearson analyses the policy imperative of 'countering violent extremism' that has received considerable attention in recent years. She examines a specific case, that of the British counter-radicalization strategy *Prevent* and women participants' navigation of the same in different regions of the country. Drawing on substantive empirical research, Pearson contends that it is limiting to see women as mere instruments in CVE community initiatives, and points to the ways in which they have come to exercise their agency and 'own' such policies.

Turning the focus to the international realm, Louise Chappell interviews Patricia Viseur Sellers, who (at the time of writing) is the Special Adviser on Gender to the Prosecutor of the International Criminal Court. They discuss the potential of international criminal law and international humanitarian law to address sexual and gender-based violence in armed conflicts, particularly in relation to the work of the International Criminal Tribunal for the former Yugoslavia (ICTY). Further, they examine the scope of the WPS resolutions in strengthening such legal mechanisms and comment on possible futures of the agenda. Finally, this section is rounded out by a conversation between Louise Allen and sam cook, who have worked with the NGO Working Group on Women, Peace and Security and the PeaceWomen project of the Women's International League for Peace and Freedom (WILPF) respectively. Drawing on their extensive advocacy experience at the UN Headquarters in New York, they consider the fraught relations that mark civil society's engagement with intergovernmental machineries, and the challenges they encountered in their efforts to hold 'feminist space' at the UN.

Part II, entitled 'Horizons', focuses primarily on issues that have traditionally either been separate from, or overlooked, in the formal WPS agenda. Toni Haastrup and Jamie Hagen open the section with a decolonial analysis of the NAPs of select countries of the global North in order to highlight the racialized hierarchies that characterize the North–South dynamics in WPS politics. Weapons control is another particularly important topic, as disarmament has been central to feminist advocacy in the peace and security arena since the early 20th century. While the WPS resolutions do not have provisions in this regard and the agenda itself has been critiqued for its militarized orientation, Anna Stavrianakis examines some recent policy successes, especially the substantive reference to gender-based violence in the UN Arms Trade Treaty. Looking into the future, she calls for the need to ensure that such developments would be inadequate unless these are inclusive of anti–racist and anti–imperialist insights. Marta Bautista Forcada and Cristina Hernández Lázaro draw attention to yet another aspect of contemporary armed conflicts in the form of the privatization of military and security services in the last few decades. The authors take note both of the threats posed by private military and security companies (PMSCs) as well as the inadequacy of existing legal mechanisms to regulate their work. They advocate for the inclusion of PMSCs as a new challenge to be considered within the WPS agenda.

In the next chapter, Gema Fernández Rodríguez de Liévana and Christine Chinkin suggest that human trafficking as an issue area has mostly been neglected within the WPS agenda and, further, that the Security Council's approach to WPS and trafficking has done a disservice to realizing the potential of the women's human rights' regime in addressing this issue. They argue for more effectively integrating a human rights-based approach into the WPS agenda. Another dimension of forced movements of people, that of climate change-induced migration, is discussed in relation to the WPS agenda by Briana Mawby and Anna Applebaum. They highlight the gendered aspects of climate change-induced migration, including as a growing threat to women's security, and provide some introductory reflections on the need to employ the WPS agenda in a context wherein its scope has remained relatively unexplored. The concluding chapter is a conversation between Joy Onyesoh, Madeleine Rees and Catia C. Confortini, all associated with WILPF in different capacities. They examine the co-option of the WPS agenda by governments and the UN, and reflect on the ways in which feminist advocates have sought to, and can, confront such challenges. WILPF has been at the forefront of international advocacy for incorporating feminist visions of peace into international policy frameworks, since its inception in 1915; it has also played a significant role in the WPS journey. As such, this conversation brings our efforts to map 'new directions' in the WPS agenda full circle.

The road ahead

To conclude our cartography, in this final section we continue to reflect on the last two decades of WPS activity and consider some of the tensions and contestations in the WPS agenda that might animate research and practice over the next two decades. We focus on two sets of tensions that are broadly illustrative of the ways in which the agenda has emerged and developed over time. First, we explore the question of boundaries: the histories of the WPS agenda are histories of territorial struggle, not only over what the WPS agenda *is* (as discussed in the previous sections) but also over what is included as a 'WPS issue' and what is not. Where those boundary lines are drawn, and what is therefore included and excluded, has clear political effects. Second, we interrogate the idea of implementation. The tension we identify here is not so much in the barriers to implementation, but in the basis on which it is decided whether implementation is happening effectively, or not. This is a question of measurement and evidence. We examine some of the claims that are made about WPS successes and failures, and critically engage with efforts to capture WPS activity using trackers, indicators and composite indices. We conclude by noting the intractable challenges faced by the WPS agenda, the 'wicked problems' (Conklin, 2005) that seem both irreducible and impervious to resolution. It is likely that these challenges will drive the agenda forward for many years to come, and thus we draw our cartography to a close by foreshadowing how these problems – and the institutional infrastructures that have grown up around them – will shape the WPS agenda in the future.

The question of boundaries is not a new issue in WPS scholarship. Although the conventional narrative of the WPS agenda suggests neat division into four 'pillars' deriving from UNSCR 1325, this coherence and consolidation was in fact a later development. The first System-Wide Action Plan for implementation of WPS at the UN identifies 12 areas of action (United Nations Security Council, 2005, p 3), which were narrowed to five thematic areas (the four pillars, plus a normative dimension) in the second System–Wide Action Plan in 2007. The five areas were reported on across four pillars in 2010, as the normative pillar was deemed to be 'cross–cutting' and was therefore incorporated into reporting on the other four pillars rather than being reported on separately (United Nations Security Council, 2010). This process of narrowing and focusing on prevention, protection, participation, and relief and recovery simultaneously *includes* the 'pillars' within the boundaries of the WPS agenda, broad as they are.

There is a growing body of work that examines 'tensions' in the WPS agenda (see, for example, Hudson, 2013; Lee-Koo, 2014; Kirby, 2015; George and Shepherd, 2016), recognizing that boundary–drawing practices drive the agenda in radically different directions. In previous work, two of us have noted a specific tension relating to the structure and organization of the agenda itself around the four 'pillars' identified earlier, and the 'subsequent narrowing of the agenda around one of these' – protection (Kirby and Shepherd, 2016, p 379). Institutionally, the creation of United Nations Action Against Sexual Violence in Conflict (UN Action) and the office of the Special Representative of the Secretary-General on Sexual Violence in Conflict (SRSG-SVC), and the absence of offices mandated to engage with women's conflict prevention work and women's participation in peace and security, lends credence to the claim that conflict-related sexual violence in conflict is *a* central – if not *the* central – part of the WPS agenda.

It is odd, then, that the agenda around sexual exploitation and abuse (SEA) by UN peacekeepers and allied actors has developed separate to WPS. Prompted by a UN Office of Internal Oversight Services investigation in 2002, the 'zero tolerance' bulletin issued by the Secretary-General in 2003 quickly became the cornerstone of SEA policy. SEA policy, however, has largely been both conceptually and practically siloed from WPS activity, to the significant detriment of both. As Jasmine-Kim Westendorf argues, 'prevention and response policies would benefit from being situated within the WPS frame of gender, power and protection issues, while accountability mechanisms would be strengthened by closer integration with CRSV frameworks' (2017, p 11). The explicit incorporation of counter-terrorism and countering violent extremism (CT/CVE) into WPS represents another example of border skirmishing in the agenda. The process of drafting the resolution outlining the need for gender-sensitive CT/CVE as part of the WPS agenda was highly contentious, with some actors involved in the negotiations arguing forcefully for the protection of the WPS agenda as a peace agenda, concerned that the inclusion of CT/CVE would securitize and ultimately militarize the agenda. Through her analysis of the institutional effects of such inclusion, Fionnuala Ní Aoláin shows that there are 'real risks of commodification, agenda hijacking and deepened gendered insecurity in some of the most precarious territories and communities in the world' incurred through the expansion of the definition of conflict in the WPS agenda to include terrorism and violent extremism (2016, p 277). In the case of both SEA and CT/CVE, whether they are included in, or excluded from, the WPS agenda, this will have material implications for the resources that flow to these areas (both human and financial), and the attention given to these areas within the accounting of WPS implementation and 'success'.

The idea of implementation forms part of the 'common sense' of WPS. It is assumed that the WPS resolutions – and plans, strategies, guidelines and protocols which invoke them – exist as policy artefacts to be implemented, by different actors across various contexts. Much of the literature on NAPs – and on the WPS agenda more broadly – focuses on the problems of, and gaps in, implementation (see, for example, Tryggestad, 2009; Shawki, 2017; Reiling, 2017). The most comprehensive, and perhaps significant, engagement with implementation was the 2015 publication entitled *Preventing Conflict, Transforming Justice, Securing the Peace: A Global Study on the Implementation of United Nations Security Council Resolution 1325* (Coomaraswamy et al, 2015); the Executive Summary affirms the focus on implementation, noting several achievements but also concluding that 'obstacles and challenges still persist and prevent the full implementation of the women, peace and security (WPS) agenda' (Coomaraswamy et al, 2015, p 14).

Questions about the factors impeding full implementation remain. The literature on WPS implementation tends to offer a range of explanations for failures of implementation that cohere around three poles: 1) lack of resources (see, for example, Willett, 2010; Dharmapuri, 2013; Shepherd and True, 2014); 2) lack of political will (see, for example, Fujio, 2008; George, 2014; Basini and Ryan, 2016); and 3) lack of understanding about the 'true' WPS principles that ought to be prioritized and thus operationalized (see, for example, Reeves, 2012; Shepherd, 2016). All of these explanations are plausible, and, arguably on the balance of evidence from the works cited here, most sites of implementation manifest one or more of these inhibitors at different times. Though plausible, and empirically verifiable, they are not, however, very revealing in terms of the degrees of contestation over WPS practices and the differentiation that occurs within various WPS contexts over time.

Further, acknowledging impediments to implementation sidesteps the question of how implementation is monitored and evaluated. Monitoring and evaluation of the evidence base on which judgements about implementation are founded is contested across many contexts of WPS practice (see, for example, Gumru and Fritz, 2009; Fritz, Doering and Gumru, 2011; Lee-Koo, 2016). There have certainly been a number of striking claims made about WPS implementation and the difference that effective implementation makes in the world: consider, for example, frequently cited data about correlation between women's participation and durability of peace agreements. The fact is that, until recently, there was very limited empirical proof of such correlation, because the numbers of women involved in peace processes at any stage were vanishingly small. UN Women and the US Council on Foreign Relations data suggests that 'women constituted only 2 per cent of mediators, 8 per cent of negotiators, and 5 per cent of witnesses and signatories in all major peace processes' between 1990 and 2017 (Council on Foreign Relations, 2019, np). A significant volume of research effort has therefore been focused on generating the evidence base from which claims about WPS implementation can be persuasively made (see, for example, O'Reilly et al, 2015; Paffenholz et al, 2016; Krause et al, 2018). These efforts have borne fruit. As the *Global Study* concludes, 'recent research ... provides concrete evidence that women's participation is linked to better outcomes in general, and that the inclusiveness of peace processes and the democratization of conflict resolution are crucial to sustained peace and stability' (Coomaraswamy et al, 2015, p 4).

In tandem with the development of robust quantitative evidence regarding WPS implementation, there has also proliferated other modes of quantifying WPS, in the form of implementation trackers and indices. A specific 'Women, Peace and Security Index', for example, was launched in October 2017 by the Georgetown Institute for Women, Peace and Security (GIWPS) in the USA and the Peace Research Institute (PRIO) in Norway. The WPS Index claims to offer a 'comprehensive measure of women's wellbeing and their empowerment in homes, communities, and societies more broadly' (GIWPS, 2019) and ranks 153 countries according to their score across three domains: inclusion, justice and security. It captures some aspects of WPS principles in an appealingly simple single digit, but the data that lies behind this digit requires careful consideration. One concern is that 'the WPS Index relies on only one measure of conflict, one that has been criticized by feminist security analysts for male bias: the number of battle deaths' (Goetz, 2018, np). Using battle deaths as an indicator skews the count of violence in favour of the global North; measures of militarization and military spending would better capture violence as it is arguably understood by supporters of WPS. A second issue relates to the absence of efforts to measure women's participation in peacework and conflict prevention. 'There is data available on the vibrancy of, and rights afforded to, civil society movements across the world, which suggests that such spaces are under threat even in so-called developed countries' (Mundkur and Shepherd, 2018, np). Given the centrality of women's civil society leadership and organization to the WPS agenda, the inability of the WPS Index to measure this dimension of WPS work is a problem.

As their advocates argue, '[g]lobal indices are increasingly popular because they can distil an array of complex information into a single number' (Klugman et al, 2018, p 2). Sometimes, however, systems are defined by complexity. Attempts to reduce complex information can lead to comparisons being drawn across contexts that are not necessarily comparable. Further, some dimensions of WPS

> are next to impossible to quantify, such as the nature of engagement by women's groups with peace negotiators and the quality of a transitional justice arrangement from a gender equality perspective. Indicators of these conflict-specific processes do exist ... [but] They are not intended to enable comparisons between cases of peace talks or recovery programmes; each one is almost too anomalous to make comparative analysis meaningful. (Goetz, 2018, np)

Including these dimensions in an Index, or even the act of creating a WPS Index itself, brings into being a vision of WPS that has certain characteristics and qualities, shaping a world in which comparisons across diverse contexts can easily be summarized in numerical form. In the search for evidence of effective WPS implementation, and the adoption of WPS provisions and principles worldwide, it seems important to take heed of Sally Engle Merry's insight that 'those who create indicators aspire to measure the world but, in practice, create the world they are measuring' (Merry, 2016, p 21).

The world of WPS, as we go forward into the next two decades, will likely retain familiar elements while developing in unexpected directions, much as it has for the past two decades. A small number of WPS issues will no doubt continue to receive the lion's share of institutional and scholarly attention, while progress on a larger number will stagnate or even be reversed. Financing, for example, remains a key concern for everyone doing WPS work: the Women's Peace and Humanitarian Fund (WPHF, formerly the Global Acceleration Instrument for Women, Peace and Security and Humanitarian Action) received US $3,026,834 from donors in 2017, representing a drop of over half a million dollars from the previous year (United Nations Multi-Partner Trust Fund Office, 2019, np). Moreover, as of the time of writing, only ten UN member states have contributed to the Fund since its creation in 2016.[5] World military spending, meanwhile, increased in real terms by 1.1% in 2017 (SIPRI, 2018, np). There is not much cause for optimism that such patterns of spending will change. Relatedly, women's economic empowerment in post-conflict and conflict-affected settings remains a priority for the WPS agenda, although not necessarily a priority shared by those involved in post-conflict reconstruction and recovery. 'The clear gender inequality in women's access to resources is not simply caused by the presence of conflict. It is also a reflection of non-prioritization of women's needs and the relegation of women to small-scale and local peripheral initiatives' (UN Women, 2018, np).

Over the past two decades, it has been tricky to generate momentum in other areas of WPS practice, such as the meaningful participation of women in peace negotiations (setting aside for a moment the question of what 'meaningful' actually means), and the protection of female human rights defenders. The latter 'are fighting a lonely battle. Many die a lonely death from weapons that are meant to protect them' (UN Women, 2018, np). Taking seriously the ways in which women participate in nurturing, ensuring and sustaining peace and enabling them to realize their human, political, civil and economics rights is the familiar terrain of the WPS agenda. As the contributions to this collection demonstrate, we have travelled a long way towards realizing WPS in the world and yet, in the words of the poet Robert Frost, we yet have promises to keep ... and miles to go before we sleep.

Notes

[1] This data is drawn from a search of records held by the Web of Science citation indexing platform. All results were generated from a search conducted on 25 February 2019 for the topics 'Women, Peace and Security agenda' or 'women, peace and security' or 'Resolution 1325' or 'UNSCR 1325' across all available databases in the 2000–2018 period. 'Topics' in the Web of Science capture references to designated terms in the title, abstract or keywords of academic articles indexed in the collection. This search returning 243 hits, which were subsequently compiled and manually checked. Where multiple book chapters were listed in the search results, these were consolidated into a single reference (such as, for example, for Hudson, 2010). Where individual chapters in edited volumes were returned, these

were included *without* also listing the volume as a whole as a separate item. Where book chapters in edited volumes explicitly referring to WPS (such as in the title) were returned, the volume as a whole was checked, leading to the inclusion of other chapters that may not have been returned by the initial search but which were clearly WPS-related by virtue of their place in the volume. Where an edited book referred only in part to WPS (for example, Heathcote [ed], 2014) only those chapters returned in the Web of Science search were listed. Where articles in special issues were not returned as part of the initial search, they were not included (for example, Nordas and Rustad on SEA in *International Interactions* SI, 2013). The resulting list includes 240 distinct WPS publications over 18 years.

[2]   That the timing is closely related to waves of *political* interest in WPS may be inferred by noting the timing of National Action Plans, which also tend to cluster around landmark anniversaries.

[3]   Pieces which do not signal their relation to the WPS agenda less directly may be included through a different strategy. A Google Scholar search for the occurrence of the exact phrase 'Women, Peace and Security agenda' in the same 2000–2018 period returns approximately 1,390 results. The Google Scholar and Web of Science collections are not directly comparable. The larger set of returns from the former reflects not just that WPS may be examined in the main body of an article, but also that the agenda has come to serve as a ready example of wider trends, and material for larger debates, on issues from inclusive statebuilding (Langhi, 2014: 205) to changing masculinities (Vess et al, 2013) to the characteristics of a feminist security studies (Wibben, 2014).

[4]   For information on the development and progression of NAPs within and across countries, see www.wpsnaps.org.

[5]   They are Australia, Austria, Canada, Ireland, Liechtenstein, Lithuania, The Netherlands, Norway, Spain and the United Kingdom.

References

Aggestam, K., Bergman Rosamond, A. and Kronsell, A. (2018) 'Theorising feminist foreign policy', *International Relations*, 33(1): 23–39.

Allen, L. and Shepherd L. (2019) 'In pursuing a new resolution on sexual violence security council significantly undermines women's reproductive rights', LSE Centre for Women, Peace and Security, Available from: https://blogs.lse.ac.uk/wps/2019/04/25/in-pursuing-a-new-resolution-on-sexual-violence-security-council-significantly-undermines-womens-reproductive-rights/.

Aroussi, S. (2011) '"Women, Peace and Security": addressing accountability for wartime sexual violence', *International Feminist Journal of Politics*, 13(4): 576–593.

Aroussi, S. (2017) 'Women, Peace, and Security and the DRC: time to rethink wartime sexual violence as gender-based violence?', *Politics and Gender*, 13(3): 488–515.

Basini, H. and Ryan, C. (2016) 'National Action Plans as an obstacle to meaningful local ownership of UNSCR 1325 in Liberia and Sierra Leone', *International Political Science Review*, 37(3): 390–403.

Basu, S. (2016) 'Civil society actors and the implementation of resolution 1325 in India', in A. Hans and S. Rajagopalan (eds) *Openings for Peace: UNSCR 1325, Women and Security in India*, New Delhi: SAGE, pp 33–50.

Bell, C. and O' Rourke, C. (2010) 'Peace agreements or pieces of paper? The impact of UNSC Resolution 1325 on peace processes and their agreements', *International & Comparative Law Quarterly*, 59(4): 941–980.

Binder, C., Lukas, K. and Schweiger, R. (2008) 'Empty words or real achievement? The impact of Security Council Resolution 1325 on women in armed conflicts', *Radical History Review*, 101: 22–41.

Cockburn, C. (2007) *From Where We Stand: War, Women's Activism & Feminist Analysis*, London and New York: Zed Books.

Cohn, C. (2008) 'Mainstreaming gender in UN security policy: a path to political transformation?', in S.M. Rai and G. Waylen (eds) *Global Governance: Feminist Perspectives*. Basingstoke: Palgrave Macmillan, pp 185–206.

Cohn, C., Kinsella, H. and Gibbings, S. (2004) 'Women, peace and security: Resolution 1325', *International Feminist Journal of Politics*, 6(1): 130–140.

Conklin, J. (2005) *Dialogue Mapping: Building a Shared Understanding of Wicked Problems*, Oxford: Wiley.

Coomaraswamy, R. et al (2015) *Preventing Conflict, Transforming Justice, Securing the Peace: A Global Study on the Implementation of United Nations Security Council Resolution 1325*, New York, NY: UN Women, Available from: http://wps.unwomen.org/pdf/en/GlobalStudy_EN_Web.pdf.

Council on Foreign Relations (2019) 'Women's participation in peace processes', Available from: www.cfr.org/interactive/womens-participation-in-peace-processes.

Davies, S.E., Teitt, S. and Nwokora, Z. (2015) 'Bridging the gap: early warning, gender and the Responsibility to Protect', *Cooperation and Conflict*, 50(2): 228–249.

Deiana, M-A. and McDonagh, K. (2018) '"It is important, but …": translating the Women Peace and Security (WPS) agenda into the planning of EU Peacekeeping Missions', *Peacebuilding*, 6(1): 34–48.

Dharmapuri, S. (2013) 'Implementing UN Security Council Resolution 1325: putting the Responsibility to Protect into practice', in S.E. Davies, Z. Nwokora, E. Stamnes and Sarah Teitt (eds) *Responsibility to Protect and Women, Peace and Security*, Boston, MA: Brill/Nijhoff Publishers, pp 121–154.

Diop, B. (2011) 'The African Union and implementation of UNSCR 1325', in F. Olonisakin, K. Barnes and E. Ikpe (eds) *Women, Peace and Security: Translating Policy into Practice*, Abingdon: Routledge.

El-Bushra, J. (2007) 'Feminism, gender, and women's peace activism', *Development and Change* 38(1): 131–147.

Fritz, J.M., Doering, S. and Gumru, F.B. (2011) 'Women, peace, security, and the National Action Plans', *Journal of Applied Social Science*, 5(1): 1–23.

Fujio, C. (2008) 'From soft to hard law: moving resolution 1325 on Women, Peace and Security across the spectrum', *Georgetown Journal of Gender and the Law*, 9(1): 215–35.

George, N. (2014) 'Promoting women, peace and security in the Pacific Islands: hot conflict/slow violence', *Australian Journal of International Affairs*, 68(3): 314–332.

George, N. and Shepherd, L.J. (2016) 'Women, Peace and Security: exploring the implementation and integration of UNSCR 1325', *International Political Science Review*, 37(3): 297–306.

GIWPS (Georgetown Institute for Women, Peace and Security) (2019) 'Women, Peace and Security Index', Available from: https://giwps.georgetown.edu/the-index/.

Gibbings, S. (2011) 'No angry women at the United Nations: political dreams and the cultural politics of United Nations Security Council Resolution 1325', *International Feminist Journal of Politics*, 13(4): 522–538.

Goetz, A.M. (2018) 'What does the new Women, Peace, and Security Index measure?', *IPI Global Observatory*, Available from: https://theglobalobservatory.org/2018/03/what-does-wps-index-measure/.

Gumru, F.B. and Fritz, J.M. (2009) 'Women, Peace and Security: an analysis of the National Action Plans developed in response to UN Security Council Resolution 1325', *Societies Without Borders*, 4(2): 209–225.

Heathcote, G. and Otto, D. (eds) (2014) *Rethinking Peacekeeping, Gender Equality and Collective Security*, Basingstoke: Palgrave Macmillan.

Hendricks, C. (2017) 'Progress and challenges in implementing the Women, Peace and Security Agenda in the African Union's peace and security architecture', *Africa Development*, 42(3): 73–98.

Henry, M. (2012) 'Peacexploitation? Interrogating labor hierarchies and global sisterhood among Indian and Uruguayan female peacekeepers?', *Globalizations*, 9(1): 15–33.

Hill, F., Aboitiz, M. and Poehlman-Doumbouya, S. (2003) 'Nongovernmental organizations' role in the build-up and implementation of Security Council Resolution 1325', *Signs: Journal of Women in Culture and Society*, 28(4): 1255–1269.

Hossain, M., Howard, N. and Singh, N. (2019) 'Opinion: a resolution without resolve – UN Security Council fails to protect women and girls in conflict', *Thomson Reuters Foundation News*, Available from: http://news.trust.org/item/20190501125141-hfzka/.

Hudson, N.F. (2009) 'Securitizing women's rights and gender equality', *Journal of Human Rights*, 8(1): 53–70.

Hudson, N.F. (2010) *Gender, Human Security and the United Nations: Security Language as a Political Framework for Women*, Abingdon: Routledge.

Hudson, N.F. (2013) 'UNSCR 1325: the challenges of framing women's rights as a security matter', *NOREF: Norwegian Centre for Conflict Resolution Policy Brief*, Available from: https://noref.no/Publications/Themes/Gender-and-inclusivity/UNSCR-1325-the-challenges-of-framing-women-s-rights-as-a-security-matter.

Kandiyoti, D. (2004) 'Political fiction meets gender myth: post-conflict reconstruction, "democratisation" and women's rights', *IDS Bulletin*, 35(4): 134–136,

Karim, S. (2017) 'Reevaluating peacekeeping effectiveness: does gender neutrality inhibit progress?', *International Interactions*, 43(5): 822–847.

Kirby, P. (2015) 'Ending sexual violence in conflict: the Preventing Sexual Violence Initiative and its critics', *International Affairs*, 91(3): 457–472.

Kirby, P. and Shepherd, L.J. (2016) 'The futures past of the Women, Peace and Security agenda', *International Affairs*, 92(2): 373–392.

Klot, J. (2002) 'Women and peace processes – an impossible match?', in L. Olsson (ed) *Gender Processes – An Impossible Match*, Uppsala: Collegium of Development Studies, pp 17–23.

Klugman, J., Dahl, M. and Bakken, I.V. (2018) 'The Women, Peace, and Security Index: a global index of women's wellbeing', *PRIO Paper*, Available from: www.prio.org/utility/DownloadFile.ashx?id=1619&type=publicationfile.

Krause, J., Krause, W. and Bränfors, P. (2018) 'Women's participation in peace negotiations and the durability of peace', *International Interactions*, 44(6): 985–1016.

Langhi, Z. (2014) 'Gender and state-building in Libya: towards a politics of inclusion', *Journal of North African Studies*, 19(2): 200–210.

Lee-Koo, K. (2014) 'Implementing Australia's National Action Plan on United Nations Security Council Resolution 1325', *Australian Journal of International Affairs*, 68(3): 300–313.

Lee-Koo, K. (2016) 'Engaging UNSCR 1325 through Australia's National Action Plan', *International Political Science Review*, 37(3): 336–349.

McLeod, L. (2011) 'Configurations of post-conflict: impacts of representations of conflict and post-conflict upon the (political) translations of gender security within UNSCR 1325', *International Feminist Journal of Politics*, 13(4): 594–611.

Merry, S.E. (2016) *The Seductions of Quantification: Measuring Human Rights, Gender Violence, and Sex Trafficking*, Chicago, IL: University of Chicago Press.

Mundkur, A. and Shepherd, L.J. (2018) 'How (not) to make WPS count', *LSE Centre for Women, Peace and Security*, Available from: https://blogs.lse.ac.uk/wps/2018/01/23/how-not-to-make-wps-count/.

Neuwirth, J. (2002) 'Women and Peace and Security: the implementation of U.N. Security Council Resolution 1325', *Duke Journal of Gender, Law and Policy*, 9: 253–260.

Ní Aoláin, F. (2016) 'The "War on Terror" and extremism: assessing the relevance of the Women, Peace and Security agenda', *International Affairs*, 92(2): 275–291.

Ní Aoláin, F. (2019) 'Gutting the substance of a Security Council resolution on sexual violence', *Just Security*, Available from: www.justsecurity.org/63750/gutting-the-substance-of-a-security-council-resolution-on-sexual-violence/.

O'Reilly, M., Ó Súilleabháin, A. and Paffenholz, T. (2015) 'Reimagining peacemaking: women's roles in peace processes', New York: International Peace Institute, Available from: www.ipinst.org/wp-content/uploads/2015/06/IPI-E-pub-Reimagining-Peacemaking.pdf.

Olonisakin, 'F., Barnes, K. and Ikpe, E. (eds) (2011) *Women, Peace and Security: Translating Policy into Practice*, Abingdon: Routledge.

Otto, D. (2009) 'The exile of inclusion: reflections on gender issues in international law over the last decade', *Melbourne Journal of International Law*, 10(1): 11–26.

Otto, D. (2010a) 'The Security Council's alliance of gender legitimacy: the symbolic capital of Resolution 1325', in H. Charlesworth and J.-M. Coicaud (eds) *Fault Lines of International Legitimacy*, Cambridge: Cambridge University Press.

Otto, D. (2010b) 'Power and danger: feminist engagement with international law through the UN Security Council', *Australian Feminist Law Journal*, 32(1): 97–121.

Owen, M. (2011) 'Widowhood issues in the context of United Nations Security Council Resolution 1325', *International Feminist Journal of Politics*, 13(4): 616–622.

Paffenholz, T., Ross, N., Dixon, S., Schluchter, A.-L. and True, J. (2016) 'Making women count – not just counting women: assessing women's inclusion and influence on peace negotiations', Geneva: Inclusive Peace and Transition Initiative (The Graduate Institute of International and Development Studies) and UN Women, Available from: www.inclusivepeace.org/sites/default/files/IPTI-UN-Women-Report-Making-Women-Count-60-Pages.pdf.

Pratt, N. and Richter-Devroe, S. (2011) 'Critically examining UNSCR 1325 on Women, Peace and Security', *International Feminist Journal of Politics*, 13(4): 489–503.

Puechguirbal, N. (2010) 'Discourses on gender, patriarchy and resolution 1325: a textual analysis of UN documents', *International Peacekeeping*, 17(2): 172–187.

Reeves, A. (2012) 'Feminist knowledge and emerging governmentality in UN peacekeeping', *International Feminist Journal of Politics*, 14(3): 348–369.

Reiling, C. (2017) 'Pragmatic scepticism in implementing the Women, Peace and Security agenda', *Global Affairs*, 3(4–5): 469–481.

Reilly, N. (2018) 'Ending impunity for conflict-related sexual violence overwhelmed the UN Women, Peace, and Security agenda: a discursive genealogy', *Violence Against Women*, 24(6): 631–649.

Shawki, N. (2017) 'Implementing the Women, Peace and Security agenda', *Global Affairs*, 3(4–5): 455–467.

Shepherd, L.J. (2008) 'Power and authority in the production of United Nations Security Council Resolution 1325', *International Studies Quarterly*, 52(2): 383–404.

Shepherd, L.J. (2011) 'Sex, security and superhero(in)es: from 1325 to 1820 and beyond', *International Feminist Journal of Politics*, 13(4): 504–521.

Shepherd, L.J. and True, J. (2014) 'The Women, Peace and Security agenda and Australian leadership in the world: from rhetoric to commitment?', *Australian Journal of International Affairs*, 68(3): 257–284.

Simic, O. (2010) 'Does the presence of women really matter? Towards combating male violence in peacekeeping operations', *International Peacekeeping*, 17(2): 188–199.

SIPRI (Stockholm International Peace Research Institute) (2018) 'Global military spending remains high at $1.7 trillion', Available from: www.sipri.org/media/press-release/2018/global-military-spending-remains-high-17-trillion.

Swaine, A. (2017) 'Globalising women, peace and security: trends in National Action Plans', in S. Aroussi (ed) *Rethinking National Action Plans on Women, Peace and Security*, Amsterdam: IOS Press.

True, J. (2016) 'Explaining the global diffusion of the Women, Peace and Security agenda', *International Political Science Review*, 37(3): 307–323.

True, J. (2019) 'Gender research and the study of institutional transfer and norm transmission', in M. Sawer and K. Baker (eds) *Gender Innovation in Political Science: New Norms, New Knowledge*, London: Palgrave Macmillan, pp 135–152.

Tryggestad, T.L. (2009) 'Trick or treat? The UN and implementation of Security Council Resolution 1325 on Women, Peace, and Security', *Global Governance: A Review of Multilateralism and International Organizations*, 15(4): 539–557.

Tryggestad, T.L. (2010) 'The UN Peacebuilding Commission and gender: a case of norm reinforcement', *International Peacekeeping*, 17(2): 159–171.

UN Women (2018) 'Executive Director remarks at the UN Security Council open debate on women, peace and security', Available from: www.unwomen.org/en/news/stories/2018/10/speech-ed-phumzile-security-council-open-debate-on-women-peace-and-security.

United Nations Multi-Partner Trust Fund Office (2019) 'Trust fund factsheet: Women's Peace and Humanitarian Fund', Available from: http://mptf.undp.org/factsheet/fund/GAI00?fund_status_month_to=8&fund_status_year_to=2017.

United Nations Security Council (2005) 'Report of the Secretary-General on Women and Peace and Security', S/2005/636, 10 October, Available from: https://undocs.org/S/2005/636.

United Nations Security Council (2010) 'Women and Peace and Security: Report of the Secretary-General', S/2010/173, 6 April, Available from: https://undocs.org/S/2010/173.

Vess, J., Barker, G., Naraghi-Anderlini, S. and Hassink, A. (2013) 'The other side of gender: men as critical agents of change', United States Institute of Peace Special Report, December, Washington, DC: United States Institute of Peace.

Westendorf, J.-K. (2017) 'WPS, CRSV and sexual exploitation and abuse in peace operations: making sense of the missing links', *LSE Centre for Women, Peace and Security Working Paper Series*, No. 9, Available from: www.lse.ac.uk/women-peace-security/assets/documents/2017/wps9Westendorf.pdf.

Wibben, A. (2014), 'Researching feminist security studies', *Australian Journal of Political Science*, 49(4): 743–755.

Willett, S. (2010) 'Introduction. Security Council Resolution 1325: assessing the impact on Women, Peace and Security', *International Peacekeeping*, 17(2): 142–158.

Wright, K.A.M. (2016) 'NATO's Adoption of UNSCR 1325 on Women, Peace and Security: making the agenda a reality', *International Political Science Review*, 37(3): 350–361.

PART I

Encounters

2

South Sudanese Women on the Move: An Account of the Women, Peace and Security Agenda

Rita M. Lopidia and Lucy Hall

Upon completing her first university degree in 2005, Rita M. Lopidia and seven other women from universities in Sudan came together to form EVE Organization for Women Development. EVE provides skills building, rights awareness and leadership training for young women in South Sudan. Since forming, EVE has broadened its scope to promote women's political participation and advocate for women's voices to be included at the peace table.

In this chapter, Rita M. Lopidia and Lucy Hall discuss Rita's first-hand experience of feminist advocacy on Women, Peace and Security (WPS) in South Sudan and transnationally. Under Rita's leadership EVE has also played a key role in monitoring the implementation of UNSCR 1325 in South Sudan. South Sudan launched its first National Action Plan (NAP) in 2016 for a period of five years (2015–2020).

Lucy Hall (LH):   Rita, I understand that you spent the majority of your childhood in Sudan as an internally displaced person (IDP). Could you tell me about how this inspires your activism?

Rita M. Lopidia (RML):   I was only eight years old when the conflict between the Sudanese government and the Sudan People's Liberation Army (SPLA) intensified in

Juba in the early 1990s. We lived through the horror of continuous shelling, students' riots, demonstrations rejecting Arabization of the curriculum, and the disappearing of civilians at the hands of Sudanese government national intelligence services for allegedly supporting rebels. It was during this period that I started to realize that something was wrong with my country. At the age of 10, I was a restless kid and amid the uprising in town, I decided to join the students' movement at St Joseph's Church in Juba and that was where the spirit of activism in me was nurtured.

My family was eventually displaced to Khartoum where I completed my undergraduate degree. I consider myself privileged to have completed my first degree, given the hardship and discrimination that South Sudanese people faced under the Sudanese government. Some South Sudanese women were not even able to complete their basic education. In 2006, my friends and I founded Eve Organization in Khartoum to support South Sudanese Women.

LH: How does your organization go about monitoring the implementation of UNSCR 1325?

RML: EVE Organization was for the first time introduced to UNSCR 1325 in 2008 by a partner organization from Sweden, Operation 1325. This was two years after the formation of EVE Organization and eight years after the landmark resolution was passed by the Security Council. That was a 'wow' moment for us. As an organization, we worked with displaced women in Khartoum on leadership, disseminating information about the 2005 Comprehensive Peace Agreement (CPA) and supporting women to repatriate to South Sudan, as well as mobilizing women in South Sudan to take part in the Sudan Census in 2008.[1] We were doing this not knowing that UNSCR 1325 existed.

From 2008, Eve Organization utilized UNSCR 1325 as a base for its work – all four of its pillars are relevant to the work we do in the context of South Sudan. We mobilized women in South Sudan to participate in the Sudan Elections in 2010 as well as the South Sudan referendum in 2011. EVE Organization increased awareness on the importance of UNSCR 1325 and called on government institutions at both national and local levels to include WPS-related activities in their programmes.

In partnership with Cordaid and the Global Network of Women Peacebuilders, Eve Organization formed the CSO (civil society organization) working group for monitoring the implementation of UNSCR 1325 in 2012 in order to hold the government, UN, donors and civil society accountable. The objective of monitoring UNSCR 1325 was to collect data and measure the implementation of the resolution in South Sudan, even though at the time South Sudan did not have a NAP. Based on 11 indicators, the monitoring was part of a global civil society initiative called 'Women Count' that was launched on the 10th anniversary of UNSCR 1325. South Sudan was among the 17 countries globally that participated in the Women Count project. These efforts resulted in some small victories for the women of South Sudan, including the development of South Sudan's first UNSCR 1325 NAP in 2015 and the participation of women in the Intergovernmental Authority on Development (IGAD) led South Sudan Peace process from 2014–2018.

LH: What was the role of UNSCR 1325 in ensuring women's access to the peace table?

RML: Although the Security Council directly tasked member states with the responsibility of consolidating and implementing UNSCR 1325, women's organizations in South Sudan took the lead and utilized the resolution as a legal framework to mobilize women to bring to light their plight, as well as demand space at the peace table.

With the return to armed conflict in 2016 and the disastrous impact it had – particularly on women and children – seeking the return to peace and stability is of great interest to the women of South Sudan. This means silencing the guns, protection of women and children, demilitarization of civilian centres, return of IDPs and refugees to their homes, restoration of livelihoods, access to humanitarian services, healing and reparations. Peace and stability, however, cannot be achieved without women's participation at the peace table. When the IGAD announced the High-Level Revitalization

Forum (HLRF) for the resolution of conflict in South Sudan in 2017, EVE Organization mobilized women's organizations and formed the South Sudan Women's Coalition for Peace. We capitalized on UNSCR 1325 as an advocacy tool to get access to the peace table in Addis Ababa, Ethiopia. Utilizing the principles and the four pillars of UNSCR 1325, members of the coalition, who were accredited delegates to the process and eventually signatories, together with other women in the process, pushed for gender provisions to be included in the revitalized agreement.

The resulting Revitalized Agreement on the Resolution of Conflict in South Sudan (R-ARCSS) signed in September 2018 included the following gender gains. In Chapter I, 'The Transitional Government', article 1.4.4 calls for a quota of 35% women representatives at all levels of governance. Initially this quota was 25%. Article 1.5.2 states that during the Transitional Period, there shall be four Vice Presidents of the Republic of South Sudan, and article 1.5.2.4 ensures that one of these four Vice Presidents is a woman. Articles 1.14.3 and 1.14.5 calls for the two deputy speakers of the upper and lower houses of the Transitional National Legislative assembly (TNLA) to be women. Chapter II, 'Permanent Ceasefire and Transitional Security Arrangements' prohibits acts and forms of sexual violence and gender-based violence, including sexual exploitation and harassment, calls for the protection of the needs of women and girls, and the demilitarization of civilian areas (articles 2.1.10.2, 2.1.10.7.5 and 2.2.3.1).

In Chapter IV, 'Resource, Economic and Financial Management', article 4.15.1.5 calls for the establishment of the Women Enterprise Development Fund. In Chapter V, 'Transitional Justice, Accountability, Reconciliation and Healing', article 5.1.1 calls for the establishment of the Commission for Truth, Reconciliation and Healing, an independent hybrid judicial body (to be known as the Hybrid Court for South Sudan) and the Compensation and Reparation Authority. Both the Commission for Truth, Reconciliation and Healing and the Compensation and Reparation Authority are required to ensure that 35% of representatives on these mechanisms are women. These institutions are tasked with the implementation of Chapter V, and article 5.3.2.1.4 states that the Hybrid Court for South Sudan shall have jurisdiction with respect to 'other serious crimes under international law and relevant laws of South Sudan, *including gender based crimes and sexual violence*'.

The R-ARCSS framework also provides for women's participation in the different implementation mechanisms of the agreement, including i) the National Pre-Transition Committee (NPTC), ii) the Revitalized National Constitution Amendment Committee (R-NCAC), iii) the Board of the Ceasefire and Transitional Security Arrangements Monitoring and Verification Mechanism (CTSAMVM), iv) The Board of the Strategic Defence and Security Review (SDSR), and v) the Revitalized Joint Monitoring and Evaluation Commission (R-JMEC).

LH: South Sudan's NAP was designed to ensure that a gender perspective is integrated into the design and implementation of all policies related to peace and security. How would you evaluate progress on this so far?

RML: South Sudan adopted its first UNSCR 1325 NAP 2015–2020 subsequent to the endorsement by the Council of Ministers in October 2015. It was developed following a vigorous participatory process. Officially launched in May 2016, the NAP covers three main strategic goals: i) increasing women's effective participation in peacebuilding and reconstruction; ii) supporting security sector reforms to implement the resolution; and iii) making efforts to prevent and protect women and girls against any form of violence. Nonetheless, operationalizing the NAP to address the daily realities of women in South Sudan in the context of ongoing conflict faces a number of challenges.

First, right from its inception, the South Sudan UNSCR 1325 NAP lacked a finance strategy to aid its implementation. While the Ministry of Gender is a lead ministry in the implementation of the NAP, other line ministries such as the Ministries of Finance, Interior, Justice and Foreign Affairs, and the Office of the President were also supposed to co-lead. However, this did not materialize and the weight of responsibility is left with the Ministry of Gender, which receives less funding than other ministries. This has hindered the rigorous implementation of the NAP and, just like other gender-related policies and frameworks, the NAP remains shelved with no clear commitment from the government.

Second, the timing of the launch of the NAP was both a challenge and an opportunity. It happened during turbulent times following the formation of the Transitional Government in 2016. Less than two months following its launch, South Sudan slipped into conflict again. This period was a litmus test for the government's commitment to the NAP. The government had the opportunity to use the NAP to show its commitment to protect women and girls; unfortunately, the world witnessed some of the most gruesome atrocities committed against women and girls in our times.

Third, with the return to violence, it is clear that the NAP was not among the priorities of the government. The belief that victory can be achieved through the barrel of the gun results in the largest amounts of government spending going into defence.

On the other hand, CSOs working on women, peace and security utilized the NAP for advocacy and to implement projects on peace, countering gender-based violence, justice, education and humanitarian aid for women and girls.

Personally, if I were to evaluate the progress of the state of South Sudan in the implementation of the NAP, I would say that it is a disappointment. If we assess the situation of women and girls in South Sudan before and after the launch of the NAP, looking at key aspects such as access to basic services relating to health, education and jobs, protection and security of women, food security and livelihood, level of participation in governance and in communities, it is obvious that the situation now is more appalling than before. This NAP's lifespan is until 2020. For any future NAP to usher in the much-needed reforms to genuinely construct meaningful opportunities for women's socio-political empowerment and for the protection of women and girls from violence, the government needs to demonstrate the necessary political will and commitment to spearhead the WPS agenda in South Sudan. Then, development partners and civil society will follow.

LH: I understand your organization works across several geographic areas, locally, nationally, transnationally and regionally. How do gender politics change depending on your location?

RML: EVE Organization operates in South Sudan and Uganda. In South Sudan we operate in five of the former ten states of South Sudan, namely Central Equatoria, Eastern Equatoria, Jongolei State, Western Bahr el Ghazal and Western Equatoria. In Uganda, we are basically engaged in the West Nile where most of the refugee settlements are located.

Across both contexts, gender politics do not differ much. In South Sudan, for instance, where patriarchy is deeply entrenched, most communities still view women largely as caregivers and men as breadwinners, providers of protection and decision makers in the family and community. Boys' education is preferred over that of girls', and early and forced marriages are part of social and cultural norms. Control over women is considered a patriarchal right. This is further demonstrated during conflict as armed groups demonstrate their might, control and defeat of enemies, by uprooting families, intimidating and abducting women and children and inflicting pain, particularly on women and girls. The socio-political sphere is male dominated, and the women who are involved in politics are still relegated to political positions and institutions that reflect their domestic roles of caregiving and nurturing.

In the Midwest and the West Nile, places where EVE Organization operates in Uganda, the situation of women and girls is not so different, as the northern part of Uganda is still recovering from the consequence of war. Women still face gender inequalities and limited access to basic rights and opportunities. The political sphere is mostly dominated by men at the district level and women occupy lower positions. Our projects in refugee settlements also include the host communities to enhance peaceful co-existence and social cohesion.

LH: Please tell me about bilateral meetings with Missions to the UN, meetings with members of the Security Council, and your experience briefing the Security Council.

RML: Nobody will tell your story better than you. Since the start of conflict in South Sudan in 2013, EVE Organization has been reaching out to the Security Council and its member states, as well as other missions to the UN to seek international involvement in the resolution of the conflict in South Sudan. In the case of knotty issues such as the conflict in South Sudan, in which regional and international interests play a significant role, it is rare to find direct solutions from the Security Council. However, the Security Council still has a voice in shaping the global agenda and responding to global issues.

Our advocacy efforts and interests at the Security Council include i) keeping the conflict in South Sudan and in particular the plight of the women of South Sudan in the spotlight and a priority on the global agenda; ii) calling on the Security Council to take tougher measures on parties to the conflict who continue to target civilians and in particular violate human rights and perpetrate violence, including sexual violence against women and girls; iii) calling for increased women's participation in the South Sudan peace process, as well as provision of support to women's organizations; and iv) seeking increased humanitarian aid for displaced civilians.

I have personally addressed the Security Council on the situation of women in South Sudan, and other countries in conflict such as Syria, Yemen and Colombia. I also participated in an Arria Formula meeting on sexual violence in 2018. Furthermore, we have held numerous bilateral meetings with different missions and particularly those with interest in South Sudan, including African Representatives to the Security Council.

Not all the meetings were productive, though. Often it depended on the interest of the mission. Some do not have a clue about what is happening on the ground while others treat it as a Twitter opportunity on South Sudan. One frustrating experience my team encountered was that their photo was circulated on social media without their consent. Nonetheless, regardless of the outcome, advocacy and lobbying the Security Council remains central to bringing issues of women in conflict areas closer to the corridors where major global decisions are taken.

LH: Do you envision a relationship between WPS and UNSCR 2250 on Youth, Peace and Security?

RML: Oh yes, there is a huge relationship between the two. At the beginning of UNSCR 2250, the Security Council recalled all the WPS resolutions and urged member states to give youth a greater voice in decision making at all levels as well as to develop mechanisms to allow youth to participate in peace processes. Young women should take advantage of both resolutions to claim their spaces at local, national, regional and global levels.

Globally, youth form the largest population and account for most civilians affected by armed conflict. In South Sudan for instance, 70% of the total population are youth under the age of 30 (UNESCO, 2019). However, you do not see young people in the corridors of power or taking part in making decisions that affect their lives. The youth are marginalized and face a lot of issues such as unemployment and high levels of illiteracy. Many become social deviants out of frustration. Old politicians use the youth to fight their wars and when it comes to decision making and getting a seat to participate at the peace table, they are told, 'your time is not now'.

This is even worse for young women and girls. They are particularly disadvantaged, as many have been displaced from their homes, have dropped out of school, been subjected to early marriage, and experienced a lot of peer pressure due to a lack of programmes and opportunities to educate them and help them to overcome some of these barriers. According to the latest UNESCO Institute of Statistics, the literacy rate among women in the age group of 15–24 years is 29.58% (UNESCO, 2019). At EVE Organization, we are very enthusiastic about empowering young women. I was 22 years old when we co-founded EVE Organization. Launched in 2018, our project, the Young Women Leadership Program – dubbed the 'Incubator' – draws from both the WPS resolutions and UNSCR 2250 on Youth, Peace and Security to develop the skills of young women in South Sudan.

LH: How would you describe the main obstacles for women's meaningful participation in the politics of peace?

RML: Instead of focusing on obstacles to women's participation in the politics of peace, I will identify the lessons learnt based on my experience in the South Sudan peace processes.

First, peace processes are fast-paced, male-dominated, and a harsh and hostile environment. One male delegate told me 'if you can't stand insults, then the peace table is not a space for you ... you should be in the church'. Warring parties perceive women as unimportant actors, because we do not carry guns and are hence less powerful. To ensure women's voices are heard, in the case of South Sudan, we had to assert ourselves.

Second, numbers matter. During the South Sudan HLRF, only a handful of women were invited in their personal capacity as experts and were repeatedly reminded of that. However, women organized and formed the South Sudan Women's Coalition for Peace, and once we got access, we lobbied for more space for other women and requested that our technical support team be given access. This helped us to spread messages across different avenues.

Third, it is very crucial to understand the context, the trends and timing of events. Planning in advance and being conceptually clear on what you table and the solutions you suggest increase credibility.

Fourth, creating allies within the process is of the utmost importance. Knowing what you can push and what you can request your allies to push for during negotiations is crucial. Women cannot do it alone. Besides you might not have the time or be given the floor to table all your issues.

Fifth, advocacy and lobbying at an early stage as well as throughout the process with parties, partners and diplomatic missions go a long way.

Sixth, resources and funds are very important. You need to raise adequate resources to be able to move from point A to B – logistics are crucial for women's effective participation. For instance, the HLRF was convened in Addis Ababa, Ethiopia. In order to participate, the women's coalition technical team needed tickets, visas and accommodation throughout the process.

Seventh, the vulnerability of women activists needs to be addressed. It is important to have some sort of protection strategy. Once you are vocal and expose the reality, you invite threats against yourself. What are the measures in place to protect women's rights activists? One strategy we successfully used in South Sudan, when we organized a women's march against sexual violence in December 2017, was that all women's organizations and activists remained anonymous in the crowd. No one knew the organizers of the march, and when the national security summoned a few individuals, all the other women from the march also showed up at their office.

Finally, be ready for backlash. Gains in peace processes are fragile. These should be carefully guarded and monitored through the implementation phase when real stuff happens.

Note

[1] The CPA, also known as the Naivasha Agreement, was an accord signed on 9 January 2005 by the the Government of The Republic of The Sudan and the Sudan People's Liberation Movement/Sudan People's Liberation Army.

References

UNESCO (2019) 'Revision to South Sudan's Youth Policy continue with support of parliamentarians', UNESCO Office in Juba, Available from: www.unesco.org/new/en/juba/about-this-office/single-view/news/revisions_to_south_sudans_youth_policy_continue_with_supp/.

UNESCO Institute for Statistics (2019) 'South Sudan', Available from: http://uis.unesco.org/country/SS.

3

The Price of Peace? Frictional Encounters on Gender, Security and the 'Economic Peace Paradigm'

Nicole George

Efforts to lift women's economic participation have recently become a more pronounced aspect of international assistance for post-conflict restoration. This has occurred as part of a growing economic orientation in liberal peacebuilding practice, reflecting what some have called the 'economic peace paradigm'. This paradigm for contemporary peacebuilding seeks to transform post-conflict economies to adopt a market orientation, assuming that more interdependent and cooperative trade and exchange relations between states and communities can temper the potential for hostile encounters. It is further argued that this approach increases economic growth within conflict-affected states and communities in ways that ensure that wealth is shared and the potential for marginalization and violence is diminished (Ydesen and Verschaeve, 2019, p 482).

Global discourse on the need to make women's economic participation a stronger focus of women, peace and security claim this will further enhance the dividends of the economic peace paradigm. For example, UN Women's 2015 global study on the implementation of UNSCR 1325 stated that the most successful cases of peaceful conflict transition occurred where women had achieved high levels of economic integration and were able to direct spending towards the needs of family and dependents and thus strengthen social cohesion (Coomaraswamy et al, 2015, p 171). A recent framing of this argument in a publication for the Georgetown Institute for Women Peace and Security went even further, contending that 'women's economic empowerment strengthens women's rights and grants them increased control over their own lives, allows them to better provide for their families, and contributes to the advancement of their communities and societies' (Hudock et al, 2016).

Curiously, these claims are rarely subjected to grounded scrutiny and often seem to be reproduced uncritically. In this chapter, I argue that it is important to question the apparent blind faith in women's capacities to generate peace and security in a 'trickle-up' fashion for themselves, their family and their broader communities because they are actively integrated within the cash economy, and ignore the rather more complex gendered realities that shape women's lives in post-conflict contexts. Drawing from research into women's experiences of peacebuilding in the Pacific Islands countries of Bougainville and Solomon Islands, I show that increased understanding is required not only of the practical limitations, but also the emplaced worldviews of conflict-affected peoples, so that we might more accurately assess where and how women are positioned within post-conflict economies and the kinds of opportunities and constraints that shape their economic participation.

I am particularly motivated to demonstrate the problems that can accrue if we simply assume that women are economically inactive, and we pay insufficient attention to the ways that women may be situated within place-based networks of exchange guided by their own relational logics. As I will demonstrate, more attention given to the 'indigenous economic logics [that] shape contemporary economic practices and values' – what Gina Koczberski and others have termed 'relational economies' or 'economics of place' (Curry and Koczberski, 2012; Curry et al, 2012, p 119) – provide important insights into the nature of women's economic relations and economic power and the dangers of uncritically accepting that the liberal language of economic rights can be linked to the peacebuilding enterprise in ways that will always be beneficial to women.

Approaching the issue of women's economic participation in this way requires us to take seriously the idea that modalities of exchange are not the same in all parts of the world and that when we make efforts to link economic participation and peacebuilding we need to appreciate how economic exchange is practised to progress collective goals and ambitions as well as individual ones. In this vein, we might look sceptically at those programmes of peacebuilding that assume that women will be swept up in an 'inevitable and linear transformation of indigenous

societies' so that they are passively incorporated into globalized economies (Curry et al, 2012, p 115). Instead, we might recognize the
presence of diverse economic principles, logics and institutions. These
may generate and reinforce forms of economic value beyond the realm
of markets or finance and that may be rooted in notions of 'emotional
well-being and life satisfaction' (Curry and Koczberski, 2012, p 379).
Of course, they may reinscribe their own gendered hierarchies and
forms of gendered obligation too and should not be romanticized as
more appropriate or more empowering for women.

By focusing upon the ways that these economic logics are present in
post-conflict environments, my objective is to expose both the opportunities and constraints that market economy integration offers women.
Abilities to participate in the cash economy may enable women to
consolidate relational connections with kin, community and the environment and thus facilitate obligations within the relational economy
(McKinnon et al, 2016). Nonetheless, I am cautious about the weight
of gendered obligation within this framework. I therefore also consider how access to cash can be a trigger for violence and see coercive
pressure put upon women to adhere to relational obligations in ways
that simply add yet another layer of gendered burden to the heavy
load that women, in the field sites I have studied, tend to shoulder.

My overall contention, therefore, is that much greater effort is
required to examine, rather than to glibly go along with, the assumption
that there is a peace dividend that accrues from women's economic
participation. Further, we need to critically engage with the claim
that with their increased integration into the market-based economy,
women become selfless distributors of wealth within their familial and
kinship networks and the broader society, a claim that tends to ignore
the gendered coercion that may often produce this result. To develop
this analysis, I focus on the 'frictions' that are generated when grounded
everyday economic practices and liberal economic programming
measures intersect in the peacebuilding context. Here I am guided
by Björkdahl and Höglund's use of 'friction' as a lens which facilitates
study of the outcomes, or in their terms, the 'light and heat', that are
generated when 'ideas and norms' prevailing in global policy discourse
on peace and security are taken up and reframed to fit local contexts
(Björkdahl, 2012, p 293; Björkdahl and Höglund, 2013).

These ideas provide an analytical framework for my own interest in
understanding how and why particular visions of a post-conflict economic order are privileged and predominate globally and how those
visions land in everyday, local spaces and are made sense of, embraced
or resisted. My contention is that the focus on frictions allows for a

closer appreciation of where and how efforts to localize the economic peace paradigm may produce gains for women, but equally allow for an investigation of the outcomes that are more contradictory, unexpected, or ultimately the cause of insecurity for women.

The chapter progresses in three stages. In the first section I reflect on the logics that support the 'economic peace paradigm' as a critical component of liberal peacebuilding and examine where and how this intersects with feminist debate on the links between women's economic security and peace. In the next section, I discuss how these programmes are typically delivered in post-conflict contexts, drawing on my familiarity with practices in the Pacific Islands. Here I develop the analytical concept of friction in more detail, showing how this lens affords a more critical appreciation of the ways that liberal logics of market and commodity transaction rub against logics of place-based and relational exchange. I then apply this lens to examine the challenges that shadow efforts to progress women's economic participation as part of broader conflict transition processes in the region. I conclude with reflections on the hidden price of peace, as it is borne by women in the research sites I have studied and, on this basis, defend a call for far more nuanced and critical feminist debate on the presumed gendered exclusions of the 'economic peace paradigm'.

Gendering the economic peace paradigm

In recent years, growing attention has been focused on the idea that when efforts are made to improve women's economic participation, an appreciable peace dividend within the conflict-affected community will result. This interest is encouraged by, and harmonizes with, broader trends in peacebuilding which emphasize economic recovery as a critical goal for the achievement of a peace that will be durable. The origins of what Ydesen and Verschaeve term the 'economic peace paradigm' (2019, p 477) stretches back to the 1700s and Montesquieu's Spirit of Laws which established the long enduring international expectation that trade between states is civilizing, reduces the likelihood that they will become hostile to one another, and inclines everyday people from locations linked by trade to relate more generously to one another. Later recognition of the devastating economic cost that states incur by waging war (Angell, 1910) also helped sustain the idea that armed conflict is illogical and that economically strong states are generally also peaceful ones. The 'greed and grievance' explanation of conflict promoted by Collier and Hoeffler (2004), provided further impetus to the economic peace paradigm, linking economic marginalization with conflict-related violence and economic stability with peace. While later subjected to contestation, it is commonly accepted today that although 'poverty, inequality and underdevelopment may not in themselves cause armed conflict and human rights abuses, ... they can be contributing or enabling factors' (Ní Aoláin et al, 2011, p 257).

For all these reasons, contemporary liberal peacebuilding agendas, as well as international financial institutions such as the OECD and the World Bank, place considerable emphasis upon economic recovery as a vital element of conflict transition programming, alongside restoration of democratic institutions of the state (Richmond, 2009; True and Svedberg, 2019). The assumption is that when the economy is stable, and the conditions for interdependent trade are enabled, localized economic growth and increased wealth will also follow; this wealth can be shared, reducing the potential for marginalization and violence (Ydesen and Verschaeve, 2019, p 482).

Gender analysis of efforts to encourage economic growth in post-conflict sites rightly demonstrates, however, that even though economic investment is quick to return and 'new' opportunities for growth become known, these conditions rarely offer direct benefit to women. While the Women, Peace and Security (WPS) agenda has emphasized 'participation' as one of its four pillars, conflict transition programming has tended to emphasize women's participation in decision making over efforts to increase women's economic participation. Thus, the 2015 UN Women report on implementation of the WPS policy agenda showed that economic investment directly aimed at assisting women's economic participation constituted only 2% of total investment funds to assist economic restoration in the wake of conflict or an annual total of US $2 billion (Coomaraswamy et al, 2015, p 171). In protesting this, the report stressed the importance of women's economic contributions to peace and security, and cited the UN Peacebuilding Commission's 2013 declaration which affirmed that where women are economically empowered, sustainable post-conflict economic development becomes more likely (Coomaraswamy et al, 2015, p 171). The report further stated that women are more likely to spend money in ways that contribute to social cohesion and recovery because their spending is focused on their own security and that of families (Coomaraswamy et al, 2015, p 171). It also stated that some of the most successful cases of post-conflict economic recovery owe success, in part, to the 'increased role' undertaken by women in 'production, trade and entrepreneurship' (Coomaraswamy, 2015, p 172).

This hopeful outlook on the benefits of women's economic participation owes much to the influential work of development economist and capabilities theorist Amartya Sen, who has long advocated the importance of women's economic participation as a means by which to enhance general levels of wellbeing and opportunity. For Sen, benefits from economic participation do not only accrue to women and their families in an immediate sense, but rather, also ensure the future wellbeing of dependents. In Sen's formulation, this is because women's earning is said to enable children to attain higher levels of education and improve their chances of accessing meaningful employment as adults (Sen, 2001). Sen's findings have influenced the direction of a range of later gender and development studies which show that when women are in control of household finances, there is a stronger likelihood that funds are spent to promote their 'family's interests' (Ní Aoláin, 2011, p 260).

These arguments point to the ways in which families and even societies might benefit if women's earning potential is improved. But questions remain as to the kinds of gendered burdens that are naturalized or obscured in this analysis. For example, countless feminist researchers have taken issue with Sen's claims about the benefits of women's economic activity, demonstrating that labour markets are far from immune to the gendered discriminations and prejudices that circulate globally and locally and these shape, and are embedded in, market economies (see, for example, Elson and Pearson, 2011; Rai and Waylen, 2013; Mohanty, 2011). Thus even though women's employment may be an important source of economic security for families, gender discriminatory influences within society also mean that women's earnings are commonly less than male workers, as is their employment status. They have also shown that women's employment remains largely demarcated by gender, with women ghettoized in low-waged, labour-intensive, casualized and insecure sectors. Although efforts are underway to open up non-traditional employment sectors to women around the globe, this in no way ensures that women are recognized as gender-equal in these professions, nor does it eradicate the risk that women will be subjected to everyday forms of gendered discrimination as well as more serious incidents of gendered and sexualized abuse (see, for example, Miller, 2004; Alvinius and Holmberg, 2019). Add to this the fact that economically-active women frequently also shoulder a double- or triple-labour burden of paid work, unpaid reproductive labour and civil society activity (often absorbing community welfare needs formally provisioned by the state), and the peace dividend that is assumed to accrue from women's economic activity starts to look like just one more gendered responsibility to be added to the list of obligations that women already shoulder (see, for example, Lind, 2011).

These arguments are well-rehearsed in the fields of feminist political economy and feminist development studies but are too rarely allowed to disrupt claims made about the need to 'gender' the liberal 'economic peace paradigm' by promoting women's economic participation (Ní Aoláin et al, 2011, p 255). Likewise, little attention is given to the particular difficulties that women might experience in navigating gendered logics of the post-conflict environment so that they can safely take advantage of economic 'opportunities' created through economic restoration processes. This is so even when, during the conflict period, women may have assumed increased responsibility as heads of households, supporting families while male breadwinners are involved in fighting or if they become casualties.

Feminist investigation of conflict transition contexts shows that in times of 'peace', women's capacity to absorb 'new identities untethered from prior gender constraints' can prove challenging (Ní Aoláin et al, 2011, p 261). Women's abilities to support dependents during conflict, and into a later period of conflict transition, may not be celebrated as evidence of women's resourcefulness, and may even become a source of resentment and shame for male family members who assume that economic authority, and the status that goes with that, should accrue naturally to them (Lwambo, 2013). Likewise, women's economic autonomy may come into tension with gendered ideas about the requirement to protect women from perceived threats; a masculine ethos of gendered control that, as Iris Marion Young (2003) has shown, is frequently intensified in conflict-affected societies. In these contexts, norms about gender-appropriate behaviour can become hardened and more restrictive and the risks of women becoming exposed to disciplinary violence if they do not subordinate themselves to the ethos of masculine protection can increase. Women whose work requires independent movement through areas where 'enemy' groups live or work, or perhaps involves close proximity to men, may be viewed as flouting this protective ethos or even actively 'inviting' violence from those within or beyond their immediate community because their actions are equated with gendered dissidence.

Thus, the extent to which conflict 'scrambles women's roles (positively and negatively)' needs careful analysis when we consider the supposed benefits of integrating women into the economic peace paradigm (Ní Aoláin et al, 2011, p 261). This requires attention paid not just to rates of women's economic participation that are evident in societies and states transitioning from conflict, but also to the meaning of that participation as it is understood by women themselves and the members of their family and community. In this way it is possible to gain a fuller picture of where women are present or absent in economic activity, as well as an appreciation of how that activity is understood within households and communities, and what all that might mean with regards to women's capacities to consolidate peace more generally.

In order to examine the gendered outcomes of peacebuilding, I have found it analytically productive to focus on the gendered frictions that are generated when international actors look to localize their initiatives designed to advance the standing of women as part of a broader post-conflict restoration agenda. This work has been inspired by Annika Björkdahl's collaborative scholarship with Johanna Mannergren Selimovic and Kristine Höglund (Björkdahl, 2012; Björkdahl and Höglund, 2013; Björkdahl and Mannergren Selimovic, 2015) which has theorized the frictional processes and agency of peace localizers (non-government organizations, peace activists, religious leaders, individuals) who take 'ideas and norms in the liberal peace' and attempt to 'reframe them ... in terms that are acceptable in the local context' (Björkdahl, 2012, 293). These frictional outcomes are shaped by variables that include the 'persuasiveness and resonance of the global norms' that are introduced in a particular context, the standing of peace localizers in the broader social, cultural and political hierarchy, and the 'attractiveness of the notions of peace derived from the local context' (Björkdahl, 2012, p 293). While Björkdahl describes the 'light and heat' outcomes that become illuminated as a result of this frictional interplay between local and external peacebuilding influences, I have additionally argued that it is important to understand the ways in which this process can also shadow and obscure other aspects of the conflict transition terrain (George, 2016).

In the following sections, I deploy this analytical lens to illustrate how frictions are generated that create light and heat that illuminates certain aspects of women's economic activity but also cast shadows over other sorts of economic exchange so that their importance in women's life is obscured from general view. To do this, I draw from research I have undertaken on gender and peacebuilding in two Pacific Island locations, Bougainville, an autonomous region of Papua New Guinea, and Solomon Islands. The objective is to explain how efforts to gender economic peace are received in socio-cultural contexts where relational networks of exchange – which have been described as 'economies of place' – are also considered important and where women may have to navigate particular obligations.

Gender, markets and economies of place

In much of the work I have done with women in conflict transition contexts in the Pacific Islands, the challenges of gendered economic disadvantage emerge as a key concern, with many women expressing their frustrations about high levels of economic marginalization. These frustrations are often misunderstood by those without first hand contemporary familiarity with this part of the world, because they contradict orientalist 'Garden of Eden' tropes that since colonial times have tended to encourage a view that Pacific Island states are places of natural abundance and easy lifestyles. These ideas are routinely depicted in present-day romantic tourist representations of the region, but were also a regular feature of 18th century expedition reports on Pacific voyages that were to precipitate later European colonization of the region (Smith, 1984). As Fiji's prominent feminist economist Claire Slatter has shown, regional economic analysis undertaken by international financial institutions such as the World Bank, continued to promote the view – well into the 1990s – that the indolence of Pacific peoples, and their political leaders' general disinclination to enthusiastically embrace liberal principles of economic growth and free trade, was a problem for the region (Slatter, 1994). Slatter's critical response is that these assessments tend to underestimate the way that Pacific peoples measure wellbeing. She goes on to argue that some political leaders, and many everyday people, reject the benefits of 'economic growth' as an abstract objective not because of indolence but because they are suspicious of individual wealth accumulation that occurs in ways that undermine kin and communal distribution networks, or 'community-based terrestrial and marine resource-use systems' (Slatter, 1994, pp 26–27). Samoan theologian Upolu Vaai has argued similarly that 'reward' in Oceanic thinking is experienced not through adherence to neoliberal models of 'detached individualism' (Rasumussen, 1993, cited in Vaai, 2017, p 25), but rather through 'the promotion and maintaining of life' that enables people to flourish as part of their community, rather than at its expense (Vaai, 2017, p 27).

These contentions are taken seriously in research that has aimed to understand how market-based models of economic transaction exist alongside other modalities of economic behaviour in the Pacific region. These studies have shed critical light upon assumptions that communally-oriented, non-market relationships of exchange are erased or subsumed by market-based modernities (Curry et al, 2012, p 115). The argument here is that alongside the logics of individualized ownership and wealth accumulation that are intrinsic to market-based economic development, the presence of relational modes of economic exchange based on alternative logics of 'reciprocity', 'sharing of wealth', easy 'incorporation of outsiders' and consolidation of 'indigenous exchange relationships' continue because they are deemed critical to the 'proper functioning of the local polity' (Curry et al, 2012, p 121).

It is important to state here that attempts to understand and analyse these alternative logics of exchange, what Curry, Koczberski and Connell (2012) term 'economies of place', should not occur in ways that underplay the significance of the cash economy nor the experiences of material deprivation that are lived by Pacific peoples. The seasonal abundance of many staple foods often means that food security challenges are underestimated in the region. But crop yields are also dependent on labour-intensive forms of cultivation (often done by women and children, but also requiring the support of men) and subject to the climatic variations – flood, drought, sea-level rise and cyclone – that are becoming more frequently reported and more intense in this region. In contexts where extractive industries such as mining, logging and fishing have been established, food security may be further diminished as a result of unsustainable environmental practices. And in urban areas, and particularly for the inhabitants of the large squatter settlements that ring most urban concentrations in the Pacific Islands, access to food gardens, or coastal areas for fishing, can be more difficult. These communities are far more likely to rely on food items available for purchase, usually from local markets and shops and often at elevated prices. Beyond the purchase of food, access to cash is also required to pay for medicines, for materials to support children's education, for the costs of transportation and the purchase of manufactured goods (such as clothing) as well as any commodities that are imported to the region. While networks of communal obligation and exchange may therefore be critical to Pacific Islanders' wellbeing, this does not occur in ways that negate their need for access to cash.

Neither should it be assumed that principles of equality and justice are more effectively or 'naturally' safeguarded within systems of exchange that emphasize communal obligation and land management. Upolu Vaai contends that while there is often a strong emphasis placed upon relationality and communal thinking as a foundation of Pacific cultures, this can result in 'vulgar relativisms' and an 'anything goes in Pacific cultures' attitude that legitimizes the 'suppression of people and their lands' (Vaai, 2017, p 32) and violence perpetrated against 'men, women and children' (Vaai, 2017, p 28). Relational thinking is therefore critical for the progression of wellbeing in Pacific communities, says Vaai, but only when it rejects oppression as a phenomenon that has both external and domestic origins in Pacific Islands communities and commits to upholding the 'intrinsic dignity and value of the "many"' (Vaai, 2017, p 24).

With all of these caveats in place, however, appreciation of the central importance of relational modes of transaction or economies of place is critical if we are to fully understand the frictions that are generated through efforts to gender the economic peace paradigm in Pacific Island contexts and create opportunities to promote women's integration into market based economies. As I will explain next, women's earnings may very well be spent in ways that fulfil the needs of dependents and thus contribute to a consolidation of familial and kinship wellbeing, in line with the expectations that are articulated globally about the peace dividends that accrue from women's economic integration. Moreover, those women may indeed be proud and happy to do this, and their status within the family and the community may be increased as a result. But my observations of women's economic participation have also led me to understand that in some conflict-affected contexts, this behaviour is produced because it is expected. Women distribute their earnings to family, kin and even the community because they are expected to uphold particular kinds of obligations to family and kin according to the protocols of economies of place, and that coercion, threats and actual violence restricts their capacity to do otherwise. In these cases, the assumed peace dividend that accrues from women's earning is not one that is paid voluntarily by women, but is produced in ways that undermine individual women's wellbeing.

Gendering the economic peace paradigm in context

The idea that women's entrepreneurship can be beneficial for peacebuilding has travelled to the Pacific as part of the broader liberal peacebuilding machinery that has guided international efforts to assist conflict transition efforts in Solomon Islands and Bougainville. The influence of this agenda is found, for example, in a recent World Bank report on women's entrepreneurship in Solomon Islands that uncritically reiterates claims circulating in international peacebuilding circles about the benefits that accrue not just to women but also to 'their families, communities and ultimately the country as a whole' when they achieve higher levels of economic empowerment (World Bank, 2011, p 20).

The challenge of building this participation is hampered in part by the fact that low numbers of female students progress through the school system in both countries and even fewer undertake tertiary education. Current statistics show that in Solomon Islands only 5% of female students complete secondary education to Form 6/7 level and only 0.4% of the country's women hold tertiary degrees (SINSO, 2014). In Bougainville these numbers are slightly improved but still low with 20% of female students completing secondary school and 7% going on to achieve university qualifications (National Statistical Office 2010). This helps to explain why in Solomon Islands women make up only 32.8% of the waged workforce (World Bank 2012) and in Bougainville only 24% of women participate in waged employment (National Statistical Office, 2010). In the squatter settlements of Honiara, the Solomon Islands capital, this number falls even further with only 18.2% of women engaged in paid employment (World Bank, 2012).

In both countries, women in paid employment have reported harsh conditions and exposure to discriminatory treatment, harassment and gendered aggression, push factors which, aside from lack of educational opportunities, also encourage women to engage in informal enterprises as an alternative means by which to access cash income (World Bank, 2012, p 27; Sharp et al, 2015, p 7). This home-based or informal income generation activity is widespread and sees women seeking to build cash earning through small-scale catering ventures, sewing, handicraft production and market trade in agricultural products such as food, vegetables and betel nut. Regional statistics suggest that roughly three quarters of economically-active women in Solomon Islands and Bougainville access cash through this kind of work. But it is a precarious form of economic participation that is generally low status, and brings women little income for its long hours and arduous conditions, and with few prospects to build increased return (Pollard 2000).

For these reasons, development programmes such as 'Markets for Change', supported by UN Women in selected Pacific Islands countries for close to a decade, have sought to increase the business acumen of women market traders as well as improving market infrastructure in urban centres to make them more secure and hospitable for women traders (UN Women (Pacific), 2011). In Honiara, the Markets for Change programme has also sought to integrate women more strongly into the post-conflict economic restoration process, and women market traders have been encouraged to form market-traders' associations so that they are better placed to advocate collectively for improved facilities and more just treatment from market managers who in some sites have engaged in corrupt practices (personal communication Honiara, October 2016).

Simultaneously, programmes on business development are also offered to women small-scale traders to improve their entrepreneurship capacities and to encourage women to think of themselves as 'small business owners'. These programmes include workshops in business skills for women traders, and are frequently delivered by small-business educators from Australia such as Australian Business Volunteers who run mentorship programmes for local participants and offer them advice (World Bank, 2011). However, my discussions with some local participants who have attended these sessions revealed that women can find these to be dispiriting experiences. Participants are given many ideas about how to plan and grow their businesses, but trainers seem to underestimate the limitations of the prevailing economic environment and the challenges women face in accessing start-up capital and affordable materials to supply their businesses. They also underestimate the general population's low capacities for economic consumption beyond everyday essentials. One woman from Honiara in the Solomon Islands had attended many of these sessions and described them to me as depressing: 'The trainers fill my head full of ideas about what I can do, but I look around me and realise I can't do any of it.' The challenge, as she explained, lay in the fact that she struggled to access the kinds of source materials needed to produce something innovative to sell beyond the usual food items that were sold by countless other women with market stalls. She also struggled to find customers with the kind of disposable income that would allow her to make a reasonable return from her labour.

Richard Eves' research on women's market participation in Bougainville has observed similar challenges (Eves et al, 2018). This work also uncovered a range of insecurities that are borne by economically-active women too, as they seek to manage the demands of their retail work and the expectations of family and kin-groups. In this context as well, 'marketing', as women's small-scale retail businesses are locally known, involves the sale of food-garden produce, small store-bought goods and cooked food. But, as Eves shows, women's earnings from this work frequently inflame tensions rather than bring peace into the household environment. This is because male family members tend to think of cash-based economic activity as their sole entitlement, and thus question the rightfulness of women's economic participation and/or resent the fact that this equates to a potential loss of control over women family members. In some cases, Eves also notes that this idea inclines men to believe that they have the right to control women's market income and may threaten or use violence to relieve women of their earnings. Even in families where women's marketing brings in a second family income, Eves notes that gains in household wealth are not collectively shared. Rather, economically-active husbands may reserve their income for their own discretionary spending and refuse to share their own earnings with their families, in the expectation that it is the role of economically-active women to pay for their children's needs and all of the family's food, including that consumed by husbands (Eves et al, 2018, p ix). These observations show how, in the post-conflict environment, indigenous logics have become hardened in ways that require women to distribute their earnings in order to adhere to their relational obligations while men retain an autonomy to spend their own earnings entirely at their own discretion.

My own efforts to understand how women navigate the realm of paid employment in the conflict-affected Pacific Island states has uncovered similar evidence of controlling violence perpetrated by conjugal part-ners against working women. This occurs alongside the discriminatory treatment that women must also navigate within the workplace and casts further doubt on the supposed dividends that accrue from the economic peace paradigm. For example, in both Solomon Islands and Bougainville, women are currently being targeted as recruits to the security sector as part of broader reform programmes which aim to rehabilitate the reputation of state enforcement agencies that became compromised during the conflict period. My observations suggest that informally institutionalized gendered logics have not been challenged by these new recruitment policies, however, and that it is women rather than male officers of a similar rank that are more frequently allocated duties that are menial and uncomfortable – traffic direction for example – and are perhaps less able to challenge this kind of treatment.

Beyond this workplace discrimination, I have also heard many different accounts of working women within government departments who have been exposed to violence from male family members who are resentful of women's earning potential, and sometimes also the fact that their work brings them into proximity with men. Officers working across a range of public service roles from policing to bureaucratic administration have shared with me harrowing stories of extreme gen-dered violence perpetrated against female staff within their homes and how this impacts on their earning capacity. In Bougainville, one officer, noting the severity of this problem, explained that she sometimes sent a departmental vehicle to more junior women officer's homes as part of efforts to combat absenteeism caused by family violence. With a departmental car and driver in front of the female officers' houses she found her employees were more able to safely extract themselves from the control of resentful and potentially violent male family members.

Of course, such measures do little to ensure that women return to a safe home environment at the conclusion of their day's work.

Research conducted with family violence support services in these post-conflict contexts has also taught me that household tensions are generated not only because employment takes women outside the home, and the realm of caring, but also because this provides women with access to cash and potential autonomy. Women who make autonomous decisions about how the money they earn should be spent may be subjected to violence and this may be especially so if their spending is judged to be 'excessive', meaning they spend money on themselves rather than family or kin. Front-line crisis care workers also explained that women in professional occupations are frequently pressured by men to hand over their cash on pay days, and the phenomena of women being beaten because they resisted pressure to hand over ATM cards was common.

Together, these observations point to the need for careful assessment of the claim that a peace dividend necessarily accrues from efforts to increase women's economic participation. The family environment is imagined to become less precarious and more peaceful when women earn, according to the economic peace paradigm, but, as I have shown, there is strong evidence that it can become a place of violence and insecurity for economically-active women. These risks are currently greatly underestimated in debates on the need to make women's economic participation a stronger focus within the WPS agenda internationally. Little account is taken of the dangerous frictions that these interventions may produce if local economies of place are discounted and how these may trouble the widely accepted global narrative that peace trickles upwards and outwards from women who are economically active because they have an enhanced capacity to disperse funds. Indeed, the economies of place perspective reveals that this capacity may not always be voluntary and can in fact be coerced or become a trigger for violence, in line with customary prescriptions that women's labour should always ultimately be for the gain for her family and community rather than for herself.

It is critical to reflect on the way that constructions of feminized 'goodness' and 'duty' provide a gendered shape to post-conflict economies and result in prohibitions that aim to prevent women from exerting 'selfish' control of their earnings or wasteful spending that does not reflect their obligations to others as 'wives, mothers, sisters and in laws' (Kozcerbski, 2002, 90). The frictions that are produced when global and local ideas about gender and economic integration intersect produce more risk for women than international policy prescriptions on the benefits of economic participation seem willing to acknowledge. They also highlight the problems that occur when the economy itself is treated as a gendered vacuum, ignoring women's roles as emplaced economic actors acting within a system guided by logics of exchange that are 'embedded in indigenous social and cultural frameworks' (Curry et al, 2012, p 122).

Conclusion

Current global discourses on the need to make women's economic participation a stronger focus of the WPS agenda globally are strongly shaped by the economic peace paradigm and posit the importance of recognizing and supporting women's entrepreneurship or waged employment as a foundation both for their empowerment as well as for the consolidation of a broader peace. But not enough energy has been devoted to understanding how these agendas land on the ground in conflict-affected societies and cultures. As I show here, efforts to integrate women into the cash economy often can produce insecurity for women and compound discriminations. This can be a particular problem if it is simply assumed that women are economically inactive, rather than examining where and how women are situated within place-based networks of exchange guided by their own relational logics.

Some studies of women's location within place-based economies have been used to challenge the view that women in developing countries are marginalized and subordinate economic actors (Graham, 2002). Gibson et al's studies of gender and economic participation in a number of Pacific countries, including Solomon Islands, assert the importance of appreciating the 'rich diversity of economic practices and forms of recognition that sustain life' above and beyond the globalized capitalist model as well as women's capacities to draw benefit from these systems (Gibson et al, 2016, p 1380). Likewise, Gina Koczberski has observed that women in the island provinces of Papua New Guinea, close to Bougainville, often derive a sense of satisfaction when they are able to redistribute cash earnings to family or broader kin in line with 'rules' of relational exchange and this activity, in itself, can be described by women as a form of relational capital significant to the 'emotional well-being and life satisfaction of individuals and communities' (Curry and Kozcerbski, 2012, p 379). But, like Upolu Vaai, Kozcerbski and her co-authors are attentive to the ways that relational obligation can also be constructed as a source of oppression for women particularly. Thus they warn that relational modalities of economic exchange should not be assumed to be intrinsically 'more equitable, fairer or nobler' simply because they are indigenous and 'place-based' (Curry and Kozcerbski, 2012, 381) and caution against invoking these in ways that 'naturalize' hierarchical and discriminatory forms of social order.

With all these caveats in place, my interest in developing an 'economies of place' perspective on women's participation in post-conflict economies lies in the productive analytical potential it offers for understanding the frictional outcomes generated when global policies are made to travel to local conflict-affected contexts. This concept opens the way for us to develop locally resonant and situated understandings of the relationship between women's economic empowerment and their security. It is too easy to glibly assume that women's economic participation acts as a catalyst for enhanced social cohesion, and unjust to place that burden on women's shoulders without also investigating where and how it can increase women's vulnerability to violence. It might be tempting to conclude that the relational rhythms, principles and practices that guide networks of exchange in everyday conflict-affected communities run directly counter to the ethos of individualized wealth that is at the heart of neoliberal economic peacebuilding and that these are outmoded traditions that have had their day. But as I hope to have made clear, globalized models of economic exchange do not sweep everything up in their path quite so comprehensively. Ignoring the insistence of alternative logics that shape economic life in conflict-affected settings means that we also ignore the gendered insecurities and cruel gendered violence that may be generated by our efforts to make women's economic participation, as it is understood in global terms, a critical component of conflict transition. That is surely too heavy a price to pay for peace.

References

Alvinius, A. and Holmberg, A. (2019) 'Silence-breaking butterfly effect: resistance towards the military within #metoo', *Gender, Work & Organization*, Available from: https://doi.org/10.1111/gwao.12349.

Angell, R.N. (1910) *The Great Illusion: A Study of the Relation of Military Power in Nations to Their Economic and Social Advantage*, London: Heinemann.

Björkdahl, A. (2012) 'A gender-just peace? Exploring the post-Dayton Peace Process in Bosnia', *Peace & Change*, 37(2): 286–317.

Björkdahl, A, and Höglund, K. (2013) 'Precarious peacebuilding: friction in global–local encounters', *Peacebuilding* 1(3): 289–299.

Björkdahl, A. and Mannergren Selimovic, J. (2015) 'Gendering agency in transitional justice', *Security Dialogue*, 46(2): 165–182.

Collier, P. and Hoeffler, A. (2004) 'Greed and grievance in civil war', *Oxford Economic Papers*, 56(4): 563–595.

Coomaraswamy, R. et al (2015) *Preventing Conflict, Transforming Justice, Securing the Peace: A Global Study on the Implementation of UNSCR 1325*, New York: UN Women, Available from: http://wps.unwomen.org/

Curry, G.N. and Koczberski, G. (2012) 'Relational economics, social embeddedness and valuing labour in agrarian change: an example from the developing world', *Geographical Research*, 50(4): 377–392.

Curry, G.N., Koczberski, G. and Connell, J. (2012) 'Introduction: enacting modernity in the Pacific?', *Australian Geographer*, 43(2): 115–125.

Elson, D. and Pearson, R. (2011) 'The subordination of women and the internationalization of factory production' in N. Visvanathan, L. Duggan, N. Wiegersma and L. Nisonoff et al (eds) *The Women, Gender and Development Handbook*, 3rd edition, London and New York: Zed Books, pp 212–224.

Eves, R., Lusby, S., Araia, T., Maeni, M. and Martin, R. (2018) *Do No Harm Research: Solomon Islands*, Canberra: Department of Pacific Affairs, Australian National University, International Women's Development Agency, Australian Aid, Available from: http://dpa.bellschool.anu.edu.au/experts-publications/publications/6002/do-no-harm-research-solomon-islands.

George, N. (2016) 'Light, heat and shadows: women's reflections on peacebuilding in post-conflict Bougainville', *Peacebuilding*, 4(2): 166–179.

Gibson, K. (2002). 'Women, identity and activism in Asian and Pacific community economies', *Development*, 45(1): 74–79.

Hudock, A. Sherman, K. and Williamson, S. (2016) 'Women's economic participation in post-conflict and fragile settings', Occasional paper series, Washington, DC: Georgetown Institute for Women, Peace and Security, Available from: https://giwps.georgetown.edu/wp-content/uploads/2017/08/Occasional-Paper-Series-Womens-Economic-Participation.pdf.

Lind, A. (2011) 'Women's community organizing in Quito: the paradoxes of survival and struggle', in N. Visvanathan et al (eds) *The Women, Gender and Development Reader*, 2nd edition, London: Zed Books, pp 417–424.

Lwambo, D. (2013) '"Before the war, I was a man": men and masculinities in the Eastern Democratic Republic of Congo', *Gender & Development*, 21(1): 47–66.

Marion Young, I. (2003) 'The logic of the masculinist protection reflections on the current security state', *Signs*, 29(1): 1–25.

McKinnon, K., Carnegie, M., Gibson, K. and Rowland, C. (2016) 'Gender equality and economic empowerment in the Solomon Islands and Fiji: a placebased approach', *Gender, Place & Culture*, 23(10): 1376–1391.

Miller, G.E. (2004) 'Frontier masculinity in the oil industry: the experience of women engineers', *Gender, Work & Organization*, 11(1): 47–73.

Mohanty, C.T. (2011) 'Under western eyes: feminist scholarship and colonial discourses', in N. Visvanathan et al (eds.) *The Women, Gender and Development Reader*, 3rd edition, London and New York: Zed Books, pp 83–88.

Ní Aoláin, F.N., Haynes, D.F. and Cahn, N. (2011) *On the Frontlines: Gender, War, and the Post-Conflict Process*, Oxford: Oxford University Press.

Papua New Guinea National Statistical Office (2010) 'Household income and expenditure survey 2009–2010', Port Moresby: National Statistical Office, Available from: www.nso.gov.pg/index.php/document-library?view=download&fileId=89.

Sen, A. (2001) *Development as Freedom*, Oxford: Oxford University Press.

Rai, S. and Waylen, G. (eds) (2013) *New Frontiers in Feminist Political Economy*, New York: Routledge.

Richmond, O. (2009) 'Beyond liberal peace? Responses to "backsliding"?', in E. Newman, R. Paris and O. Richmond (eds) *New Perspectives on Liberal Peacebuilding*, Tokyo: United Nations University Press, pp 54–77.

Pollard, A.A. (2000) *Givers of Wisdom, Labourers without Gain: Essays on Women in Solomon Islands*, Suva, Institute of Pacific Studies.

Sharp, T., Cox, J., Spark, C., Lusby, S. and Rooney, M. (2015) 'The formal, the informal and the precarious: making a living in urban Papua New Guinea', SSGM Discussion Paper 2015/2, Canberra: Australian National University, Available from: https://openresearch-repository.anu.edu.au/bitstream/1885/32429/2/01_Sharp_The_Formal,_the_Informal,_and_2015.pdf.

Slatter, C. (1994) 'Banking on the growth model? The World Bank and market policies in the Pacific', in A. Emberson-Bain (ed) *Sustainable Development or Malignant Growth? Perspectives of Pacific Island Women*, Suva: Marama Publications, pp 17–35.

SINSO (Solomon Islands National Statistics Office) (2014) 'Population and housing census: report on gender', Honiara: SINSO, Available from: www.statistics.gov.sb/sinso-documents?view=download&format=raw&fileId=527.

Smith, B. (1984) *European Vision and the South Pacific*, 2nd edition, Sydney: Harper & Row.

True, J. and Svedberg, B. (2019) 'WPS and international financial institutions', in J. True and S. Davies (eds) *The Oxford Handbook of Women, Peace and Security*, Oxford: Oxford University Press, pp 336–350.

United Nations Security Council (2000) Resolution 1325, 31 October, Available from: https://documents-dds-ny.un.org/doc/UNDOC/GEN/N00/720/18/PDF/N0072018.pdf?OpenElement.

UN Women (Pacific) (2011) 'Pacific markets and market vendors: evidence, data and knowledge in Pacific Island countries', Suva: UN Women (Pacific).

Vaai, U.L. (2017) 'Relational hermeneutics: a return to the relationality of the Pacific itulagi as a lens for understanding and interpreting life', in U.L. Vaai and A. Casimira (eds) *Relational Hermeneutics: Decolonising the Mindset of the Pacific Itulagi*, Suva: The University of the South Pacific and The Pacific Theological College, pp 17–41.

World Bank (2011) 'Increasing the participation of women entrepreneurs in the Solomon Islands aid economy', Honiara: World Bank.

World Bank (2012) 'Skills for Solomon Islands: opening new opportunities', Sydney: World Bank, Available from: https://olc.worldbank.org/sites/default/files/WB001%20BKL%20Solomon%20Skills_v3_0.pdf.

Ydesen, C. and Verschaeve, J. (2019) 'The OECD development assistance committee and peace: instituting peace by economic means', in A. Kulnazarova and W. Popovski (eds) *The Palgrave Handbook of Global Approaches to Peace*, Cham: Palgrave Macmillan, pp 477–495.

4

Difficult Encounters with the WPS Agenda in South Asia: Re-scripting Globalized Norms and Policy Frameworks for a Feminist Peace

Rita Manchanda

South Asia's ongoing conflicts and embattled 'post-conflict' transitions reveal the tensions inherent in the globalized Women, Peace and Security (WPS) agenda, between the *ritualism of recognizing* the relationship between gender inequality and violence, and the *practice of incorporating* women's plural perspectives to achieve genuine inclusion in conflict resolution and peace processes on the ground. A generation of macro- and micro-level studies of the diversity and complexity of the gendered experiences of the conflict–peace continuum in the region have shown that prescriptive norms and policy frameworks, derived from the neoliberal WPS template of peacemaking, run the risk of distorting and de-politicizing locally rooted women's peacework (Banerjee, 2008; Manchanda, 2017b). Some have argued that there is a narrowing of the original imagination of the global WPS agenda and missing in particular is the recognition of women's resistance politics and their resilience. The conceptual framing of WPS discourse undervalues the contextual understanding that the region's women's peace groups are integrally linked with broader struggles for socio-economic justice and human security (Coomaraswamy and Fonseca, 2004; Hans, 2016).

Across the region, it is apparent that post–war transitions in conflict zones have produced a contentious politics of fragile agreements. In Nepal, for instance, consociational arrangements between contending elites serve as a substitute for a transformative politics of inclusion and equal rights (Falch and Miklian, 2008). There are protracted ceasefires and pacification in northeast India (Manchanda and Bose, 2015), internal domination in Sri Lanka, occupation in Jammu and Kashmir (Duschinski et al, 2018), a 'violent peace' in Chittagong Hill Tracts (CHT) (Bangladesh) (D'Costa, 2014), and relapse to war in Afghanistan. When confronted with unjust and exclusionary peace settlements that fail to tackle root causes, reconcile divided communities, roll back militarization, bridge development deficits and promote inclusion (MacGinty, 2011; Manchanda and Bose, 2015), women's collectives have innovated an everyday resistance politics. Feminist literature has also increasingly drawn attention to women's visibility in resistance struggles, their multifaceted roles in both non–violent and violent movements (Parashar, 2014; Allison, 2003; Yami, 2007).

In this chapter, I contend that the diversity in women's responses points to the range of women's lived understanding of the plural and contested meanings of militarization, insecurity, fundamental freedoms and, above all, peace. It questions the presumed apolitical engagement of women with peace and argues for attention to be paid to the legitimacy of women's resistance politics. The argument builds upon the observations of feminist scholars Fionnuala Ní Aoláin and Nahla Valji that the concept of 'resistance' needs to be integrated into the WPS agenda as a valid exercise of power, if WPS is to be relevant to women in conflict zones (Ní Aoláin and Valji, 2019, p 59). Pushing the argument further, the chapter argues for attention to the region's contextual reality of a multifaceted and non–linear involvement of women across a continuum of peacemaking, non–violent resistance and violent politics, such as in Kashmir (Husain, 2019, pp 107–161).

In the region, global WPS norms and the policy thrust of gender equality have produced gains evident in the dramatic visibility of the numbers of women in institutional power structures, especially in the internationalized processes of Afghanistan and Nepal. Gendered audits have raised concerns about the insufficiency of the objective of participation as 'numbers' of women, and questioned which women, and whose agendas, are included, especially in high–risk militarized environments. There are unsettling questions about top-down prescriptive norms of gender equality that risk distorting local priorities and rendering women more vulnerable, as in Afghanistan (Azarbaijani-Moghaddam, 2018) or provoke a fierce backlash from local patriarchies, as in Nagaland in northeast India (Kikon, 2016; Manchanda and Kakran, 2017). The presumption of a universal WPS agenda begins to fall apart especially when, in the pursuit of gender equality and protection, women's recruitment in the security forces is promoted as the main thrust in security sector reform in Afghanistan and Nepal.

There is growing concern from critical feminist scholars about the instrumentalization of the gender equality agenda as women get incorporated in the military strategies of armies (Cockburn, 2013; Duncanson and Woodward, 2016). It argues that the militarization of the WPS agenda is reinforced by the international strategy of promoting women's roles in countering violent extremism. Not only are women caught between armed actors rendered vulnerable, but their capacity to deradicalize (or radicalize) turns on motherhood politics. It reinforces gendered binaries of women's pacifism and men's warmongering that dominate globalized WPS discourses (Aroussi, 2009).

My analysis of 'difficult encounters' with the WPS discourse largely focuses on the internationalized conflict–peace dynamics of Afghanistan and Nepal, where the WPS discourse has had normative and policy impact. Arguably, the 'ill fit' between normative frameworks and contextual local dynamics has contributed to the peripheral import-ance of UNSCR 1325 among the region's gender equality and peace activists (Goswami et al, 2017, p 75). For the WPS discourse to be of relevance to the multitude of women living in conflict zones in South Asia, global assumptions that tend to homogenize and essentialize the category of women need to be re-imagined. Here, gender identities are likely to be subsumed along the pervasive fault lines of caste, class, ethnicity and religion. Contextual diversity needs to be referenced in the framing of WPS norms and goals.

The importance of 'UNSCR 1325+', which includes subsequent WPS resolutions, in achieving a template shift with reference to the relationship of women–peace–security is well established (Naraghi Anderlini, 2007). The chapter critically reflects on the tensions in translating WPS normative frameworks as the region's women navi-gate the 'WPS-scape' and contextually adapt norms and frameworks. This chapter first explores women's everyday reality of resistance and resilience as they forge a peace politics with justice. Second, it unpacks the subtext of contradictions in the gender equality commitments of UNSCR 1325 as evident in the region's difficult transitions. Third, it reflects on women's difficult encounters with the WPS template in the context of their lived reality of continuing militarization and impunity and contested meanings of militarized security and justice. Finally, the chapter offers a word on new directions on how gender equality and peace advocates are expanding openings for feminist peace praxis in other institutional contexts, including CEDAW (Committee on the Elimination of Discrimination Against Women) and the International Criminal Court.

Post-conflict transitions and the crisis of solutions

When the moment of peacebuilding is not socially transformative and is more of a restoration of status quo (which was part of the problem in the first place), or a *peace* disrupted by everyday acts of dispersed and unpredictable violence in a persisting context of impunity, militarization and socioeconomic vulnerability how have women collectives responded to flawed peace agreements (Manchanda and Bose, 2015)? The signing of such agreements often produces a splintering of the struggle group: following the 2006 peace agreement in Nepal, some of the most prominent women Maoists broke away to continue resistance politics; and, after the signing of the CHT peace accord in 1997, the Hill Women's Federation, which had been at the forefront against militarization and resultant human rights violations, split and the vanguard joined the anti-accordists (Guhathakurta, 2001, pp 287–289).

Women's contestations of (bad) peace deals draws attention to the politics of their peacework. Kashmiri political activists Zamrooda Habib and Hameeda Nayeem were part of a 2010 delegation of 'Sisters of Peace' who were to appeal to the Indian President Pratibha Patil to end the violence in their state. They made it clear that peace was not possible without *azadi*, which Hameeda translated as freedom from repression (Manchanda, 2017a, p 33). Six years later when Kashmir's 'pacification' was ruptured after the killing of a militant icon, a Kashmiri woman activist noted that 'resistance has become mainstream' against militarized repression; a young Kashmiri women's collective called for reopening the case of the notorious incident of mass rape of Kashmiri women of their mother's generation, which happened 13 years earlier, and memorialized it in the book *Do You Remember Kunan Poshpara* (Batool et al, 2016; see also WRN, forthcoming).

In Afghanistan's series of peace parleys, gender equality activists and collectives such as the Afghan Women's Network (AWN) have been navigating the pitfalls of peace negotiations that are gender exclusionary and feared to be rights regressive. Seated at the table are not only the Taliban with their misogynist ideology but deeply patriarchal warlords and international stakeholders who seem ready to trade away advances in women's rights for a highly uncertain end to violence (Nordland et al, 2019). AWN has been critical – even hostile – to such peacemaking (AWN, 2014, pp 13–14). Further, writer activist Sippi Azarbaijani-Moghaddam has questioned the tendency to homogenize Afghan women in the peace and security discourse. Drawing upon her grounded work in Afghanistan she emphasizes the importance of factoring in contextual diversity, because for women living in the midst of violence in Afghanistan's rural areas, ending of the war takes priority over a threatened rollback of gains, which largely urban Afghan women have secured, but which remain removed from their lives (2018, p 66).

Such discursive interventions are a reminder of the risk of policy distortions that can result from flattening the diversity of contexts and promoting a prescriptive liberal feminist gender equality agenda. In the region's multi-ethnic multi-religious social space, participation is fraught with complexity of representation and belonging. The assumption that all Afghan women would unquestioningly rally around a rights-based agenda as women is highly questionable (Azarbaijani-Moghaddam, 2018, p 66). Those organizing and participating in peace talks need cautioning against homogenizing and essentializing women. As Khan points out, 'We need to recognize that women have multiple identities and the point at which their identity as a woman is privileged over the religious, caste or other identities issues' (quoted in Manchanda, 2017b, p xxvii). In Afghanistan's High Peace Council, quotas have enabled presence, but the women may be affiliated to the Mujahedeen or with their ethnic groups, and still others can be in opposition to the peace process (Duncanson and Farr, 2019, p 356).

Moreover, where women have been mobilized in ethno-national struggles, the Westphalian state-centric logic that undergirds UNSCR 1325+ problem-solving is likely to be out of sync with such movements. These struggles challenge state ideologies of a hegemonic national narrative. Viewed from a statist perspective, self-determination conflicts in Kashmir and northeast India, CHT in Bangladesh and the *Eelam* war in Sri Lanka are gaps in the state's integrationist project. Conflict resolution models betray a decisive statist bias (Manchanda and Bose, 2015). These identity struggles have been broadly Centre and Left in political orientation, not only at odds with state ideologies of nationalism, but also with the neoliberal paradigms of economic growth that are integral to the WPS agenda. Further, resolution 1325's location in the UN Security Council makes it dependent upon the 'P5 club' which, as Pakistani feminist Nighat Khan remarks, trails an 'unfortunate history of military interventions' (Goswami et al, 2017, p 74).

In identifying the makers of the regional WPS discourse, Meenakshi Gopinath and I have argued that the development discourse and issues of human security have remained an integral part of the region's WPS engagement. The normative compass provided by UNSCR 1325+ has been pushed further in the South Asian context to include struggles against forcible displacement, militarism, impunity, patriarchy, development and environmental security (Gopinath and Manchanda, 2019, p 808; Emmanuel, 2008). As funding has dried up, so too has the organizational buzz around UNSCR 1325; but recently there has been a revitalization of home-grown robustness of the peace agenda especially with a hyper-militarist culture threatening the region's peace. Activism for peace finds strength in expanding alliances with broader social movements and struggles for democratic rights.[1] South Asian women's peacework has straddled the *divides* between human rights initiatives, socio-economic movements for justice and nonviolent peace activism, too often imagined as contradictory streams in the linear WPS narrative (Gopinath and Manchanda, 2019, p 811).

Presence, participation and local patriarchies

South Asia's peace processes have been no exception to the global norm of women's absence at the peace table. The internationally-promoted Gender Subcommittee[2] during the 2002–2004 ceasefire negotiations in Sri Lanka was more an experiment in presence than participation and too short-lived to make an impact. Kumudini Samuel, a member of that subcommittee, maintains that while women's presence in official peace negotiations could place their needs and concerns on the peace agenda, their presence in and of itself would not guarantee an engendered discussion, especially if women at the high-level negotiations are distanced from their communities' grassroots peace movements (2010, pp 34–54).

South Asian feminists are critical of WPS focalization of women's agency primarily to that one indicator: number of women at peace tables. Nighat Khan, an influential voice in shaping the global South WPS discourse, argues that the 'issue was not about getting more women and expertise at the table but more about, what is it that women are negotiating or mediating for? What is on the table during peace talks and who determines what should be on the peace table?' (in Goswami et al, 2017, p 61). Quotas in Afghanistan and Nepal have vaulted women into representative politics and public office in significant numbers, but assessments show a minimal impact on decision making (Duncanson and Farr, 2019; Shrestha et al, 2017). It is beyond the scope of this chapter to probe the contextual reasons that have rendered women's political agency as 'symbolic', or reduced them to 'proxies' for powerful men.

What can be argued is that connecting with the locally-rooted rich and textured peacework of local women, can assist in counter-balancing the extreme asymmetry of power of being unarmed in the midst of armed men (Manchanda and Bose, 2015, p 131). This work is also crucial for establishing the legitimacy of representation.

The everyday resistance and resilience of women's peacework is often rendered invisible as an extension of women's caretaking role; it needs recognition as political.

> The resistances of women in what is apolitically designated as the 'private' sphere assume the magnitude of major transgressions of entrenched structures of patriarchy. These are structures that embed and legitimize cultures of militarism and impunity – the ultimate Bastille for women's peace-work. (Gopinath and Manchanda, 2019, p 812)

Recognizing the everyday resistance and incremental quality of women's peacework calls for attention to be given to the proactive approaches to peacebuilding of Afghan women working with local *shuras* to reduce civilian casualties, of women in India's northeast and Sri Lanka building reconciliations across factional and ethnic faultlines, and of Mothers of the Disappeared in Kashmir refusing to forget, demanding accountability from the state which is both protector and predator.

Women's actions and achievements as in the Afghan High Peace Council and in sustaining the long ceasefire–cold peace in Nagaland in northeast India tend to be less public and even self-abnegating from asserting a political opinion. Former President of the Naga Mothers' Association Neidonuo Angami emphasized the need for caution, lest it provoke a patriarchal backlash against women transgressing their traditional exclusion from public life (Manchanda and Kakran, 2017). Her successors in Naga women's social organizations were less reticent; they asserted their right to be included in representative bodies. Women were absent in traditional tribal structures and in modern structures of state politics. Building upon their moral authority as peacebuilders in the informal space of politics, their participation was considered essential in any civil society initiative for dialogue and reconciliation. Naga women's collectives such as Naga Mothers' Association forged a Joint Women's Front to challenge women's exclusion from formal politics.[3] As I have argued elsewhere, the Naga women's *coming out* trajectory traversed 'subsuming gender consciousness in an identity-based mobilization to pushing for inclusion and equal rights that challenged customary practices; from an apolitical engagement to political activism for transforming the nature of inequality, exploitation and exclusion' (Manchanda and Kakran, 2017, p 67).

Despite strong opposition from the all-male Naga tribal bodies, but bolstered by the Indian Supreme Court directive upholding women's quotas for Nagaland's urban and metropolitan councils, Naga women's front claimed the right to contest elections. The backlash was fierce and violent (Kikon, 2016). Women were accused of threatening the unique Naga identity, the ideological foundation of the Naga national struggle, by undermining Naga customary laws and practices. Women retreated; the gender equality agenda set back.

As scholars of gender and ethnicity have explored, women's democratic struggles are embedded in ethno-national movements of which they are an integral part (Cockburn, 2008, p 287; Das, 2008, p 56). There was no question of pursuing an independent 'gender' agenda but of negotiating for space within the community. Had the promotion of liberal feminist norms of gender equality on which the WPS discourse is premised rushed the pace? Ideas about UNSCR 1325, peacebuilding and gender equality were spreading across borders, and Naga women's peacework was a magnet for NGOs organizing around WPS (Manchanda and Kakran, 2017). Similarly, the scope for peacework in Kashmir has attracted many 'mainstream feminists' who had tried to 'superimpose their ideology and perspectives', political activist and convener of Muslim Khawateen Markaz, Zamrooda Anjum observed. It was to counter outsiders presuming to explain Kashmir's gendered narrative and to fill the vacuum of an absent Kashmiri women's movement that she had constituted a new platform (the Kashmiri Women's Movement) to assert Kashmir's own indigenous mobilization and its place within the larger movement for azadi (quoted in Husain, 2019, p 144).

More specifically, in an assessment of the impact of WPS in Afghanistan, Duncanson and Farr not only argue that its impact was limited, but quoting Azarbaijani-Moghaddam, feared that efforts to implement UNSCR 1325 have come close to doing 'more harm than good' (Duncanson and Farr, 2019, p 561). Efforts to introduce a liberal women's rights agenda of participation and protective laws against gender-based violence produced a violent backlash in a militarized environment populated by misogynist and violent men enjoying ongoing impunity. Admittedly, this assessment of WPS as 'counterproductive' is specific to the Afghanistan context.

Concerns iterated earlier in the contexts of Afghanistan and Nagaland find a disturbing echo in a study on 'Gender and Nepal's Transition from War', which strikes a note of caution about WPS-driven efforts to navigate the complex realpolitik of the conflict continuum, lest they 'be dismissed as alien, unsuitable or divisive' (Conciliation Resources, 2017, p 16). The analysis, based on the voices of women on the ground, seeks to understand the puzzle of why the significant gains in women's participation in formal politics in Nepal have not translated into impact on decision making (Conciliation Resources, 2017, p 4). In explanation, the study warns that 'Initiatives need to be (and were not) carefully aligned with local priorities and sensitivities' (Conciliation Resources, 2017, p 16). Scholarly analysis about the limited impact of the post–conflict democratization of Nepal's politics point to the resilience of local patriarchies and the presence of male–dominated kinship networks and informal all–male power structures where important decisions were made (Shrestha et al, 2017).

The importance of sensitivity to specific contexts is iterated in Punam Yadav's examination of Nepal's National Action Plan (NAP), recognized as the main instrument for implementing UNSCRs 1325 and 1820. Scepticism is evoked in the provocative title: '1325! Is that a taxi number?' Yadav juxtaposes Nepal's success in developing a highly participatory NAP and its 'minimal' impact on the ground and offers two reasons: 'a) problems at the discursive level, both knowledge construction at international level and understanding of the WPS framework at the local level; and b) reliance on experts' knowledge and co-option of the WPS agenda by the development organizations and humanitarian agencies' (2017, p 2). It should be added that the political scenario of changing governments in Nepal unhinged political ownership of the NAP, and the dwindling of donor support and international pressure further weakened its implementation.

In the case of Nepal, there is a striking contrast between the significant involvement of women in representative politics, and the silencing of the voice of the Maoist female combatant who symbolized many gendered transgressions; the latter group has been excluded from committees on rehabilitation and reintegration, and the NAP (Colekessian, 2009; Srestha et al, 2017). This points to the rapid unravelling of the Maoist social revolution and the return to the 'normalcy' of deeply entrenched pre–conflict gender norms and roles (Luna, 2019). It also reflects liberal feminism's discomfort with women in violent resistance movements (Aroussi, 2009).

Contesting meanings

Chroniclers of 'herstory' of the WPS discourse in South Asia emphasize that the region's conceptualization of WPS is rooted in the understanding that peace and security cannot be separated from broader questions of unequal relationships and development paradigms (see Goswami et al, 2017, p 66). Kumari Jayawardene, one of the region's early feminists, asserted that the robustness of the region's movements for women's rights and peace lies in its close linkages with grassroots struggles for socio-economic justice and equal rights (Jayawardena, 1986, p 10). Contestations around meanings is discussed here in two parts: militarization and militarized security; and impunity and reparations.

Militarization and militarized security

Feminist critics have expressed concern at the increasing militarization of the WPS agenda (Cockburn, 2013) and the inbuilt weakness in the foundation resolution UNSCR 1325. Laura Shepherd's analysis draws attention to the ideas and culture of the institution from which WPS emerged, the Security Council. As was to be expected, the emphasis is on the gendered impact of conflict, not on the arms and geostrategic interests that exacerbate and sustain conflict (Shepherd, 2010). The 'prevention pillar' of WPS needs foregrounding. Disarmament and demilitarization needs to be brought back into conversations about the prevention dimension of the WPS agenda (Kapur and Rees, 2019). Reflecting the concerns of women living in conflict zones, the *Global Study* to review the implementation of UNSCR 1325 exhorted that 'an attitudinal shift is needed away from a primary focus on military responses, towards investment in peaceful conflict prevention strategies' (Coomaraswamy et al, 2015, p 195). Despite feminist contributions to unpacking the gender dynamics that drive violent conflict, more resources are directed at getting more women in the security forces as an integral aspect of mainstreaming gender in WPS (see Cockburn, 2011, p 29).

Such militarization is apparent, among others, in Afghanistan; its NAP promotes more women in the security sector, as part of the protection agenda, and bypasses the issue of disarmament (Duncanson and Farr, 2019). Afghan women have insistently decried the overreach of militarized approaches to the state building project in post-conflict Afghanistan. Confronting a deteriorating security and human rights situation, women's rights activist Huma Shafi has blamed the policy choices of the international community and the Afghan government of appeasing warlords and working through irresponsible armed groups affiliated to warlords and jihadi parties, many of whom enjoy the overt and covert support of governmental agencies and the international community (Manchanda, 2017b, p xxxvi).

Tracking the shifting forms and sites of militarization in South Asia, Anuradha Chenoy, a leading scholar on women and militarization in the region, has asserted, 'This heavy securitization is felt differently by women who are at risk of being sexualized subjects and targets of control' (2017, p 101). The contention that less militarized security makes for more security, as voiced by women in the conflict affected zones, has been drowned by the militarization of the WPS agenda. There is the need for a countervailing narrative of local women resisting and surviving conflict, of the priorities of internally displaced and refugee women and of what makes women feel insecure (Gowrinathan and Cronin-Furman, 2016). Micro-level narratives have shown that the failure to seriously address demilitarization and demobilization processes, often for reasons of political expediency, has entrenched political economies of violence. The result is increased criminality, less predictable violence in the public and private sphere, and an overall culture of impunity (D'Costa, 2014; Kikon, 2016).

The dovetailing of the WPS agenda with internationally mandated frameworks of countering violent extremism has instrumentalized women in related military strategies and reinforced militarism, and insecurity. Journalist and human rights activist Anuradha Bhasin-Jamwal has warned of Kashmiri women's vulnerability to being used by both extremist ideologues and security forces, as they become 'easy targets for both sides for co-option as informers and spies' (2017, p 126). Extremism and terrorism finds no mention in resolution 1325, but subsequent resolutions 2242 (2015) and 2467 (2019) mention both extremism and terrorism.

Even as more women are being co-opted into the military system, those at the receiving end of the violent conflict are redefining security from the ground up as human security (Gopinath and Manchanda, 2019). In militarized zones such as northeast India, women's peace groups are asserting livelihood and environmental security and resisting mega hydroelectric projects and tourism projects which are often militarily enforced (Hans, 2016, pp 160–184; on CHT, see also Mohsin and Hossain, 2015). The peace agenda is nested in the larger struggle for social justice and equality, including gender equality.

Resisting impunity and reparations

The transition to a post-conflict situation hinges upon demilitarization, power sharing and crucially, truth and reconciliation for healing war-scarred societies and fighting impunity to reestablish rule of law. What kind of justice is possible when amnesties are positioned as deal breakers? What is justice for the region's women whose experiences of widespread and systematic sexualized violence are directly related to their bodies becoming markers of community identity? What and from whom can justice be demanded when women suffer the multiple harm of being a 'half widow', an IDP/Refugee, a female ex combatant, a single female, a female heading a household within the context of a political economy of violence and privations? The *Global Study* recognizes that for women 'whose experiences of violence are directly related to their unequal status, justice is as much about dealing with the past as it is about securing a better future that includes guarantees of non-recurrence' (Coomaraswamy et al, 2015, p 102).

The observation strikes at the core of the controversies that have mired some of the region's interventions for justice, including the actualization of Transitional Justice mechanisms in Nepal, Sri Lanka and Bangladesh, and their denial in Afghanistan. Nepal's much delayed accountability commissions, the Truth and Reconciliation Commission (TRC) and the Commission of Investigation on Enforced Disappeared Persons (CIEDP), continue to trail an amnesty clause despite judicial interventions. Sexual crimes are exempt but the 35-day statute of limitation renders the crime beyond the reach of the TRC. The international community, including UN institutions, had promoted these mechanisms, but now are boycotting them as they flout international norms on fighting impunity (Farasat, 2017).

Whose notion of justice does this serve? Contesting the emphasis on prosecutorial justice is a minority discourse, voiced by several Nepali victim community organizations whose priorities seem to be at odds with that of the international community's norms. They advocate critical engagement with the flawed institutional mechanism and urge that their right to truth and reparations should not be conditional on addressing impunity. Victims 'prioritize the issues of poverty and marginality that define their everyday lives' claims scholar activist Ram Bhandari (Bhandari et al, 2018). Thus relief (livelihood) and reparations gets positioned as an essential component of justice. Echoing this, the *Global Study* quotes a Nepali woman activist saying, 'just offering justice and punishment for the perpetrators is not enough, as many women want reparation and rehabilitation, without which they won't come forward' (Coomaraswamy et al, 2015, p 109). An ICRC Survey of the Families of the Disappeared found that the highest priority for most families was the need to know the truth about the fate and whereabouts of their missing relative and to receive economic support (ICRC, 2009).

Similar voices are heard in Sri Lanka in relation to the Office of Missing Persons. Notwithstanding the criticism of the international community and civil society organizations (CSOs) about the flawed process (Fonseka and Schulz, 2018), victims' families were engaging with the Office. A civil society member of the Office observed that women especially from female-headed households were coming forward, sceptically and hesitantly, for redress and relief (personal communication, Delhi, 2019). In contrast to the importance claimed for livelihood and development issues by women living in the conflict zones of the global South, transitional justice mechanisms, including those articulated within the WPS discourse, can be faulted for lack of attention to the structural inequalities that systems of war and repression exacerbate. Women's low status renders them disproportionately vulnerable to violations of socioeconomic rights (Coomaraswamy et al, 2015, p 110; see also UNSCR 2122). Within the region, women's experiences draw attention to the need to position such violations alongside concerns relating to civil and political rights.

Other international institutional contexts[4]

'It [UNSCR 1325] recognizes us [women] but it doesn't include us', notes Afghanistan's Commissioner for Human Rights, Sima Samar (cited in Manchanda, 2017b, p xxviii). This blunt statement reflects the disappointment of many of the region's eminent peace, justice and gender equality advocates. In the last two decades, the trajectory of the evolving WPS discourse, its workings within the Security Council, and the dwindling of donor support for WPS in the region, has led to civil society activists looking towards other institutional contexts. Hina Jillani, then a UN Special Rapporteur, has given voice to growing scepticism about the capacity of WPS to impact the region's lived reality. At the South Asia Women's Conference held in Kathmandu in 2013, she said, 'It is our own initiatives and movement building in the region that gives us our energy and provides more solace than the UN …. Let us build on 1325. Whatever you have on hand you use to your advantage. But it cannot be the center of our focus' (quoted in Manchanda 2017b, p xxviii).

Three of the region's leading feminist peace activists – Roshmi Goswami, Nighat Said Khan and Kumudini Samuel – have been influential in drawing attention to the limits of the relevance of the WPS framework. They had been involved in the global advocacy for a UN initiative and ideationally contributed to the original imagining of the global WPS agenda, but from the outset there were misgivings about the location of WPS in the Security Council, an institution with a masculine, militarized culture (Goswami et al, 2017). This concern was also reflected at the Asia-Pacific review of the implementation of WPS convened by the Asia Pacific Women's Alliance for Peace and Security (APWAPS) in Kathmandu in 2014. In its recommendation for the *Global Study*, APWAPS noted that UNSCR 1325+ was becoming a management tool for 'making war safe for women', rather than addressing the root causes and politics of wars and conflicts (APWAPS, 2014).[5] Moreover, the trajectory of WPS seemed to be diverging from the women's rights and social equality agenda of CEDAW. Resolutions 1325+ rarely invoked the CEDAW human rights framework of substantive equality; of the 988 Security Council resolutions adopted since the passage of UNSCR 1325 in 2000, only ten resolutions mention CEDAW (Swaine and O'Rourke, 2015).

Disillusioned over the limited relevance and impact of the evolving WPS agenda for the region, feminist activists in recent years have focused attention on country commitments under CEDAW and the Beijing Platform for Action (BPFA) to oppose militarization and support local women building human security. In particular, the adoption of CEDAW: General Recommendation 30 on 'Women in Conflict Prevention, Conflict and Post-Conflict Situations' was welcomed with enthusiasm. Taking cognisance of the diversity of conflicts, General Recommendation 30 has expanded the scope beyond the international law definition of armed conflicts to include low-intensity civil strife, ethnic and communal violence and states of emergency (CEDAW, 2013a). This was important to the region because the governments of India and Pakistan have denied the existence of 'conflicts' within their countries. India, for instance, supports UNSCR 1325 globally, but denies its relevance to officially designated 'disturbed' areas of the northeast and Kashmir.[6]

CEDAW's General Recommendation 30 and BPFA, specifically its 'Women and Armed Conflict' area of concern, bridge several of the gaps and limitations alluded to earlier, such as attention to structural causes underpinning the conflict, demilitarization and arms control, socio-economic priorities and the recognition of intersecting hierarchies that render women more vulnerable. Above all, these position women as political subjects with rights. Unlike UNSCR 1325, CEDAW has a compliance mechanism (Swaine and O'Rourke, 2015). Even before General Recommendation 30, women's groups, such as North East Network in India had used the CEDAW reporting mechanism in 2008 to leverage international accountability on sexual gender violence (Manchanda, 2017b, p xxxi). In 2014, after General Recommendation 30, cross border women's networks used the CEDAW reporting mechanism to invoke India's extra territorial obligations to protect women's rights in relation to its development assistance, including the India Housing Project in Sri Lanka. The CEDAW Committee urged an immediate review (CEDAW, 2014).

Activists in Sri Lanka and Nepal have used the UN system's human rights treaty bodies, UN Human Rights Council and its special procedures, the Special Rapporteur to protect women's rights affected by conflict. In Nepal, civil society organisations such as Advocacy Forum have turned to the Council for justice in the case of the forcible disappearance and murder of a minor by the Nepal security forces. Circumventing Nepal's impunity provisions, activists brought in vetting measures in the deployment of Nepal's peacekeepers by lobbying the UN Department of Peacekeeping Operations to recall peacekeepers accused of human rights violations in Nepal (Sharma, 2017, p 244).

Human rights defenders have invoked the Rome Statute – which led to the establishment of the International Criminal Court – to indict rape as a 'war crime' and a 'crime against humanity' in informal and formal systems of justice. More recently, Rohingya refugee activists looked to the ICC as the collective judicial system for establishing international accountability for 'genocidal like' crimes including widespread targeted sexualized violence, to drive out more than 700,000 Rohingya across the international border into Bangladesh.

It is important to note that CEDAW, BPFA, UNSCR 1325 and the Universal Periodic Review of the Human Rights Council have large and sustained civil society constituencies in the region (see Manchanda and Vaishnava/UN Women, 2014). However, the flagging organizational momentum, since the 2015 mobilization around the *Global Study* process, is a reminder of the dependence on donor assistance to sustain national as well as regional activism. Moreover, official displeasure, even punitive action against funded NGOs that internationalize 'internal' conflicts,[7] has discouraged women's groups from engaging with international instruments such as UNSCR 1325+ (Manchanda, 2017b). The shrinking of space for civil society, the branding of critical voices as 'anti-national' and punitive action of cancelling licences for receiving foreign contributions has constrained activism (Civicus, 2017, pp 2–5). Here it is worth emphasizing that women's everyday forms of resistance and resilience against oppression and militarization and their local initiatives to build peace with justice predates UNSCR 1325 and continues.

Conclusion

UNSCR 1325+ and the acknowledgement of the linkage between women, peace and security, the recognition of the relationship between gender equality and violent conflict, and the promotion of the protection and participation pillars of the WPS agenda have been significant for global policy and praxis. But if the WPS discourse is to have sustained relevance to the lived reality of women in myriad conflict zones, its global prescriptive norms and priorities need to be mediated by sensitivity to contextual differences and diversities. Women's plural positioning vis-à-vis parties to the conflict needs to be understood, their divergent perspectives emanating from their multiple identities and social hierarchies need to be incorporated. More attention is required on the significance of the social, political and cultural factors that create the condition of vulnerabilities, physical (and sexual), economic and social. The crisis of solutions and women's everyday resistance and resilience in the conflict continuum needs to be recognized within a dialectic of victimhood and agency (Gopinath and Manchanda, 2019).

Women's resistance politics need to be recognized as a legitimate aspect of the WPS peace–conflict dynamic and understood as contextual, multifaceted and non-linear. It spans women's agency across a continuum of peacemaking, non-violent resistance and involvement in violent politics against oppressive systems. Fundamental is the understanding that women's negotiations with peace and violence is political. The scope and nature of local women's peacework in the region has expanded the contours of the WPS policy framework to prioritize issues of demilitarization and denuclearization, development and socio-economic needs, and to focus on new issue areas such as multiple human rights violations of women in situations of forcible displacement. The region's gender equality activists have demonstrated the value and effectiveness of linking two separate streams of women's human rights and women-peace-security by working together with international instruments such as CEDAW, BPFA, UNSCR 1325+ and the Human Rights Council to expand openings for peace with equality and justice.

The critical observations iterated earlier are moved by the desire to revitalize the original imagination that inspired WPS advocacy for demilitarization and conflict prevention, alongside protection and participation. WPS discourse posed the question of whose security counts. The voices of women from the region loudly proclaim that more militarization does not lead to more security. In responding to the challenges of countering violent extremism and terrorism within the WPS framework, there is a need to explore the potential of non-violent approaches, building upon feminist understanding of the gendered dynamics of conflict and the construction of violent masculinities and passive femininities. If UNSCR 1325+ is to expand beyond an elite women-driven project of peripheral value, especially in non-internationalized conflict zones, the contextual reality of the region's diverse experiences and the political economy of militarization in the conflict–peace continuum needs to more effectively shape WPS policy discussions and normative frameworks. This is all the more crucial as funding support for WPS dwindles and overall space for civil society, especially activism, and for meaningful peace shrinks.

Notes

[1]   Women collectives' advocacy against war, militarism and communal hatred has been highly visible in civil society mobilizations against the rise of hyper national jingoism around the India–Pakistan conflict axis and its domestic proxy communal violence. These include, for example: Artists for Unity at the iconic Red Fort in Delhi, March 2019; women's assembly of *Hameen se Sanvidhan* ('Constitution belongs to us') convened by (among others) One Billion Rising, Act Now for Harmony and Democracy and People's Union for Civil Liberties in Delhi, February 2019; women's rally in defence of the constitution by *Aman ki Baatein* (Peace talks) in 200 cities, launched in 2018; and rural women's discussion on peace and security in Punjab in October 2019, mobilizing as part of the *Kashmiri Quami Sangharsh Himayat Committee* against the undemocratic change of the legal status of Jammu and Kashmir.

[2]   In the Norwegian-facilitated Sri Lanka peace talks, a Subcommittee on Gender Issues was appointed ten months after the Ceasefire Agreement and four months after the formal peace talks commenced. The SGI was part of a subordinate peace table to 'explore the effective inclusion of gender concerns in the peace process'. Comprising of ten women nominated by the government and the Liberation Tigers of Tamil Eelam (LTTE), it was the first effort by the Sri Lankan government and the LTTE to recognize the involvement of women in peacebuilding and peace-making (Samuel, 2010, 2017).

[3]   The Naga conflict in northeast India is the country's oldest self-determination conflict. The Naga Mothers Association (NMA) transited from a women's welfare body to becoming a stakeholder in the peace process through its campaign of 'shed no blood' that called for an end to violence among splintered Naga armed groups (Manchanda, 2004, p 39). Over these seven decades Naga women's collectives have attempted to move their work beyond the apolitical archetype of 'mother's sorrow' to political activism aimed at challenging women's exclusion from the Naga public sphere traditional and modern.

[4]   This section draws on my 'Introduction' in *Women and the Politics of Peace* (2017).

[5]   This construction references the famous phrase widely attributed to Cora Weiss, who noted in a speech in 2011 that the primary aim of eliminating conflict-related sexualized violence must not be to 'make war safe for women'.

[6]   India's Foreign Ministry demonstrably rejects international references to and intrusion into its internal conflict areas as evidenced in India's Permanent Representative to the UN Hardeep Puri's strongly-worded protest against the inclusion of India's Naxal affected areas under the rubric of 'armed conflict' in the 2010 UN *Report on Children in Armed Conflict* (Times of India, 2010).

[7]   The Indian government has been hostile to women's groups from the northeast raising the contentious Armed Forces (Special Powers) Act with CEDAW and at

other international fora. A woman activist from the northeast who spoke up against militarization and women's human rights violations in the NGO convenings around the country review processes in New York and Geneva was pulled up by a senior Indian diplomat (personal communication Delhi 2015).

References

Afghan Women's Network (2014) *UN Security Council Resolution 1325 in Afghanistan: Civil Society Monitoring Report 2014*, Kabul: Afghan Women's Network.

Allison, M. (2003) 'Cogs in the wheel? Women in the liberation tigers of Tamil Eelam', *Civil Wars*, 6(4): 37–54.

Azarbaijani-Moghaddam, S. (2018) 'Escaping the ghosts of the past: women's participation in peace talks', *Accord: An International Review of Peace Initiatives*, 27: 63–67.

Banerjee, P. (ed) (2008) *Women in Peace Politics*, Delhi: SAGE.

Batool, E. Butt, I., Mushtaq, S., Rashid, M. and Rather, N. et al (2016) *Do You Remember Kunan Poshpora?*, Delhi: Zubaan.

Bhandari, R.K., Chaudhary, B. and Chaudhary, S. (2018) 'Social justice for families of the disappeared in Nepal: notes from the field', *Practicing Anthropology*, 40(2): 14–18.

Bhasin, A. (2017) 'Gender and patriarchy in militarized Kashmir', in R. Manchanda (ed) *Women and Politics of Peace*, Delhi: SAGE, pp 124–136.

CEDAW (Committee on the Elimination of Discrimination Against Women) (2013a) General Recommendation No. 30 on women in conflict prevention, conflict and post-conflict situations, Available from: www.ohchr.org/documents/hrbodies/cedaw/gcomments/cedaw.c.cg.30.pdf.

CEDAW (Committee on the Elimination of Discrimination Against Women) (2013b) 'Concluding observations on the combined fourth and fifth periodic reports of India', C/IND/CO/4–5, 25 July.

Chenoy, A. (2017) 'Militarization values, attitudes, and practices in South Asia', in R. Manchanda (ed) *Women and Politics of Peace*, Delhi: SAGE, pp 99–122.

CIVICUS (2017) *India: Democracy Threatened by Growing Attacks on Civil Society*, November, Available from: civicus.org/images/India_Democracy_Threatened_Nov2017.pdf.

Cockburn, C. (2008) 'Drawing lines, erasing lines: feminism as a resource in opposing xenophobia and separatism', in P. Banerjee (ed) *Women in Peace Politics*, Delhi: SAGE, pp 274–288.

Cockburn, C. (2011) 'Gender relations as causal in militarization and war: a feminist standpoint', in A. Kronsell and E. Svedberg (eds) *Making Gender, Making War*, Abingdon: Routledge, pp 29–46, Available from: portal.research.lu.se/portal/files/5501673/5155687. pdf.

Cockburn, C. (2013) 'War and security, women and gender: an overview of the issues', *Gender and Development*, 21(3): 433–452.

Colekessian, A. (2009) 'Reintegrating gender: a gender analysis of the Nepali rehabilitation process', INSTRAW Gender, Peace and Security series working paper, Available from: https://reliefweb.int/sites/reliefweb.int/files/resources/4DF98D25D63E5852852577CA00683717-Full_Report.pdf.

Conciliation Resources (2017) *Gender and Nepal's Transition from War*, Accord Spotlight, London: Conciliation Resources.

Coomaraswamy, R. and Fonseca, D. (eds) (2004) *Peace-Work*, Colombo: ICES/Kali for Women.

Coomaraswamy, R. et al (2015) *Preventing Conflict, Transforming Justice, Securing the Peace: A Global Study on the Implementation of United Nations Security Council Resolution 1325*, New York, NY: UN Women, Available from: http://wps.unwomen.org/pdf/en/GlobalStudy_EN_Web.pdf.

Das, S. (2008) 'Ethnicity and democracy meet when mothers protest', in P. Banerjee (ed) *Women and Peace Politics*, New Delhi: SAGE, pp 54–77.

D'Costa, B (2014) 'Marginalisation and impunity: violence among women and girls in the Chittagong Hill Tracts', Dhaka: Chittagong Hill Tracts Commission.

Duncanson, C. and Woodward, R. (2016) 'Regendering the military: theorizing women's military participation', *Security Dialogue*, 47(1): 3–21.

Duncanson, C. and Farr, V. (2019) 'Where pillars intersect (or fail): the case of WPS in Afghanistan', S. Davies and J. True (eds) *The Oxford Handbook of Women, Peace, and Security*, Oxford: Oxford University Press, pp 553–568.

Duschinski, H., Bhan, M., Zia, A. and Mahmood, C. (eds) (2018) *Resisting Occupation in Kashmir*, Philadelphia, PA: University of Pennsylvania Press.

Emmanuel, S. (2008) *Strategic Mapping of Women's Peace Activism in Sri Lanka*, Colombo: Women and Media Collective, Available from: womenandmedia.org/.

Falch, A. and Miklian, J. (2008) 'A transitional success story: the Nepali experience with power-sharing', Oslo: CSCW/PRIO CSCW, Available from: files.ethz.ch/isn/117620/Nepal%20Policy%20Brief. pdf.

Farasat, W. (2017) 'Challenges for transitional justice in South Asia', in R. Manchanda (ed) *Women and Politics of Peace*, New Delhi: SAGE.

Fonseka, B. and Schulz, E. (2008) 'Gender and transformative justice in Sri Lanka', Available from: lse.ac.uk/women-peace-security/assets/ documents/2018/WPS18Fonseka.pdf.

Gopinath, M. and Manchanda, R. (2019) 'Women's peacemaking in South Asia', in S. Davies and J. True (eds) *The Oxford Handbook of Women, Peace, and Security*, Oxford: Oxford University Press.

Goswami, R., Samuel K. and Khan, N.S. (2017) 'Herstory: peace movements in South Asia', in R. Manchanda (ed) *Women and Politics of Peace*, New Delhi: SAGE, pp 59–79.

Gowrinathan, N. and Cronin-Furman, K. (2015) *The Forever Victims? Tamil Women in Post-War Sri Lanka*, New York: Colin Powell School.

Guhathakurta, M. (2001) 'Women's narratives from the Chittagong Hill Tracts', in R. Manchanda (ed) *Women, War and Peace in South Asia: Beyond Victimhood to Agency*, New Delhi: SAGE.

Hans, A. (2016) 'Women of Manipur: a space for UNSCR 1325', in A. Hans and S. Rajagopalan (eds) *Openings for Peace: UNSCR 1325 Women and Security in India*, New Delhi: SAGE, pp 160–184.

Husain, S. (2019) *Love, Loss, and Longing in Kashmir*, New Delhi: Zubaan.

ICRC (International Committee of the Red Cross) (2009) 'Families of missing persons in Nepal: a study of their needs', Kathmandu: ICRC, Available from: icrc.org/en/doc/assets/files/2011/families-of-missing-persons-nepal-report.pdf.

Jayawardena, K. (1986) *Feminism and Nationalism in the Third World*, London: Zed Books.

Kapur, B. and Rees, M. (2019) 'WPS and conflict prevention', in S. Davies and J. True (eds) *The Oxford Handbook of Women Peace and Security*, Oxford: Oxford University Press, pp 135–147.

Kikon, D. (2016) 'Memories of rape: the banality of violence and impunity in Naga society', in U. Chakravarti (ed) *Fault Lines of History – The India Papers II*, New Delhi: Zubaan.

Luna, K.C. (2019) 'Everyday realities of reintegration: experiences of Maoist "verified" women ex-combatants in Nepal', *Conflict, Security & Development*, 19(5): 453–474.

MacGinty, R. (2011) *International Peacebuilding and Local Resistance*, Basingstoke: Palgrave Macmillan.

Manchanda, R. (2004) *We Do More Because We Can: Naga Women in the Peace Process*, Kathmandu: South Asia Forum for Human Rights.

Manchanda, R. (2017a) 'Gender, power and peace politics' in R. Manchanda (ed) *Women and Politics of Peace*, New Delhi: SAGE, pp 31–57.

Manchanda, R. (2017b) 'Introduction', in R. Manchanda (ed) *Women and Politics of Peace*, New Delhi: SAGE, pp xvii–xlii.

Manchanda, R. and Bose, T. (2015) *Making War, Making Peace*, SAGE Human Rights and Peace Audits, Vol 1, New Delhi: SAGE.

Manchanda, R. and Kakran, S. (2017) 'Gendered power transformations in India's northeast', *Cultural Dynamics*, 29(1–2): 63–82.

Manchanda, R. and Vaishnava, S./UN Women (2014) *India Civil Society Beijing Platform for Action: 20 Year Review*, New Delhi: UN Women.

Mohsin, A. and Hossain, D. (2015) *Conflict and Partition: Chittagong Hill Tracts, Bangladesh*, New Delhi: SAGE.

Naraghi Anderlini, S. (2007) *Women Building Peace: What They Do, Why It Matters*, Boulder and London: Lynne Rienner.

Ní Aoláin, F. and Nahla, V. (2019) 'Scholarly debates and contested meanings of WPS', in S. Davies and J. True (eds) *The Oxford Handbook of Women Peace and Security*, Oxford: Oxford University Press, pp 53–66.

Nordland, R., Faizi, F. and Abed, F. (2019) 'Afghan women fear peace with Taliban may mean war on them', *The New York Times*, 27 January, Available from: www.nytimes.com/2019/01/27/world/asia/taliban-peace-deal-women-afghanistan.html.

Parashar, S. (2014) *Women and Militant Wars: The Politics of Injury*, Abingdon and New York: Routledge

Samuel, K. (2010) *The Centrality of Gender in Securing Peace*, New Delhi: WISCOMP/Rupa.

Samuel, K. (2017) 'Women's activism and the search for peace in Sri Lanka', in R. Manchanda (ed) *Women and Politics of Peace*, New Delhi: SAGE, pp 80–96.

Sharma, M. (2017) 'Beyond transitional justice: accountability initiatives in Nepal', in R. Manchanda (ed) *Women and Politics of Peace*, New Delhi: SAGE, pp 237–247.

Shepherd, L.J. (2010) 'Women, armed conflict and language – gender, violence and discourse', *International Review of the Red Cross*, 92(877): 143–159

Shrestha, G., Upreti, B.R. and Kolås, Å (2017) 'Women, peace and security: the case of Nepal', in Å Kolås (ed) *Women, Peace and Security in Nepal: From Civil War to Post-Conflict Reconstruction*, Abingdon: Routledge, pp 99–123.

Swaine, A. and O'Rourke, C. (2015) *Guidebook on CEDAW General Recommendation No. 30 and the UN Security Council Resolutions on Women, Peace and Security*, New York: UN Women.

Times of India (2010) 'Naxal problem not an armed conflict, India tells UN', *Times of India*, 18 June, Available from: https://timesofindia. indiatimes.com/india/Naxal-problem-not-an-armed-conflict-India-tells-UN/articleshow/6063604.cms.

WRN (Women's Regional Network) (2014a) 'Unequal citizens: women's narratives of resistance, militarization, corruption and security', compiled by R. Manchanda, Delhi: WRN.

WRN (Women's Regional Network) (2014b) 'Surviving war and transition in Afghanistan', Kabul: WRN.

WRN (Women's Regional Network) (forthcoming) 'Not everyone picks up stones: plural forms of resistance', New Delhi: WRN.

Yadav, P. (2017) '1325 – is that a taxi number? Implementation of the National Action Plan on 1325 and 1820 in Nepal', *LSE Working Paper Series,* Available from: https://blogs.lse.ac.uk/wps/2017/05/03/1325-is-that-a-taxi-number-implementation-of-the-national-action-plan-on-1325-and-1820-in-nepal-punam-yadav-42017/

Yami, H. (2007) *People's War and Women's Liberation in Nepal*, Kathmandu: Janadhwani Publication.

5

Best Practice Diplomacy and Feminist Killjoys in the Strategic State: Exploring the Affective Politics of Women, Peace and Security

Minna Lyytikäinen and Marjaana Jauhola

From NAPping to sNAPping

How does it feel to snap at the Ministry for Foreign Affairs, at a meeting taking stock of the progress of the Women, Peace and Security (WPS) National Action Planning (NAP)? This auto-ethnographic reflection (Martini and Jauhola 2014) on the affective sites of WPS NAPping is a result of a dialogue and writing process between two feminist international relations scholars who share a career trajectory of having been aid intervention project managers, gender experts and advocates for UNSCR 1325 during the two decades of its implementation in various international and foreign affairs spheres. We focus on the analysis of affects created around our participation in the preparation and launch of the third WPS National Action Plan (2018–21) in Finland, particularly in view of the claims by Finnish diplomats that this was 'the world's best NAP'. We weigh these claims against the intimate resonance of the NAP process with the wider turn to neoliberalism, conservatism and nationalism (Elomäki and Kantola, 2018) where the NAP emerges as a tool of global neoliberal governmentality of gendered foreign affairs, defence policies and expertise on such themes.

We suggest that affective moments of feminist killjoyism (Ahmed, 2010), which we in this context call 'sNAPping', can allow the emergence of a critical and radical democratic feminist space that draws from difference, dissent and antagonisms (Laclau and Mouffe, 1985) rather than consensus–driven gender equality policies of the neoliberal strategic state (Brown, 2015). They offer openings for new directions in feminist activist-scholarship on WPS as it turns the focus from the shame of being a feminist killjoy towards feminist creativity and the creation of alternative feminist spaces and knowledges on WPS.

NAPping makes the strategic state become real

Finland started drafting its third NAP towards the end of 2016 and the Ministry for Foreign Affairs (MFA) contracted an external facilitator – a US-based gender equality organization with a track record in facilitating WPS NAP development processes around the world – to take forward the process. The process was designed as a series of three interactive workshops in late 2016 and early 2017 with participation from several ministries and agencies, civil society organizations and a handful of university researchers, including ourselves. The first workshops began with presentations by the consultants. The presentations had three main topics: an introduction to recent global trends in the WPS agenda (such as violent extremism, forced migration and climate change); a description of the consultants' preferred approach to NAPs (based on best practice in results-based management) and an overview of Finland's strengths and weaknesses to date.

> Minna: *I found it curious that no-one from the Finnish participants had been asked to reflect on achievements and learning from previous work on 1325 NAPs. After all, there were most, if not all, of the experienced 1325 people in the same room for two days. It seemed like a shame to miss that opportunity for collective stock-taking.*

Instead, the time and energies of the civil servants and other experts in the room was harnessed during those workshops to learn about a specific project management tool, the log frame. Finland's specific needs were identified by an evaluation that had been carried out earlier by the consultants. Challenges identified by the consultants were related to how well the Finnish agencies followed international best practice in NAPs. They included the need for concrete, operational documents, overarching coordination structures, identification of specific activities and responsibilities, monitoring and evaluation, and resource allocation.

The consultants had also found some best practices in Finland that 'should be documented' and thus disseminated to other countries; 'twinning' between Finland and development aid partner countries was identified as such a practice.

As we proceeded to learn about the practice of drafting logical, results-based plans, we were instructed to split into smaller working groups and to work first on problem identification (all working groups came up with nearly identical lists of six or seven problem areas for the NAP to address) and then identification of specific short- and long-term objectives for each problem area. We were instructed to 'Speak results language!' In learning to become better results-based managers we were compelled to 'focus on problem solving through team-based and consensus-based efforts' (Brown, 2015, p 141). Resorting to such a highly consultant-led process to ensure that Finland would meet established international best practice exemplifies depoliticized neo-liberal governmentalities at the heart of WPS politics. Best practices, according to Wendy Brown, conceal their normative nature by their

> ostensibly general applicability, by their emergence from the combination of consensus and objective research, and by their formally neutral status as practices, rather than purposes or missions. Best practices can be effectively contested only by postulating better practices, not by objecting to what they promulgate. (Brown, 2015, pp 135–136)

The assumption with best practices is that they can easily be lifted from one context to another. You would, in fact, be hard pressed to guess that we were talking about women's rights, let alone issues of peace and security, just on the basis of the list of recommendations made by the consultants. One poignant example came when we noticed that while countering violent extremism (CVE) came up as a problem area on quite a few of the lists developed by the small groups, none of the participants volunteered to work on developing specific objectives for that section. That wouldn't be a problem, however, as the consultants promised to put forward some 'recommended language' for this area. Throughout the process we felt, however, that NAPping in English and with a facilitator who was not familiar with the domestic govern-ance and policy/legal framework created an obstacle for the kinds of discussions we would have wanted to see.

> Marjaana: *I remember spending a lot of time just documenting already existing legislation and policy processes and literally*

translating those processes into English so that references could be made in the formal NAP later. Yet, it feels that the moment the language is changed into English, the connection is lost to Finnish debates and activism that is simultaneously going on, for example, on forced deportations, asylum seeking processes, and changes in key legislation that governs such questions. NAPping seems to take place in another world. One that is detached from the politicization of racialized and gendered bodies entering the EU and Finland and refugee detention centres.

Government agencies responsible for refugee, asylum or immigration policies were not present in the planning workshops, despite invitations to attend. In the first workshop, it was the CSO and academic participants who took up the task of developing 'results' language on safeguarding the rights of refugees and asylum seekers, without any formal expertise (after all, we were 'just' WPS experts!) or mandate within government agencies.

Minna: At this point, I was already growing frustrated with the technical, context-free approach to the NAP process, but in this non-governmental working group, I felt a shared excitement about coming up with creative ideas and addressing political problems that were felt strongly by all of us in our everyday lives. Perhaps we all felt a bit subversive writing down our 'radical' ideas on a flip chart sheet in these meeting rooms of power.

Since 2015, the right-wing populist Finns Party had been in government for the first time and their founder and then leader, Timo Soini, was the Foreign Minister in charge of the WPS agenda. It was our gut feeling that from the start this NAPping process would require concerted action to protect the human rights of refugees and asylum seekers. However, in retrospect, WPS remains unrelated to the realities of the rest of the government programme vis-à-vis deportations, removal of humanitarian protection as a basis for asylum and the inadequate efforts to tackle human trafficking, just to name a few. Furthermore, the Finnish Immigration Service was notably absent in the initial NAP process.

SNAPping as a creative force for feminist alternative knowledge production

Two to three months into NAPping, one of the items on the agenda at a national 1325 coordination meeting was taking stock of the ongoing

NAPping process. The MFA representatives concluded that three 'log frame workshops' were completed and the results had been compiled into a logical framework matrix.

> Marjaana: *When a colleague and I asked why the draft had not yet been shared, in order to see the big picture or provide feedback, the Chair bluntly replied that the document was not in fact a draft yet, as it had been only an exercise for the sake of learning the log frame as a tool, and that experts in the field would still have to be consulted. With a rush of frustration and anger running through my body, I could no longer stop myself. Being told off like that created feelings of shame and humiliation in front of the government officials. It felt that the days we had spent in workshops, developing content for the log frame as experts on UNSCR 1325 and key policy fields in Finland was not considered to be actual input into the NAP. In short, the message was that the workshops lacked 'real' expertise on 1325 core themes. In my angry response, I said that such a belittling of feminist research has become unbearable – the participation of vocal representatives of civil society and the researcher community is not considered as 'expert enough' even though among us are those who have followed the emergence of the WPS agenda since 2000.*

Months passed, and another workshop was held without the consultants, as their contracts had run out. In this workshop, the first official draft was presented on a big screen. No copies were shared beforehand, nor were they handed over at the meeting. Participants were asked to form small groups based on the draft NAP priority areas.

> Marjaana: *It was a stunning meeting. Some of the civil society participants seemed to know the contents of the draft, whereas others, including myself, were seeing the contents for the first time. It was ironic, as the group I had joined was focused on peace processes (peace mediation), my own area of research expertise. When I asked some of the other group participants from key NGO partners of the Ministry, they admitted that an informal group had been formed by the Ministry after the last official coordination meeting to draft the contents. The feeling of exclusion got worse, as the civil society participants had in particular been working on 1325-related research goal setting – without a single full-time university-based researcher present.*

Later, in informal meetings with other civil society participants it became clear that those who had raised their critical voices during the process – in other words, those who had sNAPped – were outed from the process. Instead, representatives of core grant-receiving non-governmental organizations – the same ones that had already been identified and marked as the implementers of the NAP – had formed a task force to develop the draft.

Slowly, the anger, feelings of exclusion, and dealing with the affects of sNAPping was channelled into taking a distance from the drafting process, and instead focusing on creating space for researchers to come forward with their research-based review of the NAP. A wider circle of feminist and gender studies researcher colleagues were invited, first, to identify the researchers in Finland who contribute with critical scholarship to WPS discussions, either directly by framing their research as WPS research, or indirectly. Second, when the NAP draft was circulated formally for comments, an online document was created allowing the drafting of a collective response with concrete suggestions and critique.

Here, the voice of the researcher community was reinstated. The comments by the researchers focused on the gaps between the draft NAP and the wider WPS resolution family and existing research on the topic, starting from the basic confusion in the use of concepts such as gender, gender impact assessment and gender-sensitivity and the lack of consultation of existing feminist research on the topic. This collective response was signed by 26 researchers at various stages, from professors to early career researchers and PhD students. Its annex included, first, a list of over 40 WPS-related research topics and some 60 researchers in Finland working on such topics. Second, it identified current WPS-related research projects, and research collaboration between Finland-based researchers and researchers from conflict regions. It was disseminated to all members of the parliamentary Foreign Affairs Committee and key NAP ministries. It was also published as an online commentary at the Finnish Political Science Association's online portal that aims to popularize scientific research.

We suggest that creating such a temporary virtual feminist collective and gaining a collective voice had a number of healing effects: despite being excluded as 'not-strategic-enough' partners to the state in forming the NAP, the creation of a collective made the existence of a vibrant, active and thematically-diverse feminist researcher community visible in our own terms. Using the online tools where colleagues could provide inputs to their areas of expertise and comment on the draft texts also provided a material connectedness to activism and formed a virtual space for collective feminist solidarity that is often lost in the neoliberal university that brands individual researchers and constantly focuses on individual researcher's value in the citation market.

From co-optation towards the practice of feminist alternative politics

The WPS NAP process discussed in this chapter successfully blended the languages of project management and use of 'results language', diplomatic conventions and collective euphoria around producing 'the world's best NAP'. In our reflections, we have focused on the affects of research-policy dialogue, the pressures to showcase that feminist research has 'real world' relevance, the simple desire and need to be recognized as WPS experts, through research-based knowledge production, and the paranoia around being co-opted, excluded or marginalized in the NAPping process.

We recognize the temptation for feminist advocates within the state (and outside it) to be co-opted by the promise of results, accountability and the feeling of being at the forefront of developing new approaches to WPS, but there are considerable trade-offs. Facilitated workshops give the appearance of consultation and participation but can result in predictable texts that could be quite easily swapped with another country or organization. Moreover, the neoliberal logic of best practice NAPs chooses its priorities through the language of rationality, accountability and teamwork and as such excludes those injustices that cannot be framed in the language of consensus and results. It may well be that in the context of the conservative strategic state, critical feminist scholarship will not be considered as a valuable partner to NAPping. However, taking part in processes that make conflicts, dissonance and diversity visible should be seen as crucial elements of deliberation, as they take part in forming feminist alternatives and forms of solidarity and connectivity.

References

Ahmed, S. (2010) *The Promise of Happiness*, London: Duke University Press.

Brown, W. (2015) *Undoing the Demos, Neoliberalism's Stealth Revolution*, New York: Zone Books.

Elomäki, A. and Kantola, J. (2018) 'Theorizing feminist struggles in the triangle of neoliberalism, conservatism and nationalism,' *Social Politics: International Studies in Gender, State & Society*, 25(3): 337–370.

Laclau, E. and Mouffe, C. (1985) *Hegemony and Socialist Strategy: Towards a Radical Democratic Politics*, Verso: London.

Martini, E. and Jauhola, M. (2014) 'Journeys in Aidland: an autobiographic exploration of resistance to development aid,' *Journal of Narrative Politics* 1(1): http://journalofnarrativepolitics.com/wp-content/uploads/2014/09/JNP-Vol-1-Jahoula-and-Martini1.pdf.

6

Between Protection and Participation: Affect, Countering Violent Extremism and the Possibility for Agency

Elizabeth Pearson

In 2007, the mandate of the United Nation's Special Rapporteur on human rights and counter-terrorism was amended, requiring the role to integrate a gender perspective (Scheinin, 2009). International human rights law additionally stipulated that gender equality should be respected in counter-terrorism, in both civil and political rights (Satterthwaite and Huckerby, 2013). Then in 2015, when a range of community-based responses to counter violent extremism (CVE) were already well-instituted in a variety of global contexts, and in addition to kinetic and military actions, UNSCR 2242 was adopted to recognize the need for a gendered approach within responses to violent extremism and CVE itself (UNSCR 2242, Preamble). Since 2015, critics have suggested both UNSCR 2242 and the concept of CVE have done no more than instrumentalize the Women Peace and Security (WPS) agenda, subordinating women's rights to the security needs of states and denying women agency.

This chapter addresses another side of this story. Using the UK counter-radicalization strategy *Prevent* as a case study, it explores the ways in which CVE both relies on, and reproduces, affective relationships in grassroots communities; and it reveals the ways in which women participating in *Prevent* have an ambiguously agential role. As such, CVE efforts are a site of women's leadership, as well as women's participation; such efforts can also act as a site of Muslim women's resistance. In particular, *Prevent* relies on communities in order to function, and within these communities, women's groups have both local knowledge and power. Additionally, Muslim women represented in this chapter describe choosing to engage in *Prevent* in ways that they believe advantage them both personally and collectively. The chapter suggests that recognition of the ways in which women own CVE, as well as the ways they are co-opted by it, presents a new direction for understandings of the WPS agenda in the counter-terrorism space.

Much of the existing work on gender and CVE practices has taken a critical perspective. The analysis presented here acknowledges those critiques, but seeks to look beyond them, to the stories women tell of their own relationships with countering violent extremism within their own community practice. Critiques of UNSCR 2242 mirror those of the WPS agenda, highlighting the tensions apparent between the various roles women are allotted in policy, and between policy and its effects in practice. The WPS agenda has four core pillars – protection, participation, prevention, relief and recovery – yet Kirby and Shepherd (2016) have noted the prominence of the *protection* of women above efforts to include them at a leadership level. UNSCR 2242 meanwhile has emphasized the need to engage women in participation and leadership roles, where they can assert agency. When UNSCR 2242 was formulated in 2015, it aimed to integrate the WPS agenda into counter-terrorism work, as a 'cross-cutting' subject (UNSCR 2242, Preamble). Ní Aoláin (2016) has argued that, in practice, this aligned UNSCR 2242 more firmly to states' counter-terrorism needs than women, peace and security priorities. In essence, women's empowerment was reproduced by states, not simply as empowerment towards gender equality, as envisaged in UNSCR 1325 or 2242, but as empowerment towards roles as good Muslim citizens, who would support and enable the state in contesting particular forms of terrorism. This is the core critique.

While the chapter concludes that there is much reason for ongoing concern at women's instrumentalization and securitization within CVE, which sees them exploited by states as a means to an end (see Brown, 2013; Rashid, 2014; Ní Aoláin, 2016), the picture is not uniformly bleak. As the 'soft' side of counter-terrorism, the logic of CVE is predicated on partnering pre-existing (Muslim) communities to build resilience. Conceptually therefore, projects aimed at engaging women in countering violent extremism necessitate – and exploit – collective female participation and grassroots women's affective relationships, within a local community. This makes power in the UK's *Prevent* programme ambiguous. Yet policy is also practice, and in practice, the women *Prevent* targets or partners (depending on perspective) are able not just to exercise agency and resist exploitation, but even to shape policy. This chapter seeks to reveal the 'local acts of resistance to universalizing narratives' and see the 'places people carve out for themselves as they endeavour to decide their identities' (Sylvester, 1994, p 324).

UNSCR 2242 and countering violent extremism: gendered critiques

The opening paragraphs of UNSCR 2242 situate it firmly alongside UNSCR 1325 and the six preceding resolutions specifically addressing gender equality and women's rights (UNSCR 2242, Preamble). While the resolution addresses a variety of issues – refugees, climate change and health pandemics – its key role is to address WPS in a 'changing global context of peace and security', and 'rising violent extremism, which can be conducive to terrorism' (UNSCR 2242, Preamble). The WPS agenda is posited as a 'cross-cutting subject in all relevant thematic areas of work on its agenda, including threats to international peace and security caused by terrorist acts' (UNSCR 2242, Preamble). Addressing this core theme, UNSCR 2242 then advocates for the inclusion of WPS goals in counter-terrorism and CVE approaches, based on consultation with women; gender-sensitive data collection; and an emphasis on the goals of women's participation, empowerment and leadership, as consistent with UNSCR 1325 (UNSCR 2242, paras. 11–13). UNSCR 2242 offers a path for CVE in a global context to better acknowledge the WPS agenda outlined in previous UN resolutions.

Increasingly, CVE has been adopted and adapted by countries worldwide, and many explicitly engage with women. Nominally, CVE interventions aimed at 'empowering Muslim women' or protecting them from the oppression of men incorporate the core themes of WPS: protection, prevention of harms against women, encouragement of the participation of women, and a gender equality framework. They frequently do so, however, without consideration of possible harms to the women encountered, or the underlying gendered logics of CVE. While UNSCR 2242 belongs to the WPS agenda in that it contributes to global women's rights, scholars have also explored the ways in which it embodies another, conflicting, agenda: that of the 'War on Terror' (Puar and Rai, 2002; Nesiah, 2012). This has had a lasting legacy for Muslim women, thanks in part to the explicit adoption of narratives of women's liberation as a justification for the invasion of Afghanistan (Bush, 2001; Shepherd, 2006; von der Lippe and Väyrynen, 2011).

Since the War on Terror, western countries which regarded al-Qaeda (and latterly Daesh-inspired) terrorism as a priority have increasingly adopted CVE strategies within Muslim communities as a corner-stone of the prevention of Islamist extremism and terrorism. Western governments implemented hearts-and-minds interventions as part of military operations abroad; and they introduced programmes to counter violent extremism as a feature of home security, to moderate Muslim populations of primarily immigrant backgrounds in the West. If state security practices embody a masculinist agenda (Cohn, 1999; Tickner, 2002; Cohn and Enloe, 2003), then CVE can be understood as consistent with this.

CVE implementation and UNSCR 2242 raise tensions between state and local needs, a dynamic familiar to critics of the implemen-tation of the WPS agenda itself (Kirby and Shepherd, 2016; Cook, 2019). A range of CVE programmes aimed at preventing Islamist extremism can be understood as both racialized and gendered, even if gender is not routinely explicitly evoked. Brown (2013, p 41) iden-tifies a 'maternalist logic' in programming in diverse global contexts, which reads Muslim women according to 'their expected gender and racialized role as mothers'. Mothers became a particular keystone of interventions with training programmes to improve their confidence, teach them communication skills and train them in how to spot the signs of radicalization (Winterbotham, 2018). Moreover, CVE strat-egies frequently use the WPS goal of gender equality to suggest the necessity of empowering Muslim women, in order to aid government in preventing the radicalization of Muslim men. Gender equality has become incorporated into CVE policy in the UK and US as a 'litmus test' of assimilation and a lack of gender equality in Muslim com-munities is often read as an indicator of male potential for violence (Huckerby, 2011). These critiques suggest that CVE practices serve to neglect and negate women's agency through the prioritization of what states want, and how states read the Muslim women who are frequently the objects or 'targets' of participation efforts.

CVE, communities and an ambiguous agency

Nonetheless, neither UNSCR 2242, nor CVE, are entirely mascu-linist creations. Critiques of strategies to counter violent extremism emphasize state maternalism, but can neglect another aspect of their key logic: community. CVE is a communities-based concept, which understands radicalization and violent extremism as a primarily social problem. This has implications for the implementation of the Women,

Peace and Security agenda. Indeed, there are two core principles underlying the concept of countering violent extremism programming: first, that kinetic military solutions – which are often read as masculinist – are insufficient to prevent terrorism and radicalization; and second, that communities matter in stopping violent extremism. In particular, they matter because it is assumed that violent extremism and radicalization are primarily rooted in the issues that communities face, such as grievances, relative deprivation, racial and economic discrimination and local radical connections (Wiktorowicz, 2005; Smelser, 2010; Kundnani, 2012; Klausen, 2019). CVE is sometimes described as a hearts-and-minds or 'soft' approach, and in this regard, it is not new (Elworthy and Rifkind, 2005). The British employed community strategies as part of counter-insurgency operations as long ago as the 1950s and the Malayan Emergency (Smith, 2001; Dixon, 2009).

CVE represents an interface between government security agendas, and communities, generally defined in terms of ethnicity or faith. As such, CVE practitioners must commit to a degree of work to gain the trust of communities, given that CVE goals may not align with community values. For instance, policies neither envisaged Muslim women's own potential support of community norms regarded by the state as problematic, nor their support of Islamist ideologies (Brown, 2015; Ní Aoláin, 2016; Pearson and Winterbotham, 2017). Additionally, CVE legitimizes some sub-communities (Muslim women), while seeking to suppress others (particular Muslim men) (Prior et al, 2006; Spalek, 2008). If the idea of 'radicalization' represents a risky transformation from good citizen to dangerous radical, CVE was its antidote, reconfiguring marginalized communities in line with broader norms. Women were imagined within this as allies, a means to enable community transformation towards normative state values.

Nonetheless, following Hudson, CVE practice defies simple readings as targeting or oppressing communities. Considering the practical implementation of UNSCR 1325 at country level, Hudson suggests that this is not a straightforward case of improving women's rights; yet, nor are women always damaged. Instead, there is the possibility for 'transformational purposes' despite coexistence with 'patriarchal and/ or deeply politicised contexts' (Hudson, 2017, p 4). Similarly, there are tensions in the practice of CVE. Prevention initiatives are predicated on the engagement and participation of already existing grassroots communities. While CVE strategy may seek to exploit communities to mollify them, its logic also enables women to own a separate self-assertion, resisting and subverting state and local agendas, even as CVE seeks to assert these. The gendered logic of CVE interventions as community-based strategies engaging at grassroots with (Muslim) women also often enables women to exploit interventions in ways they choose. Women who choose to participate in CVE in their communities can do so because of what they see as the benefits or rewards for themselves: a chance to meet other women, to discuss parenting, to ask for information on entirely separate issues, for instance. These perceived advantages may or may not match the aims of CVE practitioners. Projects like *Prevent* need community relations to work. If the success of countering violent extremism is predicated on the constitution of community in local relationships, interventions engaging women rely on women's own pre-existing and empathetically constituted networks. This advances a core goal of UNSCR 1325, local ownership, recognized in UNSCR 2242 with the need to address violent extremism from an empowerment and capacity-building (communities) perspective (UNSCR 1325, para. 8; UNSCR 2242, para. 13).

In practice, countering violent extremism initiatives seek to engage with existing networks of women, in order to educate and then mobilize them against terrorism. CVE operates according to what can be thought of as an 'affective logic'. Affect is central to an understanding of CVE and its attempts at transformation through partnership between government and community. This transformation occurs in unexpected ways. Affect is a complex term, often understood as emotion generated in interactions. It is dynamic and communicative; it produces change in perception and bodily states, and it does so in ways that have specific cultural meaning. It can be inherently politicizing (Thrift, 2004; Wetherell, 2012; Ahmed, 2014). For Ahmed (2014), affective responses create political actors and mobilize them into resistance. Collins (1990, 27–28) describes emotion as the 'glue' of solidarity, 'what holds a society together … and what mobilizes conflict'. When two distinct groups come together in friendship or partnership, Jaspers (cited in Polletta et al, 2001, 20) suggests that both reciprocal emotions and shared emotions are at play, the former bonding distinct communities of practice, and the latter aimed at the Other. Both directions of emotion (intra- and inter-group) are part of the libidinal constitution of a movement, the love-based emotions that are generated to either facilitate or hinder collective action. The constitution of initiatives with women through grassroots networks raises the possibility of other forms of collective action and affect, itself politicizing and transformative (Hammack, 2011; Hemmings, 2005; Head, 2016).

Looking at policy, it is not clear to what degree UNSCR 2242 actually seeks to enable local ownership, or promotes this only as participation in imposed regimes, as with the WPS agenda more broadly

(Basini and Ryan, 2016). To see the possibilities of CVE, as well as the limitations, it is necessary to explore the practice. As the next section explores, in the context of CVE, the constitution of communities of practice through women's own grassroots connections offers the potential for the expression of a feminist agenda beyond the pernicious logics and government co-optation emphasized in critiques of UNSCR 2242. Instead, Muslim women I have encountered in the course of my research self-empower through taking ownership of CVE, in turn transforming state practices. The process takes place via women's resistance, and the interpersonal relations at play, which can both mitigate and subvert the racialized, gendered and orientalist structural effects of CVE intervention. This potentially gives them power over state security itself, and through affective mechanisms that produce an expression of political agency, directly relating countering violent extremism initiatives to the WPS agenda. It is through agency, the ability to make choices and enact them, that women's empowerment should be understood. Accounts of women's relationships with countering violent extremism interventions have positioned them as victims of pernicious government policy. There is, however, a more complex relationship with policy that relates directly to the aims of WPS: participation, leadership and empowerment. Despite the 'baggage' that policy imposes on women, they are capable of 'local acts of resistance' which in turn enable transformation towards new identities (Sylvester, 1994). It is this more ambiguous dynamic that is explored in the next empirical section, focused on the UK.

Women, peace and security and the UK's *Prevent* strategy

The UK launched its fourth and latest National Action Plan on UNSCR 1325 in 2018 (Kirby and Shepherd, 2016; UK Foreign and Commonwealth Office, 2018). Following UNSCR 2242, this NAP also engages with counter-terrorism and CVE initiatives. Led by the Foreign and Commonwealth Office, the NAP adopts an external and international focus: the strategy engages only with gender in interventions supported in conflict zones *outside* of the UK (Stone and Parke, 2016). Nonetheless, the UK has also developed a strategy to counter violent extremism and radicalization within its borders, *Prevent*, as part of its CONTEST counter-terrorism policy (Briggs, 2010; Brown, 2010). In the various iterations of *Prevent*, the WPS agenda is, however, not explicitly referenced and there is no action plan to ensure that domestic interventions recognize UNSCR 1325.

Prevent adopts a gendered approach consistent with Brown's (2013) maternalist logic. *Prevent* engages with Muslim women as at the 'heart' of communities understood as separate, and it regards women as the means by which those communities might be subsumed into what is positioned as wider British society. A cohort of prominent British Muslim women were consulted on the gendered stance government would take, as a key engagement group. Building on this consultation, initial *Prevent* delivery in 2006/7 saw a variety of classes organized to empower women, educate them on the dangers of radicalization, and build the trust necessary to report any suspicious behaviour to authorities. Elements of UNSCR 1325 such as empowerment and participation were apparent in strategy, although not acknowledged as such. For instance, the *Preventing Violent Extremism: Winning Hearts and Minds* (2007) report suggested that it was important to 'strengthen the role that women can play within their communities. Women can play a vital role in … tackling violent extremism'. Initial interventions took any form required, be that sports, parenting groups, training, workshops, coffee mornings or dances. Some *Prevent* delivery fell to local non-governmental organizations (NGOs), funded by the Home Office. Other delivery providers have included the police, community groups and faith groups.

Prevent has twice been reformulated (in 2011 and 2018) since its initial introduction, mainly in response to community complaints about implementation, some of which addressed gender. For many British Muslims, *Prevent*'s aim of community engagement, led by the police, appeared little more than a resource from which the UK government could implement its own, racialized security agenda (Kundnani, 2009; Choudhury and Fenwick, 2011; Awan, 2012). For women affected, a key critique was that policy attempted to engage with them as 'spies' on their families, and within their communities. This accusation was however rejected by a government report on the consultation (HM Government, 2011). As such, much of the response from communities affected by *Prevent* in the UK has been negative and consistent with the critiques earlier outlined.

Ambiguous agency: UK women, resistance and the possibility of feminist practice

As previously explored, critiques of countering violent extremism programmes and UNSCR 2242 suggest the effects of both are the opposite of the intentions of UNSCR 1325. Instead of empowerment, there is exploitation; instead of participation, there is co-option.

This section offers a disruption to this – limiting – narrative, and in two ways. First, CVE lives through and is enabled by communities of grassroots women, who, despite reservations about government, exhibit local ownership of programmes. This can empower women in ways that governments do not anticipate. Second, women can enact new identities and find new status and community positions, through participation in CVE programmes. Conversations with Muslim women engaged both in CVE delivery, and as recipients of interventions to prevent Islamist radicalization in the UK, reveal a complex picture, and a range of alternative perspectives. These perspectives present *Prevent* as an unexpected site of women's self-realization, principally through women's subversion of its agenda. Their affective participation enables forms of feminist resistance, to government and to patriarchy. This resistance has in turn had material effects, shaping government CVE practice and policy. The act of resistance also constitutes an assertion of the pain caused to Muslim women in the UK by Islamophobic others, including state institutions, and a – limited – recognition of this by government in response. The approach taken in this section suggests a new direction for understanding the gendered effects of CVE, UNSCR 2242 and the ways in which both can yet offer a means for the authentic expression of UNSCR 1325.

Interviews were conducted with women engaged in CVE as part of separate research projects to explore gender in CVE practices from 2013 to 2018, and in a variety of UK locations. This is not an exhaustive or quantitative study of *Prevent* delivery, and I make no universal claims; the intention is to raise the existence of an important disruption to the victim narrative of Muslim women's participation in the types of counter-terrorism practices dealt with in UNSCR 2242. Specific locations and identities are anonymized, and a different pseudonym used for each participant. Needless to say, Muslim women, like all women, have a variety of different beliefs and opinions around CVE, faith and society; I reflect views here that emerged as themes in my research.

Community and ownership

In a series of interviews with women in a range of locations, women repeatedly contested the idea that *Prevent* is owned by government alone. They asserted their own agency in their active participation in the counter-radicalization programme, and activities organized as part of its remit. They emphasized the ways in which they chose to engage in *Prevent* in order to benefit them personally; and they discussed how, in practice, *Prevent* is constituted through the active participation of women in their own communities. The women's narratives suggested that *Prevent* functioned in ways consistent with the (empowerment) objectives of UNSCR 1325. Their participation additionally shapes strategy implementation and enables women to exercise a form of empowerment that goes beyond the exploitation noted in critiques. It is important to note that all of the women interviewed voiced varying degrees of criticism of *Prevent* as a 'toxic brand'. They shared in Muslim communities' suspicion of its motives, and its effects, viewing it largely as a tool of Islamophobia designed to 'target' Muslims. However, this perception did not universally limit their participation; nor did it constrain the ways in which some women told me they felt empowered by interventions. It is this tension that this section explores. Muslim women told stories that challenged the narrative of co-option and exploitation, and asserted agency.

Muslim women's participation in *Prevent* was rooted in a sense of the possibility engagement offered for an authentic representation of their own community, and its priorities. Crucially, this was enabled through the affective networks constituting community, which enables *Prevent* interventions in the first place and gave them ownership of *Prevent* in practice. This ownership operates through pre-existing community dynamics: women leaders emerge from communities and straddle dual roles of state and community representation; and participation grows through grassroots word of mouth. Women also actively embrace aspects of CVE implementation seen in critiques as problematic, such as its maternalist logic. This produces agency, local ownership and a co-option of *Prevent* by women, not the other way around.

First, the local ownership emphasized in the Women, Peace and Security agenda is enabled through CVE delivery via leaders who genuinely belong to Muslim women's communities, have status within them, and are trusted by them. Aisha, for example, works on the provision of a variety of services for women in her local area, one of which is counter-radicalization, funded by *Prevent*. Her original community role developed organically, as local women came to her independently for help. She explained that, as she had gone to university, women perceived her as knowledgeable and authoritative. Approaches by other women for her help relied on her own bonds with the communities locally, of which she was a part. Eventually she began to work on shared issues with local agencies, who 'found it hard to get into the communities that we got into'. While cooperating with government, of which communities are suspicious, she remained trusted, as she is first and foremost seen as a local leader, embodying a local perspective. Her relationship was one of trust and authentic knowledge of 'cultural factors', factors which, she said, 'can't be taught'. Khadija, a local *Prevent* officer in another part of the UK, told a similar story. She knew a number of women like Aisha and said that they were trusted because, 'It's really personal for them. They're not just doing it for work … It's everything they do, it's their life.' Personal relationships and trust produced this view, not any job title endowed either by government or *Prevent*.

A Muslim woman herself, Khadija engaged with a variety of different NGOs, mostly led and established by local women, responding to the needs of the pre-existing communities of which they were part. These communities were fundamental to women's survival, 'women who spend time together, drop off their kids to school … I know women's networks here, where someone has got into financial trouble, they've taken money out of their grocery budget to help that woman.' Of her *Prevent* work she said, 'Those networks are there, and I think it would be a waste if we didn't tap into [them].' This 'tapping into' could be regarded locally as exploitation, but was not, Khadija suggested, because Muslim women were essentially tapping into their own networks. Aisha, for instance, explained that her success was evident in the ways in which interventions snowballed, and through word of mouth recommendations. A number of other intervention providers and users also stressed the importance of word of mouth contacts in conversations with me, with some women attending CVE workshops only because other participants they knew told them they were 'worth going to'. Women here create their own networks of trust in *Prevent*, via trust in individuals running courses, and in turn, in existing community links.

Prevent's operation, whether in local groups, or in access to local communities of women, in the identification of women's needs, in knowledge of local practices, habitus and cultural meaning, is entirely built on local relationships of trust. While CVE does arguably exploit these relationships to enable interventions, the localization of CVE programming through women's own community links problematizes claims that intervention is imposed. Instead, policy is in tension with local ownership. As another intervention provider, Fatima, suggested, ownership of *Prevent* activities with Muslim women by 'people on the ground' was the opposite of 'tick box' provision of CVE, because it was implemented by communities, and from within communities, even as those same communities largely opposed CVE's institutional intentions. Women instead found 'common scripts' between community and authority (Sylvester, 1994, p 331), often linked through empathetic connections to the community itself via Muslim intervention providers. Women found these common scripts, and they also sometimes exploited them.

On the one hand, government's relocation of responsibility for CVE to local NGOs represents an admission of an institutional lack of knowledge of local Muslim communities that are the 'targets' of intervention; on the other, it places power in the hands of local people as intervention providers. In one London borough, the *Prevent* team uses parenting workshops developed by the Race Equality Commission, 'Strengthening Families, Strengthening Communities', to raise issues of radicalization with groups of approximately a dozen mothers and, separately, the same number of fathers in a Somali community. The local authority handed ownership to local people, who willingly accepted this, evident in a number of ways. First, the course is voluntary, and many participants self-refer, enabling women to express agency around participation. Second, classes are led by trained Somali facilitators in an informal lunch setting. Although most women speak some English, classes are mostly conducted in Somali and therefore inaccessible to the *Prevent* teams. At least two of the weekly sessions include a guest speaker, on topics selected by the parents. The counter-radicalization content is additionally tailored to parents' expressed needs. While I was there these included: improving parents' social media knowledge, to safeguard against online radicalization; educating parents of their rights and responsibilities; improving parenting skills; and teaching them how to spot potential indicators of radicalization.

The women's ownership of the class enables their formulation of new identities, as well as the reformulation of existing ones. Importantly, women were able to reimagine their roles as mothers, uniformly welcoming the 'maternalist logic' through which programming was constructed. Women used the classes to negotiate unfamiliar situations, such as the loss of traditional collective parenting, sudden roles as breadwinner, heads of households, divorcees and mothers of children whom they perceived as 'foreign'. As Zeinab said, 'Children here don't have responsibilities. They don't do household chores; they are very immature compared to when we were their age. As a child I wanted to please my mother and do the right things. They don't.' All the women participating suggested such differences were hard to navigate, and the classes enabled them to deal with emotional issues, reformulating what motherhood entailed, in ways consistent with more relational and Islamic understandings of identity, foregrounding family responsibilities and values (Malik, 2006; Rizvi, 2007). All parents sought advice to help them enact positive change in their personal and family lives. They also sought advice for themselves, one woman telling me her attendance was 'something for me', in a schedule that was filled with obligations to others. Women took ownership of classes to create new identities and develop existing ones; *Prevent* teams facilitated this through a process of listening to facilitator and participant feedback alike.

Consistent with UNSCR 1325, women are engaged in decision making and consultation throughout the delivery of the intervention. This local ownership is vital to their ongoing participation, and articulation of the intervention's meaning to them. The project certainly seeks to impose a counter-radicalization narrative; however, this constitutes only one part of the practice, and the women participants themselves perceived this as a minor aspect of the classes. They mostly appeared to tolerate discussion of radicalization, which was of more limited interest to them, while focusing their own questions on advice on disciplining children, and their key concerns of drugs and crime.

Affect and resistance

CVE programmes aimed at women's participation rely on – and indeed reproduce – women's affective relationships within a distinctly localized terrain. Following Ahmed (2014), empathetic collective engagement, owned locally and constituted during *Prevent* programming, produces an affective and politicizing transformation. This happens through women sharing experiences which they would not otherwise express to institutional figures. This enables the subversion of interventions and their outcomes. This is perhaps most evident in the ways in which women both taking part in CVE initiatives, and delivering them, nonetheless articulate resistance to CVE and its gendered effects. Trust constituted at the micro-level, in the empathetic bonds between intervention providers and women in the communities to which they belong, is in constant conflict with women's lack of trust in the structures of CVE, frequently perceived as an expression of gendered Islamophobia.

This participation and ownership also enabled another important strand of the Women Peace and Security agenda, leadership and genuine empowerment. Many Muslim women highlighted the ways in which *Prevent* groups provided spaces for them to challenge local patriarchy, through affect generated in women's discussion. Women employed the political space provided through *Prevent* to express anger around issues which they could not raise in a mixed setting, and thus to raise the affective temperature of meetings. Mariam told me that she began to attend workshops on extremism as she was 'sick of men talking all the time'. On the subject of radicalization, she told me that men 'don't say what they were doing about it … the way women network is a very different dynamic'. Meanwhile, women in the Somali parenting group frequently expressed dissatisfaction at their husbands' perceived inability to cope with British life, and their inadequacies, and to contest this. Similarly, Khadija used her work as a *Prevent* officer to assert Muslim female leadership at a local level, telling me that in her community, 'Men are still seen through the lens of patriarchy, they are still considered leaders just by virtue of their penis – to put it crudely – they don't have to prove anything.' She worked to counter this, exploiting her CVE workshops to express agency according to her own agenda, a resistance to local patriarchal powers.

In line with previous findings, all the women I encountered also expressed reservations about and resistance to the goals of *Prevent* and CVE, and the ways in which it was perceived to target Muslims (HM Government, 2011; Rashid, 2014; Winterbotham and Pearson, 2016). Because they belonged to the partner communities, Muslim women intervention providers deliberately sought to create space for women to articulate anger at government policy, or fears around it. Mina, who worked in an NGO focused on women's rights and counter-radicalization (but without *Prevent* funding) was typical in suggesting that women wanted to openly discuss the ways in which they felt 'victimized' by *Prevent*. *Prevent* provider Fatima, mentioned earlier, suggested that *Prevent* was a 'dirty word' for women she knew; yet this did not stop them engaging. It did, however, frame their discussion priorities. In this way, resistance – to men, to patriarchy, to government – paradoxically became a feature of women's participation.

The picture of women's engagement in *Prevent* delivery is therefore more complex than one of simple victimization. Women expressed agency through CVE. They used the opportunity of discussion on al-Qaeda or Daesh-related extremism to produce collective affective change. Crucially, they also used it to testify to the effects of the far-right and broader Islamophobic prejudice and abuse. Indeed, as *Prevent* leaders fed this back to government, this insistence on the forms of extremism Muslim women themselves prioritized saw a degree of state transformation, although this would not wholly satisfy communities (Home Affairs Select Committee, 2016). In 2011, *Prevent* was rebranded, partly in response to concerns from British Muslims, including women's complaints that the policy unfairly targeted them as potential spies on their families. A government consultation (HM Government, 2011, 6) reported that the strategy should 'focus on all threats of violence, not just those from Al Qa'ida', and the rebranded *Prevent* therefore explicitly introduced the theme of far-right extremism, even if this was arguably tokenism (Githens-Mazer, 2012, 9). The 2018 counter-terrorism strategy CONTEST also adapted policy language to respond to concerns from British Muslims that they were being 'targeted', now adopting a 'safeguarding' discourse (see Home Office, 2018). These changes do not alter the fundamental assertion that government counter-radicalization strategies disproportionately focus on British Muslims in ways that both racialize and problematize them according to gendered scripts. Nonetheless, the ability of Muslim women to impact strategy suggests a more complex gender relationship between state and community than one of straightforward domination. This transformation is made possible by the affective nature of community engagement.

Conclusions

In the UK, only interventions to counter violent extremism abroad are approached through the lens of WPS and UNSCR 2242. However, key terms of the WPS agenda are evident in the domestic CVE programme *Prevent*, including participation, leadership and empowerment. Their inclusion has been critiqued according to the logic of critiques of UNSCR 2242 itself: that such interventions exploit women's rights in order to enable state security agendas, and they also objectify Muslim women. Via a long-standing active engagement with British Muslim women as a distinct group, conceived primarily as both mothers and allies, *Prevent* demonstrates a gendered and well-critiqued rationale. However, through an empirical exploration of the UK's *Prevent* strategy, this piece has suggested that the policy's gender rationale is less straightforward at a grass-roots level, where it produces possibilities for Muslim women that go beyond the many important critiques of UNSCRs 1325, 2242, and the WPS agenda within CVE practice, which link these to women's securitization and instrumentalization. This chapter argued for the ambiguities in women's roles in gendered CVE, which yet contains the possibility for women to exercise agency, through their affective connections with each other.

Where policy often acts as a site of domination, practice offers the possibility for both resistance and subversion. Where policy is neat and orderly, practice – through its reliance on human relations of empathy between Muslim women, *Prevent* officials and community – is messy and disordered, challenging easy distinctions between community and state. This chapter has argued for what Muslim women repeatedly tell me: that their participation in CVE intervention is complex, and is a site of agency, as well as oppression. While they insist that racialized and gendered state logics must be contested, this contestation should not exclude the perspective of those women able to subvert security agendas, and exercise a political subjectivity capable of bending, if not transforming, government policy and their own identities.

This affective response to policy as well as to local patriarchy, as Ahmed (2014) has noted, facilitates the constitution of political identity and resistance. Women do this through a selective and extractive relationship with the policy, which they critique, in tandem with genuine and meaningful relationships with those who provide it. The logic of CVE therefore both encompasses and goes beyond the 'maternalism' that Brown (2013) has rightly noted, or the instrumentalization of WPS outlined by Ní Aoláin (2016). In particular, community and affect are constituted in the micro-level, and it is here that the success or failure of the UK's counter-radicalization strategy *Prevent* is apparent, even as its structures and macro manifestations are resisted.

The macro-level resistance offered by Muslim women to *Prevent* is not trivial. Muslim women's critiques have arguably contributed to the reformulation of UK *Prevent* policy to include the far-right, and to reframe intervention as safeguarding (even as this might be a cynical state move). The effects on local patriarchal structures of women's activism within CVE are yet to be measured. Basini and Ryan (2016, 391) note that WPS 'discourse alone will tell us little about how [the] NAPs actually function on the ground'. The same is true of CVE programming. The UK NAP ignores the UK's attempts to counter extremism at home; there is no reason for this, as gender and the WPS agenda are clearly evident in *Prevent*, and in unexpected ways. This chapter sought to reveal ways in which women's own community relations produce agency, ownership and empowerment through CVE practice, in spite of all its challenges. This, in turn, suggests a new path for the WPS agenda in UK CVE, working with Muslim women's resistance and agency. The mechanisms are already there, if government is willing to acknowledge them.

References

Ahmed, S. (2014) *The Cultural Politics of Emotion*, 2nd revised edition, Edinburgh: Edinburgh University Press.

Awan, I. (2012) ' "I am a Muslim not an extremist": how the prevent strategy has constructed a "suspect" community', *Politics & Policy*, 40(6): 1158–85, doi:10.1111/j.1747-1346.2012.00397.x.

Basini, H. and Ryan, C. (2016) 'National Action Plans as an obstacle to meaningful local ownership of UNSCR 1325 in Liberia and Sierra Leone', *International Political Science Review*, 37(3): 390–403, doi:10.1177/0192512116636121.

Briggs, R. (2010) 'Community engagement for counter-terrorism: lessons from the United Kingdom', 4 (July): 971–981.

Brown, K.E. (2010) 'Gender and counter-terrorism: UK prevent and de-radicalisation strategies', in Washington, DC: British Politics Group, Available from: www.britishpoliticsgroup.org/BPG%20 2010-Brown.pdf.

Brown, K.E. (2013) 'Gender and counter-radicalization: women and emerging counter-terror measures', in M.L. Satterthwaite and J.C. Huckerby (eds) *Gender, National Security and Counter-Terrorism*, Abingdon and New York: Routledge.

Brown, K.E. (2015) 'How IS message lures Western women', *BBC News*, Available from: www.bbc.co.uk/news/world-middle-east-32208217.

Bush, L.W. (2001). 'Radio Address by Mrs. Laura W. Bush, Crawford, TX, November 17, 2001', Available from: www.bushcenter.org/ publications/articles/2013/02/radio-address-by-mrs-laura-w-bush-crawford-tx-november-17-2001.html.

Choudhury, T. and Fenwick, H. (2011) 'The impact of counter-terrorism measures on Muslim communities', *International Review of Law, Computers & Technology*, 25(3): 151–81, doi:10.1080/1360086 9.2011.617491.

Cohn, C. (1999) 'Missions, men and masculinities', *International Feminist Journal of Politics*, 1(3): 460–475, doi:10.1080/146167499359835.

Cohn, C. and Enloe, E. (2003) 'A conversation with Cynthia Enloe: feminists look at masculinity and the men who wage war', *Signs: Journal of Women in Culture and Society*, 28(4): 1187–1107, doi:10.1086/368326.

Collins, R. (1990) 'Stratification, emotional energy, and the transient emotions', in T.D. Kemper (ed) *Research Agendas in the Sociology of Emotions*, New York: SUNY Press.

Cook, S. (2019) 'Marking failure, making space: feminist interventions in Security Council policy', *International Affairs*, 95(6): 1289–1306.

Dixon, P. (2009) '"Hearts and minds"? British counter-insurgency from Malaya to Iraq', *Journal of Strategic Studies*, 32(3): 353–81, doi:10.1080/01402390902928172.

Elworthy, S. and Rifkind, G. (2005) *Hearts and Minds: Human Security Approaches to Political Violence*, London: Demos.

Githens-Mazer, J. (2012) 'The rhetoric and reality: radicalisation and political discourse', *International Political Science Review*, 33(5): 556–67, doi:10.1177/0192512112454416.

Hammack, P.L. (2011) *Narrative and the Politics of Identity: The Cultural Psychology of Israeli and Palestinian Youth*, New York: Oxford University Press.

Head, N. (2016) 'A politics of empathy: encounters with empathy in Israel and Palestine', *Review of International Studies*, 42(1): 95–113, doi:10.1017/S0260210515000108.

Hemmings, C. (2005) 'Telling feminist stories', *Feminist Theory*, 6(2): 115–139, doi:10.1177/1464700105053690.

HM Government (2011) 'Prevent review: summary of responses to the consultation', London, Available from: www.gov.uk/government/uploads/system/uploads/attachment_data/file/97978/prevent-summary-consultation.pdf.

Home Affairs Select Committee (2016) 'Radicalisation: the counter-narrative and identifying the tipping point', London: House of Commons Home Affairs Select Committee, House of Commons, Available from: www.publications.parliament.uk/pa/cm201617/cmselect/cmhaff/135/135.pdf.

Huckerby, J. (2011) 'Women and preventing violent extremism: the U.S. and U.K. experiences'. Briefing Paper. New York: Center for Human Rights and Global Justice (CHRGJ), Available from: https://chrgj.org/wp-content/uploads/2016/09/Women-and-Violent-Extremism-The-US-and-UK-Experiences.pdf.

Hudson, H. (2017) 'The power of mixed messages: women, peace, and security language in National Action Plans from Africa', *Africa Spectrum*, 52(3): 3–29.

Kirby, P. and Shepherd, L.J. (2016) 'The futures past of the Women, Peace and Security agenda', *International Affairs*, 92(2): 373–392.

Klausen, J. (2019) 'Neighbourhood effects – how Jihadist recruitment really works', in A. Richards, D. Margolin, and N. Scremin (eds) *Jihadist Terror: New Threats, New Responses*, London and New York: I. B. Tauris.

Kundnani, A. (2009) *Spooked*, Institute of Race Relations, Available from: www.irr.org.uk/pdf2/spooked.pdf.

Kundnani, A. (2012) 'Radicalisation: the journey of a concept', *Race & Class*, 54(2): 3–25.

Malik, M. (2006) ' "The branch on which we sit": multiculturalism, minority women and family law', in A. Diduck and K. O'Donovan (eds) *Feminist Perspectives on Family Law*, Abingdon and New York: Routledge-Cavendish, pp 211–231.

Nesiah, V. (2013) 'Feminism as counter-terrorism: the seduction of power', in M.L. Satterthwaite and J.C. Huckerby (eds) *Gender, National Security, and Counter-Terrorism: Human Rights Perspectives*, Abingdon and New York: Routledge.

Ní Aoláin, F. (2016) 'The "War on Terror" and extremism: assessing the relevance of the Women, Peace and Security agenda', *International Affairs*, 92(2): 275–291.

Pearson, E. and Winterbotham, E. (2017) 'Women, gender and Daesh radicalisation', *The RUSI Journal*, 162(3): 60–72.

Polletta, F., Jasper, J.M. and Goodwin, J. (eds) (2001) *Passionate Politics: Emotions and Social Movements*, Chicago, IL: University of Chicago Press.

Prior, D., Spalek, B., Farrow, F. and Barnes. M. (2006) 'Can anti-social behaviour interventions help to contribute to civil renewal?', in T. Brannan, G. Stoker and P. John (eds) *Re-Energizing Citizenship – Strategies for Civil Renewal*, London: Palgrave Macmillan, pp 91–111.

Puar, J.K. and Rai, A.S. (2002) 'Monster, terrorist, fag: The War on Terrorism and the production of docile patriots', *Social Text 72*, 20(3): 117–148.

Rashid, N. (2014) 'Giving the silent majority a stronger voice? Initiatives to empower Muslim women as part of the UK's "War on Terror"', *Ethnic and Racial Studies*, 37(4): 589–604.

Rizvi, S. (2007) 'News cultures, security and transnational belonging cross-generational perspectives among British Pakistani women', *European Journal of Cultural Studies*, 10(3): 327–342.

Satterthwaite, M.L. and Huckerby, J.C. (2013) 'Introduction', in M.L. Satterthwaite and J.C. Huckerby (eds) *Gender, National Security and Counter-terrorism: Human Rights Perspectives*, Abingdon and New York: Routledge.

Scheinin, M. (2009) *Report of the Special Rapporteur on the promotion and protection of human rights and fundamental freedoms while countering terrorism*, Human Rights Council. A/HRC/13/37, 13th Session Agenda Item 3, 28 December.

Shepherd, L.J. (2006) 'Veiled references: constructions of gender in the Bush administration discourse on the attacks on Afghanistan post-9/11', *International Feminist Journal of Politics*, 8(1): 19–41.

Smelser, N.J. (2010) *The Faces of Terrorism: Social and Psychological Dimensions*, Princeton, NJ: Princeton University Press.

Smith, S. (2001) 'General Templer and counter-insurgency in Malaya: hearts and minds, intelligence, and propaganda', *Intelligence and National Security*, 16(3): 60–78.

Spalek, B. (2008) 'Muslim communities post-9/11 – citizenship, security and social justice', *International Journal of Law, Crime and Justice*, 36(4): 211–214.

Stone, L. and Parke, A. (2016) *UK National Action Plan on Women, Peace and Security: Midline Report*, London: Department for International Development.

Sylvester, C. (1994) 'Empathetic cooperation: a feminist method for IR', *Millennium – Journal of International Studies*, 23(2): 315–334.

Thrift, N. (2004) 'Intensities of feeling: towards a spatial politics of affect', *Geografiska Annaler: Series B, Human Geography*, 86(1): 57–78.

Tickner, J.A. (2002) 'Feminist perspectives on 9/11', *International Studies Perspectives*, 3(4): 333–350.

UK Foreign and Commonwealth Office (2018) *UK National Action Plan on Women, Peace Security 2018–2022*, Available from: https://assets.publishing.service.gov.uk/government/uploads/system/uploads/attachment_data/file/677586/FCO1215-NAP-Women-Peace-Security-ONLINE_V2.pdf.

UK Government (2007) *Preventing Violent Extremism: Winning Hearts and Minds*, London: Department for Communities and Local Government.

von der Lippe, B. and Väyrynen, T. (2011) 'Co-opting feminist voices for the War on Terror: Laura Bush meets Nordic feminism', *European Journal of Women's Studies*, 18(1): 19–33.

Wetherell, M. (2012) *Affect and Emotion*, Los Angeles and London: SAGE Publications.

Wiktorowicz, Q. (2005) *Radical Islam Rising: Muslim Extremism in the West*, Lanham, MD: Rowman & Littlefield Publishers, Inc.

Winterbotham, E. (2018) 'Do mothers know best? How assumptions harm CVE', Tony Blair Institute for Global Change, Available from: http://institute.global/insight/co-existence/do-mothers-know-best-how-assumptions-harm-cve.

Winterbotham, E. and Pearson, E. (2016) 'Different cities, shared stories: a five-country study challenging assumptions around Muslim women and CVE interventions', *RUSI Journal*, 161(5), Available from: https://rusi.org/publication/rusi-journal/different-cities-shared-stories-five-country-study-challenging-assumptions.

7

Lessons Lived in Gender and International Criminal Law

Patricia Viseur Sellers and Louise Chappell

Accountability for gender-based crimes has been discussed as an important feature of the Women, Peace and Security agenda. However, too often there has been a significant gap between the ideal of such accountability and its operation. This has been demonstrated over the past decade or so in the operations of the International Criminal Court (ICC) and other tribunals such as those for conflicts in the former Yugoslavia, Rwanda, Sierra Leone. In the form of a conversation between Patricia Viseur Sellers, the Special Advisor for Gender for the Office of the Prosecutor of the International Criminal Court and Louise Chappell, Director of the Australian Human Rights Institute at UNSW Sydney and an expert on the ICC, this chapter explores the challenges of, and lessons learned about, achieving accountability for gender crimes through international criminal tribunals, the steps forward towards new accountability practices and strategies and for strengthening the relationship between these tribunals and the broader international WPS agenda.

Louise Chappell (LC):   Patricia, can I start by asking what influenced you to enter the field of law, and in particular international criminal law?

Patricia Viseur Sellers (PVS):   I went to law school intending to practice criminal law. I attended the Law School of the University of Pennsylvania. After graduation, I joined the Public Defender Office in Philadelphia where I represented indigent defendants who were mainly African American and Latino in criminal proceedings. In addition to defence work, I'd always nurtured an interest in international subjects, whether it was learning languages or travelling outside of the United States. The fact that my father was an officer in the US Army meant that I travelled as a child, spending several years abroad in Germany and living on several army bases within the United States. So I had a conceptualization of the world outside of the United States, along with the breadth of the world inside the United States. For a year during my undergraduate studies at Rutgers, I lived in Mexico and attended the Autonomous University of Mexico. Between undergraduate studies and law school, I moved to Puerto Rico to work on human rights issues.

As an African American growing up in the 1960s and the 1970s, my interest in the law naturally combined with a sense of social justice. The Civil Rights Movement along with other notions of justice and equality permeated our communities, and my family discussions. Thurgood Marshall, the first African American appointed to the US Supreme Court, along with other justice-minded attorneys such as Paul Robeson, also guided my choice toward law as a profession. In addition, coming from Philadelphia, where the Quakers have a strong presence, allowed me to be engaged in issues of racial and social justice. For many years as a young attorney, I sat on their Latin America and International boards.

After practising as a Public Defender for several years, I accepted an offer from the Ford Foundation to be a human rights programme officer at their office in Rio de Janeiro, Brazil. It was during this stay in Latin America that issues about gender became a prominent part of my work and my worldview. Women's rights, together with projects concerning racial, social and economic justice, were the mainstay of my human rights portfolio. In the mid-1980s, as Brazil transited out of dictatorship, a wave of feminism emerged and accompanied the return to democratic electoral politics. The human rights context in Brazil could be analysed through the new voices of feminism including those of

Afro-Brazilian women. Hence, I was able to develop a poignant understanding of feminism, politically, professionally and personally. During this period, many of the Latin-American feminist movements reignited and became very vibrant, much as they are now, offering perceptive critiques about their societies. Their advocacy greatly influenced me.

LC: How did you come to work at the International Criminal Tribunal for the former Yugoslavia (ICTY)?

PVS: After three years in Brazil, I relocated to Brussels, Belgium. In 1994, seven years later, I discovered that the Yugoslav Tribunal [ICTY] would be established. The Tribunal combined my attraction to criminal law and to international law. In reality, tales of torture, imprisonment, disappearances, persecution, what could be termed as crimes against humanity, that had occurred during the years of dictatorship intersected with my human rights portfolio in Brazil. Also, in the 1980s, instruments against torture, recent international conventions, such as CEDAW, and UN conferences addressing women's rights began to permeate the international legal sphere. So, for me, the Yugoslav tribunal had the potential of uniting my interests and my experiences. Clearly, I relished the possibility to return to the practice of criminal law.

In July of 1994, I joined the Office of the Prosecutor (OTP), after first having contemplated working as a law clerk for the US Judge, Gabrielle Kirk McDonald. She became my mentor. A few months into my tenure, the Deputy Prosecutor – Graham Blewitt, an Australian – and the Prosecutor, Justice Richard Goldstone, from South Africa, asked if would I would become the Legal Advisor for Gender and handle the sexual violence portfolio for the OTP. In retrospect, the skills acquired from my human rights work in Brazil and as a Public Defender in the United States prepared me to assume the daunting role. Ad hoc tribunals were a new, almost experimental judicial creation. The Legal Advisor for Gender, heretofore, was an unheard-of responsibility, especially for a criminal court. However, the sex-based crimes and the victim/survivors from the armed conflict in the former Yugoslavia were devastatingly real. Certainly, most thought that the ICTY must be responsive and investigate, prosecute and adjudicate the sexual crimes.

LC: So, when you started in this role at the ICTY, what would you say were the biggest challenges you faced in trying to bring a gender focus to international criminal law?

PVS: Well, multiple challenges existed. Some were purely legal: how would the OTP plead customary law, as directed by the ICTY Statute, to address sexual violence? What were the accepted customary law bases for the elements of the crimes in the Statute? Also, how could the lawyers and investigators secure the best evidence and reliable witness testimony to support any charges for sexual crimes? What operational and policy priorities would translate, eventually, into successful case law? These practical questions were at the heart of the endeavour.

It must be acknowledged that challenges also revolved around the prevailing mindset within the ICTY and the OTP. Many colleagues initially assigned to work at the ICTY came from national war-crime departments that investigated crimes that dated from the Second World War. Others were seconded or 'loaned' FBI investigators or federal or high-ranking state attorneys. Some were recruited from major crime divisions, and had worked on serial murders, or white-collar fraud, what they termed 'complex investigations'. Others were military lawyers on loan to the OTP. Even though all were highly qualified professionals, for most, investigating or prosecuting sexual violence hadn't been in their remit 'back home'. They arrived ready to contribute to the ICTY, primed to deal, literally, with death and destruction, not rape or other sexual crimes. Consciously or subconsciously, they viewed sexual violence as crimes that were addressed in family – read, inferior – courts, by family court lawyers. Certain investigators and prosecutors – and, indeed, certain judges – acknowledged the toll of sexual violence as unfortunate, but did not necessarily see them as war crimes related to the armed conflict. When deemed susceptible to redress by the law, it was often thought that sexual violence should not be over-emphasized since it would be very difficult to amass the proof.

As for the international lawyers, sexual violence did not figure within their conception of international criminal law or international humanitarian law. In the mid-1990s, the perceived absence of international law jurisprudence and dearth of academic literature on the subject of sex-based international crimes or humanitarian prohibitions seemed to be 'proof' that most sexual violence was unconnected to war. As a matter of fact, some international lawyers queried whether concerted attention to sexual violence would actually belittle the seriousness of international humanitarian and criminal law.

Notwithstanding this, in the Yugoslav armed conflict detention facilities, the take-over of towns and forced transfers of civilians featured prominently. Within those contexts and circumstances, deaths, torture, imprisonment, expulsion, rapes and other sexual violence occurred repeatedly. That mindset infused the early days of the ICTY. Navigating its complexity proved difficult. One needed to generate sufficient personnel resources and to create a supportive office environment in order to redress crimes of sexual violence, a mandate clearly contained in the Secretary-General's Reports on this topic and in the ICTY Statute.

LC: These are huge hurdles to overcome. Why do you think it was possible to bring a focus to sexual violence crimes at the ICTY?

PVS: An important factor consisted of Richard Goldstone and Graham Blewit's foresight to dedicate one person to assist in devising investigative and legal strategies and then developing accompanying policies on sexual violence. They also understood the value of interrogating the internal workings of the OTP to ensure a gender-competent work product. For example, it was decided to form gender-mixed investigation teams so that all teams would focus on the sexual violence committed in their geographical area, even though for a limited time, one investigation team 'specialized' in sexual violence and acted as a resource for other teams. Without Goldstone's and Blewit's leadership and commitment to this part of our mandate, the initial successful rulings on gender jurisprudence would have been delayed or missed. This experience taught me the lesson that the tone concerning the pursuit of sexual violence cases must be set at the top and carried out by everyone.

After I was appointed Legal Advisor for Gender, other lawyers, investigators and analysts made it clear that they too wanted to participate in addressing these crimes. People such as Nancy Patterson, who self-identified as having a concern about gender justice would approach me and say, 'Okay, let's try and make this work'. Jointly, we undertook projects. Some colleagues were professional who *had* worked on sexual-assault crimes in their national jurisdictions and were ready to take on the challenge presented by the egregious acts committed in the former Yugoslavia. A sense of collegiality and camaraderie, akin to an internal constituency, developed and was fundamental to forwarding the OTP's sincere engagement in this area.

Unofficially, I became a lightning rod. In other words, the pain in the *derrière*, who spoke up, ad nauseam, about sexual violence legal matters and evidence during investigation and legal meetings. However, in hindsight, my posturing allowed others a greater leeway to speak and act on issues of sexual violence within their respective teams. It further legitimized analysing sexual assault evidence and engrained the need to locate witnesses – both of which were vital to our mandate. Personally, my background made me comfortable in playing what was at times an unpopular role, although I made good friends among my colleagues.

Other supportive factors were crucial. Coalitions of feminists, who advocated that the patterns of wartime rapes uncovered in the UN Commission of Experts Report should be included in Secretary-General's Report to the Security Council, continued their constructive engagement with the OTP once the Yugoslav Tribunal was created. I recall holding a series of meetings at the OTP very early on, with such committed advocates as feminist academic and practitioner, Rhonda Copeland. Also, feminist groups based in the former Yugoslavia, such as Medica Mondiale, critically supported the OTP's work, introducing investigators to civil society actors and to individuals who could identify potential witnesses or provide survivors with psycho–social/medical services. And then, there were the other organs of the ICTY. In the Registry, the Witness Protection Unit, eventually led by Wendy Lobwein – another Australian – implemented a series of policies and undertook projects to ensure that sexual assault witnesses could securely present their testimony. In the chambers, certain judges, such as Judge Kirk McDonald, Judge Odio-Benito and Judge Mumba, drafted the Rules of Procedure and Evidence that addressed sexual assault victims. The *de nova* stance of these complex procedural rules pertaining to sexual violence is little recognized in the international law literature. Rule 96 stated that a victim's testimony did not have to be corroborated to be admissible and that prior sexual conduct was inadmissible. The rules of procedure and evidence of the ad hoc tribunals descend from the general flexibility given to evidentiary matters in the London and Tokyo Charters of the Second World War. Notwithstanding, Rule 96's astute drafting inevitably strengthened the Statute's ability to redress of sexual assault crimes.

LC: In your view, what has been the value of the ICTY and other ad hoc tribunals to the future of the ICC and to international criminal law in general?

PVS: The ICTY and the International Criminal Tribunal for Rwanda (ICTR), as well as the Special Court of Sierra Leone (SCSL) and the Extraordinary Criminal Chambers of Cambodia (ECCC) demonstrate that sexual violence committed in armed conflict, genocide or periods of crimes against humanity are justiciable. Outside the Rome Statute's framework [which has restricted temporal jurisdiction], these tribunals investigate, prosecute and adjudicate contemporaneous crimes, crimes occurring in the recent past or crimes committed decades ago. The ECCC jurisprudence validates that impunity that has reigned for 30 or 40 years can be redressed using customary international law. The time-deferred justice for Chadians, using international customary law, was finally tried in the Habré case, conducted by the Extraordinary African Chambers in 2017. In the wake of the ad hoc tribunals, national courts, whether in Argentina or Guatemala, Bosnia or

Rwanda, tried conflict-related and genocide-related sexual violence. The ad hoc tribunals created a watershed moment ushering in a judicial revival of international humanitarian and criminal law.

Today it's impermissible for a top politician or military general to simply shrug his or her shoulders and comment, 'Well, what can we do? Rape happens in war, you know. You can't stop it because it is human nature.' The increasingly normative legal framework no longer regards sexual violence as a problem of human nature but as pursuable criminal conduct.

The recognition of sexual violence as a constituent act of genocide, or as the underlying bases of crimes against humanity or war crime has been fortified by rigorous jurisprudence. This has been monumental, legally, as far as policy is concerned as well as from a human rights perspective. I believe that we're still absorbing the breadth of these decisions. Doing so allows us to fathom the unaddressed sexual violence in the Nuremburg or Tokyo Military Tribunals, or during periods of colonization or slavery. Our current analysis of sex-based international crimes and the impunity allotted them is more precise. Impunity is unacceptable, yet eradication of such conduct still appears to lie in the distant future. Enforcement remains the preeminent predicament.

The International Criminal Court, a permanent institution, exercises prospective and complementary jurisdiction over international crimes in 122 countries. This contrasts substantially from the ICTY, ICTR, SCSL, ECCC and the EAC, which exercise primary jurisdiction over a single country or geographical area during a specific time period of atrocities. The ICTR, for example, has conducted 75 trials in relation to the genocide of 1994. The ICC might conduct a limited number of trials per atrocity; however, its greater geographical reach requires it to deal with a myriad of armed conflicts or genocides simultaneously. Accordingly, one must caveat any direct comparisons between the ICC and ad hoc judicial mechanisms. Notwithstanding, the ICC benefits from the substantive and procedural jurisprudence and practice of the ad hoc regimes that have armed it with a body of international judicial decisions that prime it to interpret the Rome Statute's unique sex-based crimes, including gender as a form of persecution. The ICC's disappointing conviction rates for sexual conduct has, in part, been tethered more to the interpretation of the modes of liability than to the interpretation of the enumerated sex crimes.

LC: I want to focus on the links with the Women, Peace and Security agenda, which has been developing alongside international criminal law over the past two decades. Is there a need for a closer engagement between the two, especially concerning issues of accountability?

PVS: Clearly, links exist between the two agendas. The Security Council formulations of sexual violence basically originate from the armed conflicts in Sierra Leone, DRC or the former Yugoslavia, or the genocide in Rwanda and now in Iraq, Myanmar and Syria. The Security Council resolutions have drawn upon the judgments handed down by the international tribunals as well as the annual reports of the Special Representatives of the Secretary General for Sexual Violence in Armed Conflict and Children Affected by Armed Conflict.

The WPS agenda rests in part upon the Security Council's acceptance of jurisprudence affirming how sexual violence contravenes international humanitarian law and international criminal law. The broader, inter-related context or links between WPS and international criminal law is evinced in the Security Council's mandate under Chapter 7 of the UN Charter, to restore, maintain or detect breaches of international peace. The mandate now configures the Security Council's acceptance of the legal characterization of rape, enslavement and sexual slavery, recruitment of child soldiers, sexualized torture and sexual violence as an act of genocide, and so on. International crimes, as manifested via sexual violence, threaten the maintenance or restoration of the peace, and thus confound, if not prohibit, the provision of security. They are therefore a key component of the WPS agenda. The Security Council's peace purview necessarily entails a responsive political agenda, which is often communicated through resolutions that impress upon UN member states – and even non-state actors – to prohibit or redress these sex-based international crimes.

The various WPS-related resolutions are integral to this responsive political agenda. UNSCR 2106 specifically 'calls upon Member States to comply with their relevant obligations to continue to fight impunity by investigating and prosecuting those subject to their jurisdiction who are responsible for such crimes'.

With regard to accountability, even though a legal submission arguing the nexus between sexual violence and restoration of the peace might seem untenable, the WPS Security Council resolutions presumably speak to the crystallization or a certain 'codification' of international customary law. The resolutions represent a form of *opinio juris* for which obligations are owed by (the community of) states for the sexual violent conduct overseen by the Security Council. Hence, the political agenda of the Security Council, as demonstrated by WPS resolutions, was informed by international criminal law judicial mechanisms. In turn, WPS resolutions are supportive of legal submissions to secure individual responsibility or confront state-sponsored impunity, such as illegal amnesties, for sex-based atrocity crimes. Therein, the WPS political agenda and international criminal law converge at critical junctures.

LC: That's really interesting. So they're working already from a foundation where they're acknowledging sex-based atrocities: they're not trying to retrofit it, if you like, which has been the trouble for ICL in the past.

PVS: Yes, as an international criminal lawyer and an academic, I view the foundational remit of the international judicial mechanism – to adjudicate crimes – and the UN Security Council – to politically oversee peace and security – as coalescing. This is unsurprising given that the ad hoc tribunals were established under the Chapter 7 mandate as a means to restore peace in the face of the armed conflict in the former Yugoslavia and of the genocide in Rwanda. Thus, WPS-related resolutions and their agenda, the operational execution of the Chapter 7 mandate, are imbued with both approaches.

LC: And would you say that in the work at the ICC, in developing arguments, that the WPS agenda is a useful hook or means to make a point?

PVS: As I stated earlier, certain arguments, usually based on emerging or codified customary law prompted by the WPS agenda might provide a hook. Security Council resolutions issued under the Chapter 7 mandate – such as UNSCR 2173 concerning Sudan – cite and thus employ the precepts of the WPS resolutions. To the extent that these evince *opinion juris* and urge states to undertake concomitant action or practice, such WPS-grounded resolutions would be relevant for arguments in national or international courts to fetter out the customary law basis of state obligations and of individual responsibility for sex-based crimes.

    Even though WPS is often juxtaposed with the ICC's Rome Statute, its precepts exist as a means of eventual interpretation of international criminal or humanitarian law cases brought before national courts.

LC: So, what would you see as critical way forward to engage serious adherence to international criminal law at the national level? Do you draw on the idea of 'complementarity' to strengthen domestic capacity?

PVS: The short answer to your question is yes. However, I would go beyond Rome Statute-inspired complementarity. Prior to the establishment of the ICC or the ad hoc tribunals, cooperative international obligations already existed for atrocity crimes, especially crimes against humanity, war crimes and genocide. However, states rarely triggered jurisdiction in their national courts to try international crimes. Any implementation was conducted in national courts, either via national or universal jurisdiction, and was inconsistent or ineffective. Most redressal of war crimes took place as a disciplinary matter in national military courts. It is important to recall that cooperative states' obligations to redress international crimes continue to exist. States that ratified the Rome Statute presumably have fortified their capacity to act under the prongs of complementarity. Nevertheless, pre-existing obligations to pursue international crimes at the national level have neither been erased nor diminished for states that are not signatories to the Rome Statute.

    International customary law, as well as treaty law, remains key to the enforcement of international criminal law in national judicial systems. Even states that partake in the formal complementarity under the Rome legal regime remain obliged to customary law. Also, there is an, albeit slight, resurgence in the recourse to universal jurisdiction, which often relies upon custom. Owed partially to the inability of crimes committed in Syria, Iraq or Myanmar to come within the jurisdiction of the ICC, some cases are being brought into national courts. Germany, Spain, Switzerland and France have potential cases based upon international crimes under their national criminal codes or upon forms of universal jurisdiction. In the US, crimes related to the armed conflict in Liberia were litigated in a civil case. It's exciting to witness national courts assume these international law obligations. States have a type of contract or pact with international crimes, starting with piracy, but certainly including slavery and the slave trade, war crimes, crimes against humanity and genocide. The international community of states are obliged to act on each other's behalf to redress international crimes. If the state obligations were met consistently and effectively, there might be a reduced need – or no need at all – for ad hoc tribunals or an international court. As a political scientist, you understand that we have ebbs and flows – but mostly ebbs – in our ability to deter and redress international crimes. The WPS agenda, in my view, represents a flow.

8

Holding Feminist Space

sam cook and Louise Allen

Although each of us has engaged in a range of women, peace and security (WPS)-related work, our most immediate point of connection is that we each have acted as NGO policy advocates in the WPS policy space of the UN Security Council: sam cook, from 2005 to 2010 for the Women's International League for Peace and Freedom as the PeaceWomen Project Director and Louise Allen as the Executive Director Coordinator of the NGO Working Group on WPS from 2014–2018. The contours of this policy space have shifted profoundly across the nine years of our combined experience – many of these changes are quite explicitly addressed by this volume. In this conversation we focus on the role of NGOs and some of the challenges of working in coalition in this particular space. The role of NGOs in policy formation (especially in relation to the adoption of UNSCR 1325) has been widely acknowledged, but the nature of ongoing engagement has received quite limited attention. As the body of WPS policy has expanded and developed, many feminist critiques of WPS policy have treated unsatisfactory policies as indicative of a failure in NGO representation. A common accusation is that those who occupy positions as NGO representatives in the policy space have been co-opted or have abandoned their commitment to feminist principles (cook, 2018). Here we think through what NGO engagement involves, the risks of co-optation, and the challenges and rewards of working in feminist coalition.

sam cook (SC):   The landscape of NGO policy advocacy we each faced is quite different. When I started at PeaceWomen in 2005, the Council had adopted one

WPS resolution – UNSCR 1325. Our focus was on this one resolution, on expanding the Security Council's own understanding of peace and security and on getting it to pay attention to WPS issues in its day-to-day work. By 2015 there were eight resolutions and the membership of the NGO Working Group itself had radically expanded. What do you see as the role of NGOs, and more specifically of the Working Group, in relation to the Security Council's WPS policy?

Louise Allen (LA): The Working Group is the only group which undertakes gender analysis of the Security Council's full decision-making cycle and it has been a key facilitator of briefings of the Security Council by women civil society representatives from conflict-affected countries. But the work of the coalition has also changed as the normative framework has developed. While the Council remains the primary target, the group expanded its monitoring and advocacy work to capture how the UN's key peace and security entities and humanitarian agencies implement their WPS obligations. We also increased our country-specific advocacy when it was apparent that the commitments made at the October Open Debate did not actually translate into gender perspectives being considered in country-specific situations. These developments have been possible in part because of the diversity of our membership.

SC: This brings up what I see as a critical aspect of feminist work on WPS – working in coalition. I think each of the organizational positions we occupied made a difference to how we had to operate. Although I would often also represent the views of the coalitions we worked in, my primary guide was WILPF's (Women's International League for Peace and Freedom) own policies and its membership's directives. You worked as an advocate on behalf of an entire coalition of organizations with diverse priorities which, at its inception in 2000, consisted of only five members [Amnesty International, Hague Appeal for Peace, Women's Commission for Refugee Women and Children, International Alert and the Women's International League for Peace and Freedom].

LA: When I started, there were 12 member organizations. During my tenure, four organizations left the group – three as a result of significant changes to their operational landscape, meaning that New York-based WPS advocacy was no longer within their capacity. The other organization left after a re-structuring of its women's rights team to focus on other areas outside of WPS. When I left, in 2018, it was a coalition of 18 organizations.

SC: Has the expansion in the group's membership, and concomitant shifts in priorities, had an effect on its advocacy work?

LA: The bolstering of membership was the result of a deliberate decision aimed at strengthening our collective impact and the reputation of the working group as an authority on WPS monitoring and advocacy. It is also important that its composition be diverse and that it brings together groups from various sectors including women's human rights and humanitarian organizations, working on different components of the WPS agenda. Oxfam International, MADRE and CARE International joined the group early in 2015 in the leadup to UNSCR 1325's 15th anniversary. In 2017, the group again expanded with the addition of Cordaid, the Global Network of Women Peacebuilders, Plan International and OutRight International. There is strength in numbers and the group's size gave my advocacy messages significant weight. I always reminded UN decision makers and diplomats that the Working Group was a consensus coalition of 18 organizations spanning a range of sectors.

        The addition of OutRight International as our first LGBTIQ organization followed a deliberate decision by the Working Group to expand our policies and analyses to better address the specific risks, persecution and discrimination faced by LGBTIQ individuals and other marginalized groups. For the coalition to genuinely be progressive and feminist, it is important for its membership to be inclusive and diverse.

SC: So, the group's expansion in membership has accompanied an expansion in the scope of its work. Have these shifts added to the challenges of working in coalition?

LA: I won't pretend that coalitions are easy, especially consensus ones! As the membership grew it remained important that all members continued to feel their positions or concerns were equally considered whether founding or newer members. Developing new policy areas or our position on emerging crisis situations always had to carefully balance the in-country perspectives of our humanitarian colleagues with the calls from human rights advocacy organizations. We developed – and would revisit when needed – operational guidelines outlining our processes and how we might reach consensus in a respectful way. While some positions might require more extensive or nuanced negotiations, what really helped was the common understanding members had of the group and its strategic objective of advancing a feminist and progressive WPS agenda. For instance, one issue was coming to consensus on security sector reform considering the groups positions on anti-militarization. We knew this was an important area that we could not overlook. In the end, our agreed call was for member states to commit to raise the recruitment, retention and professionalization of women across all justice and security sector components in order to improve and advance rule of law-based institutions that are gender-sensitive and effective at an operational level. This process, while sometimes lengthy, helped us come to an agreed position we could represent as endorsed by all members.

My responsibility was to our members and ensuring I was representing the views of the coalition and the consensus positions we had reached. Having the trust of the membership is vital and being consultative and transparent are key to this. Diplomats and UN officials knew that I was representing a coalition. When I was meeting one-on-one with decision makers, I would convey as clearly as possible that while I might not specify details from conversations, information from meetings would be relayed back to our members and inform our strategic approach to new developments.

SC: Are there other ethical challenges that arise in working in a space like the UN or, more specifically, the Security Council space?

LA: One issue that always really concerned me was the possibility that female civil society speakers who briefed

126

the Security Council were being instrumentalized (Allen, 2018; Cook, 2016; Gibbings 2011). In 2015, the Security Council (in UNSCR 2242) committed to considering civil society briefings during country-specific meetings. This was a significant and positive step which saw an increasing number of women being able to speak directly to Security Council members and provide their recommendations. It also meant that greater care was needed to ensure that their statements were not co-opted. First, it was imperative that the women felt empowered to deliver the statement that they needed to give and which reflected the needs of their communities and the priorities of their own organizations. Second, it was also important for us to continually convey to Council members the importance of preserving the independence of this new space for civil society.

Council members would frequently request speakers who could recount their personal, often harrowing, stories and who would focus on their personal experiences rather than providing their local analysis and recommendations. This was often coupled with requests for women who were strong English speakers and for those who would avoid discussing politically sensitive issues. The most concerning example of this trend was when a diplomat relayed their ambassador's request that I identify a civil society speaker who had either been raped or was born of rape, had lived through the stigma of their ordeal and had then had risen to become a leader in their community. Their aim was to have someone who could 'move' the Council with her story. This type of request reduces civil society participation to entertainment, of a potentially exploitative or voyeuristic kind. It is not a partnership and we certainly pushed back against these types of requests and any external attempts to 'massage' the statements of civil society speakers. These attempts completely miss the significance and purpose of civil society statements. They are also part of a broader pattern and there are concerns over how it is always the same individuals who are invited to attend international meetings and forums on peace and security – usually those considered to be representing 'elite' and national organizations.

Working with women from conflict-affected areas, my primary job was to assist them in navigating the space – a daunting prospect for those who have never been to New York or to the UN. My responsibility was to ensure that they were able to deliver their messages and to help them focus their speaking points according to whom they were meeting. It would have undermined my own feminist principles if these women either felt compelled to say things which did not reflect their own priorities, or to not raise particular issues at the behest of New York partners. It was incredibly important to me that women human rights defenders be given the platform to speak directly to decision makers and to raise the issues they needed to raise. Preserving that independence must remain a priority.

SC: I think this is also related to a critique that I struggled with in my own practice – that we who are privileged enough to be present in these policy spaces are not sufficiently transparent with our constituents. Some allege that those who work on the inside of institutions like the UN are inevitably co-opted by its dominant practices. I see the role of feminist advocates as working with those practices in order to advance our ends and it seems almost impossible to do without taking on those practices. How do you see the challenges of doing effective advocacy while maintaining a commitment to feminist principles such as transparency or being consultative?

LA: I agree with your view that those who work within these policy spaces must remain staunch advocates and their proximity to senior decision makers does not mean that they are being co-opted per se. In fact, I think advocates in these spaces have a responsibility to call out negative developments and outline issues which are being overlooked. It was an amazing experience to work alongside incredible advocates representing a range of NGOs who were both polite and respectful but also extremely firm in their delivery of blunt or targeted messages.

In terms of transparency, the Working Group made a deliberate decision to publish all of its monitoring and analysis online to enable global colleagues to draw on our findings related to the Security Council's

decision-making processes. This serves as an accountability mechanism for the Security Council and the UN
but hopefully also provides information that other NGOs
and local activists can use in their own advocacy. We
also expanded our consultative processes. For example,
the open letters sent to all member states ahead of WPS
Open Debates used to only be signed by Working Group
members. In 2015, in preparation for the 15th anniversary High Level Review, this letter was opened to
other organizations as a way to include a more extensive
group of colleagues in our efforts. In 2015, our advocacy
letter had 111 organizations signing; by 2017, this had
expanded to 391 organizations from 98 countries, and
was available in English, French, Spanish and Arabic.

SC: Did working in this policy space shift your sense of
feminist solidarity or what it means to work as part of
a feminist community?

LA: I came to the Working Group as a feminist and human
rights advocate who had worked on women's rights
advocacy campaigns and alongside formidable women
human rights defenders. My time at the Working
Group and in the WPS space in New York significantly
enhanced my passion and commitment for working on
advancing women's rights. It was both a humbling and
inspiring experience to work next to women from across
15 conflict- and crisis-affected countries and facilitating
their statements to the Security Council. Many risk
their lives every day campaigning to end the violent
conflicts gripping their countries; standing up against
armed groups and extremists; insisting they have a seat
at the table; and calling for gender equality and justice
for crimes against humanity. Speaking out so publicly
on the highest international platform is often even more
dangerous but they do so to be heard and talk directly
to decision makers. It was their resolve that spurred me
on when I felt frustrated at Security Council inaction,
and they further cemented my belief in the importance
of the WPS agenda.

SC: Are there things that you see as particularly important
in thinking through future efforts?

LA: We would ask every peacebuilder we worked alongside
what UNSCR 1325 meant to her and how she used it

in her daily work. Women whose range of experiences concerned conflict, post-conflict and fragile states all recounted how important the resolution was to them; it provided them with an international instrument that they could use in demanding their inclusion in security and political processes at all levels. I think it is in efforts to further localize the agenda at the grassroots level and empower local women's organizations to develop and implement their own community-based programmes and initiatives where we will continue to see the most transformative results.

Focused attention is also needed at the UN Headquarters in New York. While the WPS agenda has expanded beyond the machinations of the UN system in New York, this is where the majority of the normative developments occur. We're seeing strong pushback against women's rights. Protecting the gains of the last two decades will be incredibly important as we know that they can be unravelled pretty quickly.

References

Allen, L. (2018) 'Why the United Nations must let women speak freely', *Open Democracy 50/50*, 22 October, Available from: www.opendemocracy.net/en/5050/united-nations-security-council-must-let-women-speak-freely/.

cook, s. (2016) 'The "woman-in-conflict" at the UN Security Council: a subject of practice', *International Affairs*, 92(2): 353–372.

cook, s. (2018) 'Encountering metis in the Security Council', *LSE WPS Working Paper Series*, 15: 1–12.

Gibbings, S.L. (2011) 'No angry women at the United Nations: political dreams and the cultural politics of United Nations Security Council Resolution 1325', *International Feminist Journal of Politics*, 13(4): 522–538.

PART II

Horizons

9

Global Racial Hierarchies and the Limits of Localization via National Action Plans

Toni Haastrup and Jamie J. Hagen

We locate our reflections about the practices of the Women, Peace and Security (WPS) agenda in contemporary scholarship about race and racism in global politics. Our contribution reflects on how whiteness and white privilege are refracted in the narratives and practices of the WPS agenda through a focus on National Action Plans (NAPs). We consider who the WPS agenda is *about*, and who it is *for*, on the international stage. A central part of this investigation is interrogating whether certain NAPs are truly able to localize the international project of WPS or whether, because of global racial hierarchies, they actually simply reinforce the status quo. If the latter, NAPs – particularly those originating in the global North – can then be seen to perpetuate an image wherein the peaceful North (which nevertheless employs and relies on militarism for its practices of peace and security) is obliged to 'rescue' the insecure global South. Further, we examine the imagery used by different countries within their NAPs and the implications for WPS messaging by countries in the global North.

We explore the ways in which these NAPs consider violent conflicts and gendered violence in the global South against responses to similar concerns within the borders of originating countries. We contend that the WPS agenda despite its potential for emancipation, and given its framing as a universal/global normative framework, is steeped in racialized hierarchies manifested in whiteness. George Yancy (2004, pp 7–8) writes that

> whiteness [is] a synergistic system of transversal relationships of privileges, norms, rights, modes of self-perception and the perception of others, unquestioned presumptions, deceptions, beliefs, 'truths,' behaviors, advantages, modes of comportment, and sites of power and hegemony that benefits whites individually and institutionally.

There is a lot of complexity in the idea of whiteness. But it is nevertheless enough to know that it is a system that reifies the status quo of 'White privileges, protections, and material advantages over People of Color' (Sartori, 2018; see also Lipsitz, 2006; Leonardo, 2009). Whiteness born of global white supremacy was crystalized through colonization and the post-colonization relations that have been forged between the global North and global South (see Mills, 1998; Allen, 2004). In this chapter, we follow Dados and Connell's (2012) understanding of the global South as a way of accounting for the geopolitical power relations within which much of global governance occurs. Although an imperfect delineation, as Sartori (2018, p 28) observes, it does the job that the concepts of 'Third World' (an outdated cold war-era term that focuses on only former colonies) and 'developing countries' (that implies a teleology culminating in western models) do not capture. The global North is thus defined in juxtaposition to the global South.

The ever-present co-optation of the narrative framework of the need for a feminist-informed gender analysis of women's experiences in conflict-related environments also takes insidious forms. These may be about essentializing women as better at making peace than men, or co-opting women's work to resist militarization to instead see women's inclusion in peacebuilding as making war safe for women (Shepherd 2016). Perhaps the most persistent hegemonic process at work in the WPS architecture, though least discussed, is that of racialized hierarchies steeped in whiteness.

Race and global policymaking: whiteness at work in WPS

In this chapter, race and the function of whiteness is recognized in how WPS practices are situated in a dynamic relationship between the global North and global South narrated as global. In this relationship, the countries that dominate the WPS agenda by virtue of their wealth, and their position in international relations 'do' WPS to the 'Other' mainly outside the borders of the global North. This process of creating the Other or othering is 'a colonial tool … reflecting a pattern where the

Self first establishes dominance by making the colonial Other aware of who holds the power ... [entrenching] the Other's inferiority' (Hudson, 2016, p 5). This process is evident in the language used, and in the visual depiction of some of the women included in NAP documentation. It is also visible in the inconsistencies in internal responses to the plight of women in some global North countries when compared to the commitments articulated in NAPs. Like much of the existing scholarship on NAPs and the policy push to establish NAPs, we see them as important artefacts of the WPS agenda.

Overall, we offer a different critique of the WPS agenda as a contribution to feminist security studies and studies in International Relations that takes race seriously. Moreover, we add to the ongoing discourses that demonstrate unease with the way in which the dominant practices of WPS serves to perpetuate 'white saviour' narratives around peace and security interventions, without adequate reflection on what this might mean within the borders of the global North. NAPs, we argue, provide a valuable lens for assessing the way that racialized hierarchies persist in global policymaking and doing, even by those with the best intention including civil society organizations (CSOs) that are invested in women's engagement in peace processes. In conclusion, the chapter articulates limits to the practices of localization offered by NAPs when funded from the global North, as well as the complications of using the NAPs as an indicator of proper implementation of WPS.

In the following sections, we identify 22 countries who have had at least one NAP and fit the description of the global North, understood in opposition to the global South as described earlier. By focusing on the NAPs of the global North, we do not seek to reify or legitimize their power in the WPS field; rather, we seek to expose the ways in which broader hierarchies of race in international relations are played out in the WPS agenda. We sourced all the NAPs from PeaceWomen, an initiative of the Women International League for Peace and Freedom (WILPF). PeaceWomen includes a comprehensive database of NAPs, with 83 countries having adopted at least one NAP as of December 2019 (PeaceWomen, nd).

We build our analysis of the NAPs by drawing on the insights of black feminists such as bell hooks (1989) and Kimberlé Crenshaw (1989), and the decolonial feminist scholarship of Chandra Mohanty (2003), Inderpal Grewal (2017), Sara Ahmed (2012) and Jasbir Puar (2007). These scholars contribute to the critical readings of transnational feminist engagements that dangerously re-marginalize those whom they claim to liberate, thus stalling gender justice and social change. Moreover, as in the analysis offered by scholars who have engaged in racial or postcolonial critique of WPS including Marjaana Jauhola (2016), Nicola Pratt (2013), María Martín De Almagro (2017) and Swati Parashar (2019), our contribution reinforces the idea that race matters in understanding global North and global South WPS knowledge and resource exchange as well as transnational collaborations. We draw on critical work by decolonial and black feminist scholars to reflect on race as it shapes who are viewed as actors and who are viewed as victims in the grand narratives of the WPS agenda.

Chandra Mohanty writes, 'I believe one of the greatest challenges we (feminists) face is this task of recognizing and undoing the ways in which we colonize and objectify our different histories and cultures, thus colluding with hegemonic processes of domination and rule' (2003, p 125). In this chapter, we seek to examine the colonial histories that persist in WPS by more closely considering the possibilities and limitations of the NAP as a tool of gender justice.

Why look at NAPs?

NAPs offer a valuable point of intervention to reflect on the WPS architecture for a number of reasons. NAPs are a result of a Security Council recommendation in 2002 (United Nations Security Council, 2002). According to Shepherd, NAPs are 'one of the ways that states can indicate a commitment to the WPS agenda and articulate strategies for implementation' (2016, p 325). Jacevic describes NAPs as 'official government policy' that combines the national and international dimensions of a country's WPS legal and policy framework (2019, p 274).

Moreover, civil society initiatives such as the PeaceWomen project of the WILPF have turned to NAPs as a means of tracking the degree to which states meet their WPS obligations. Additionally, because of the purpose they are intended to serve, NAPs can illustrate how states intend to fund WPS initiatives and determine which initiatives will receive funding. With this in mind, CSOs are seen as an important aspect of capacity building for localization in the form of helping to draft, update and share the NAP. This is true in countries in both the global North and the global South. To a certain extent then, a NAP can also serve as a tool for civil society to both shape and critique the WPS agenda. Swati Parashar argues, however, that NAPs can be counterproductive for postcolonial subjects when they simply endorse 'the state's narratives of the conflict and its marginalizations and discrimination' (2019, p 5).

The politics of how these narratives are selected, and by whom, are not often discussed. Similarly, narratives about which issues are prioritized within NAPs are understudied. Inherent then in the work that NAPs are intended to do are questions around who has power, and the possibilities of instrumentalizing NAPs to the advantage of those in power. In our analysis, however, we narrow in on three modes of analysis. We first consider which countries have NAPs and how those plans are funded. Relatedly we take note of countries that have multiple NAPs. Our second mode of analysis is to identify what gets counted as a matter of conflict by each country. This interrogation is motivated by the persistence of global North countries' ability to use NAPs to continue to engage in the WPS agenda as being about the 'Other' without internal self-reflection. The third mode of analysis we consider in relation to the narratives of NAPs is that told by the images of women featured in NAPs primarily on the cover of the documents. As Bleiker (2018, p 3) notes, we live in a visual age and images tell us about how the world is seen; in that sense, images in NAPs tell us about how the relevant actors see the WPS agenda in the world. Together, these three modes of analysis offer a way to consider the way in which racial hierarchies are perpetuated by global North WPS actors who have tended to, at least discursively, dominate the WPS landscape.

What can NAPs really indicate?

In 2005, five years after the passage of the first WPS Security Council resolution (UNSCR 1325 in 2000), Denmark became the first country to adopt a NAP. Since then, Denmark has refined and adopted two more NAPs bringing its total to three. Overwhelmingly, the countries that have more than one NAP are those located in the global North[1] although this is by no means exclusively the case. The volume of NAPs coming from the global North and their content reinforces the dominant narrative of the global North as the originator of the WPS agenda and the South as the recipients (Basu, 2016). This, as Swati Parashar (2019) argues, further underscores the WPS agenda's lack of attention to the realities of the global South as a place from which knowledge is derived, potentially producing racialized erasures.

Here, we show the ways in which these narratives of racialized dominance are reproduced via the NAPs. To do this, we ask three questions: 1) How do NAPs represent WPS?; 2) Whose needs are being foregrounded in the NAPs of the global North?; and 3) In what ways do NAPs reinforce or challenge racialized global North/global South binaries? To answer these questions, we first assess the realities of the funding landscape focusing on the funding commitments articulated by NAPs of global North countries as part of their foreign policies. Specifically, we look at the extent to which these commitments reproduce problematic hierarchies between the global North and global South even while working to support the localization of WPS through civil society engagement on the ground. Second, while the majority of the global North's NAPs are tied to foreign policy practices, we examine the focus of these practices as they are directed mainly at the countries in the global South. We argue that these external foci of WPS that targets the global South performs an 'othering' function.

A closer look at localization

We focus on civil society as this space generally provides a form of hybrid engagement between the international and the local that aims to make post-conflict peacebuilding projects legitimate when it comes to localization (Björkdahl and Hoglund, 2013; Donais, 2009). As Amitav Acharya defines it, localization is, 'the active construction (through discourse, framing, grafting and cultural selection) of foreign ideals by local actors, which results in the former developing significant congruence with local beliefs and practices' (2004, p 245). We consider whether the more transformational potential of the WPS agenda relies on a hybrid practice of localization that also requires the global North to be transformative in thinking through what it means to apply NAPs domestically. What would it mean to apply the WPS agenda within the borders of the United States, the UK, Canada or Sweden?

In our narrative analysis we first observe which countries have NAPs as well as which countries have multiple NAPs. We then turn to the content of the NAPs as a way to examine which WPS initiatives are funded; further, we analyse the imagined subjects of the NAPs, asking which women are being made secure. Specifically, we ask which women are racialized as foreign in the language of the NAPs. By assessing the funding focus including to civil society in the countries of the global North, we see a WPS agenda that is increasingly moving away from the possibility of a transformation framework that is built on mutual respect, partnership and equality within global governance and rather one that unsurprisingly reinforces the status quo.

PeaceWomen suggests that each NAP should: 1) reflect on the holistic intention of UNSCR 1325 (participation, protection and conflict prevention); 2) be measurable, including a dedicated budget, indicators/output results, set timeframes and plan periods; 3) have a participatory, transparent process of drafting, implementation and monitoring involving civil society and women's organizations; and 4) focus on the prevention of conflict, extending to the resolution of the arms trade and disarmament to fully remedy violations of women's human rights in conflict (2013, p 8).

The word 'holistic' is important here. A holistic vision for UNSCR 1325 invites questions about access to economic, political and social opportunities. It raises questions, for instance, about whether or not a military in the global North engages in gender equal budgeting. It also invites questions about how women are affected by issues such as climate change, migration, asylum and religious freedom. As Claire Duncanson explains, 'Peace is not thus just the absence of war. For feminists, it includes the economic and social empowerment of women and other marginalized groups: freedom from want as well as from fear' (2016, p 63). An expansive understanding of the WPS agenda requires attention to a myriad of gendered dimensions of peace and security rather than simply working towards an absence of conflict.

Who gets funded and how?

The majority of the countries we examined paid attention to the four pillars of the WPS agenda: participation, prevention, protection and relief and recovery. Overwhelmingly, however, most of the 22 countries have committed mainly to the protection pillar. According to a PeaceWomen report, the protection pillar refers to 'specific protection rights and needs of women and girls in conflict and post-conflict settings, including … gender-based violence' (PeaceWomen, 2013, p 5).

The constant refrain from those who advocate for the implementation of the WPS agenda is that it is underfunded. The *Global Study* (UN Women, 2015), identified chronic underfunding of the WPS agenda as 'the most serious and unrelenting obstacle to implementation of women, peace and security commitments' (UN Women, 2015, p 16). The study asked that a minimum of 15% of all allocations to peace and security be committed to WPS as a way to ensure sustainability and predictability in funding.

NAP funding in the context of the countries of the global North is important for a couple of interrelated reasons. First, these countries are among the wealthiest countries in the world. The reality, then, is that these particular countries are in a better position to provide the bulk of the funding towards WPS initiatives. It is no surprise that international CSOs, especially, campaign and rely on the global North to fund WPS-related programmes. Second, it is precisely because of these levels of wealth that countries in the global North are positioned as donors, while those in the global South are positioned as recipients. As donors, countries in the global North invariably have an impact on how WPS 'happens' in some countries in the global South.

Moreover, because much of the doing of WPS is embedded within the foreign policy domain, it is unsurprising that funding commitments to WPS specifically is externally oriented. We assess the funding priorities of the countries based in the global North and the extent to which the mechanisms for funding those priorities are clear and fulfil relevant actions.

From our reading of NAPs of global North countries, 22 of them recognize the importance of civil society stakeholders for ensuring an inclusive UNSCR 1325 process. Canada's most recent NAP, for instance, states:

> Recognizing the important role of civil society in advancing the WPS agenda internationally, the government is increasing its support to local women's groups and movements, working toward achieving gender equality and the human rights of women and girls. (Canadian NAP, 2017, p 1)

While all other countries make the same commitment in a variety of ways, they are less explicit about funding civil society. The latest German NAP commits to supporting 'civil society projects for a comprehensive, gender-specific and cross generational understanding of peace' (German NAP, 2017, p 16). The only reference to a specific funding mechanism in this NAP is the contribution to the UN Women Trust Fund and there is no specification of how much is contributed. The UK reveals more as it is clear the focus for funding in its latest action plan is on Afghanistan, Burma, Democratic Republic of Congo, Iraq, Libya, Nigeria, Somalia, South Sudan and Syria (UK NAP, 2018, pp 21–22). Similarly, Norway makes Afghanistan, Colombia, Myanmar, Palestine and South Sudan its main priorities in addition to the Middle East, because this is considered a region 'where the conflict situation is constantly changing' (Norwegian NAP, 2015, p 41).

Both the UK and Norway pay particular attention to funding mechanisms. Norway commits specific funding for WPS and especially to NGOs to be disbursed by the civil society department of the Norwegian Agency for Development Cooperation. France, too, targets its funding towards Africa and 'the Arab world'. In Africa, this is dominated by its former colonies including Mali and Senegal (French

NAP, 2015), while Belgium has similarly targeted Afghanistan, the Democratic Republic of Congo and Mali (Belgian NAP, 2013 p 6). The Netherlands has tended to focus on direct funding to national programmes and CSOs in Afghanistan, Burundi, Colombia, the DRC, South Sudan and Sudan (Dutch NAP, 2016, p 17). Denmark focuses its latest NAP on Afghanistan, Kenya, Lebanon, Mali, Myanmar, Nepal, the Occupied Palestinian Territories, South Sudan, Zimbabwe and Syria (Danish NAP, 2014, pp 12–16).

The United States, more so than the other countries under consideration, overwhelmingly supports WPS-linked programmes to countering violent extremism in 'sub-Saharan Africa, the Middle East and North Africa, and South Asia' although these fall within its promotion of strategies for conflict prevention (USA NAP, 2016, p 11). On protection, the US also supports civil society initiatives in countries such as Cameroon, Central African Republic, Democratic Republic of the Congo, Iraq, Liberia, Mali, Niger, Nigeria, Somalia, South Sudan, Sudan and Syria (USA NAP 2016, p 9). Canada is vague about which countries its targets, although fragile states and conflict contexts dominate – and stand in as proxies for similar countries in the global South (Canadian NAP, 2017, p 9).

Across all these NAPs, we see consistent overlaps. There are not only regional overlaps but also specific country overlaps. Arguably, this may simply be about the current conditions in those countries. They are poorer, they are experiencing ongoing conflict-related insecurity, and their NAPs are developed in response to the funding calls made and articulated in the *Global Study*. Yet, one could also read these NAPs as evidence of WPS being done to the global South. Parashar's recent analysis of how WPS functions is very apt, and we see this well captured by the NAPs. Parashar (2019), drawing on Pratt (2013), notes that the direction of funding serves to represent the global South as 'conflict affected' and consequently in need of rescuing. What is more, the structure and targets of funding serve to link negative perceptions of insecurity with particular countries. For instance, Afghanistan, South Sudan and the Democratic Republic of Congo are very visible as objects needing intervention from the global North on WPS.

Foreign policy for whom?

From the analysis of global North NAPs, we see that not all countries in the global North identify a particular region of their policy target. Yet, through inference, we observe framings and narratives that undoubtedly serve as appropriate proxies for the global South. There is a tendency for states to externalize the WPS agenda which leads to an 'othering' of mainly women in the global South (Pratt 2013). As we have noted, this has embedded the notion that WPS is primary applied in the realm of foreign policy. But in taking into account the NAPs, it is clear that WPS as foreign policy is not applied evenly across the foreign policy practices of the global North countries.

We find the case of Canada to be very interesting given that the implementation of the WPS agenda is most resonant in its Feminist International Assistance Policy. At the same time, Canada under Justin Trudeau has made rhetorical moves about being more reflective about its racist colonial past (Markusoff, 2017). Its latest NAP states that the NAP is 'at the heart of Canada's Feminist International Assistance Policy and Defence Policy' (Canadian NAP, 2017, p ii). Yet, the specific context for action is to countries affected by 'fragility, conflict and violence' (Canadian NAP, 2017, p 2) not to all of Canada's external partners. This is similar to the case of Sweden whose NAP is situated as part of its broader feminist foreign policy. This focus on these particular types of countries is perhaps buoyed by what Parashar (2019) describes as 'pressure to improve the lot of the women "out there"', often advocated by members of international CSOs.

An interesting caveat within the latest Canadian NAP is the acknowledgement of the condition of indigenous women as targets of the WPS agenda implementation. The focus on the historical neglect and erosion of indigenous people's – and especially women's – lives is a welcome consideration and is in keeping with the feminist aspiration of the Canadian government of Prime Minister Justin Trudeau. Yet while it commits to initiatives like establishing an independent National Inquiry into Missing and Murdered Indigenous Women and Girls to tackle the 'disproportionately high rate of missing and murdered Indigenous women and girls' (Canadian NAP, 2017, p 5), there is no clear articulation of how this would be done, or how it fits into the WPS agenda.

What is clear, however, is that indigenous women and girls in particular are 'othered' in specific ways. On the one hand, by including indigenous women specifically in the NAP, they are presented as needing separate interventions to which the externalized WPS framework caters. At the same time, the lived experiences of indigenous women and the broader context of these challenges are treated as separate to conditions in so-called 'fragile' contexts. The NAP states:

Although Canada is not a fragile or conflict affected state, women in Canada face a variety of challenges including

gender-based violence. Indigenous women and girls in particular face intersecting discrimination and violence based
on gender, race, socioeconomic status and other identity
factors, as well as underlying historic causes – in particular
the legacy of colonialism. (Canadian NAP, 2017, p 4)

There is no consideration here of the intersections of violence including
the historical colonialism on conditions in the external global South
even though a general definition of gender-based violence (GBV)
acknowledges that GBV is intensified by various forms of discrimination including colonialism (Canadian NAP, 2017, p 19). Thus,
while the acknowledgement of the precarious position of indigenous
people in Canada and especially women and girls is very important,
the lack of integration of the proposed interventions is at best awk-
ward. At the same time, it is unsurprising since WPS as articulated in
this NAP is for those 'foreign' 'Others' in fragile or conflict-affected
states. Moreover, and as Heidi Hudson reflects on the need to decol-
onize gender mainstreaming in peacebuilding,

> knowledge produced about gendering peacebuilding gains
> respectability by virtue of being produced in the West, as
> part of the liberal family. In this scenario, it does not mean
> that local knowledge is always ignored, but rather that local
> contexts are 'domesticate' as sites of empirical knowledge
> where Western theory is applied. (2016, p 5)

This is in contrast to Ireland's approach as articulated in the last two NAPs
(2015, 2019). Among the NAPs of the global North that we analysed,
Ireland is unique in that its NAP is both an internal and external policy
agenda. In this sense, it is both about domestic and foreign policy. Ireland
acknowledges its own history of conflict and as part of its obligations
and relationship to Northern Ireland. In the NAP, Ireland too acknowledges the implications of coloniality based on that past experience but
also in solidarity with its international partners. Moreover, while Ireland
does not have the equivalent of Canada's indigenous peoples, Ireland
acknowledges that its immigrant population who have escaped conflict
are also governed by the WPS agenda.

In analysing the current NAP of Portugal, we see that it targets its
actions primarily towards Lusophone countries in Africa rather than
Portugal. Overall, then, WPS as articulated in this NAP provides
another method through which Portugal's renewed quest for engaging
in the former colonies can be realized since the broader context of

the Portuguese foreign policy cannot be ignored. This focus on the foreign is also underscored in the images depicted within NAPs as we elaborate in the next section.

Overall, we see this context of existing donor–recipient relationships as based on colonial and racialized power hierarchies. Furthermore, through these relationships, we see manifestations of whiteness that render the countries and peoples of the global South without agency. We show how the WPS agenda can reproduce 'racialised colonial histories' (Sartori, 2018, p 28). An analysis that captures the priorities and modes of funding can help to determine the extent to which these allow for agency that is gender-just in the global South.

Southern imagery in northern NAPs

In *Mapping Visual Global Politics*, Roland Bleiker noted that images 'shape international events and our understanding of them' (2018, p 1). Moreover, artefacts such as photographs influence how we view and approach diverse phenomena. Indeed, we'd argue that these sorts of artefacts are intended to influence *how* we view certain phenomenon. So how do certain images, in this case photographs, reproduce whiteness/racialized hierarchies within the WPS through the NAP documentation?

First, not all of the 22 NAPs we examined include photographic images. The most recent English language versions of the NAPs of Germany, Belgium, Portugal, Spain and Japan have only text, and include stock images of national emblems rather than specific photographs. The majority of those that have these images include one photograph, on the title page of the NAP (see Figure 9.1). This positioning of a photo image on the title page may be interpreted as a signifier of the central message of the NAPs. As Bleiker notes, images shape as much as they depict politics (Bleiker, 2018). While each NAP photograph is distinct, there is a recurrent theme in these images. With the exception of the latest Swedish NAP, NAPs of countries located in the global North and with images on the title pages often depict women of colour located in Africa and/or the Middle East. These black and brown women are of the global South, the object of the WPS. The locality of these women is signified in a variety of ways – their national or religious dress, the immediate background environment, in other words, the physical space they occupy.

In some cases, these images of the women from the global South are juxtaposed against the women of the global North, the latter of whom are often depicted in military apparel, or some other sort of

Figure 9.1: *Title Pages of 8 Global North NAPs*

Top, L-R: UK NAP; Austrian NAP; Ireland NAP; Middle, L-R: Canada NAP; Switzerland NAP; Bottom, L-R: Australian NAP; New Zealand NAP; Iceland NAP

military apparatus. This is the case for the latest NAPs of Australia, France, Canada, Iceland and Austria. While the United States has no such image on its title page, one exists in the text. The images on the other NAPs like those of the UK, the Netherlands and Ireland is solely of the 'other' woman. Across all of these, although the 'other' woman is centred, they are also positioned as being 'saved' by the interventions of white people through militaries. In these images, the role of the global North is depicted as interventionist while the performances of receiving assistance is done by those women in the global South.

These images reinforce the 'Otherness' of women located outside the global North. Perhaps with the exception of Ireland, the women who are to be the subjects of WPS practices designed by those countries in the global North are portrayed so as to underscore that their positionalities are external to those of the countries where the NAPs themselves originate.

Conclusion

National Action Plans are the primary means by which countries articulate how they intend to instrumentalize and localize the Women, Peace and Security agenda through hybrid peace processes. Often they allow civil society actors to be agents in realizing a global North agenda in the peace and security contexts of countries in the global South. In this sense, they are important artefacts of states' gender, security and foreign policies. Each NAP outlines how the state understands what WPS is and who WPS is for. In this chapter, we set out to trouble localization and to understand what localization work funded from abroad tells us about race through an interrogation of whiteness within the NAPs. In so doing, we were able to gauge the narratives of security and their racialized representations and implications of donor states who currently fund many WPS initiatives.

While some global North countries aspire to integrate more women in their foreign policy and security apparatus, primarily, the focus of most of these NAPs have been on 'Other' women located in the global South. In this way, NAPs produced by countries in the global North exacerbate the racialized norms of international relations and of conflict/insecurity being something that happens in other places, while refusing the gendered violence within their own borders.

In conclusion, our analysis has also allowed us to reflect on the push for localization in WPS practices. In reality, this call for localization only seems to be about the global South, and in a way that is heavily shaped by the outside and more powerful actors, including civil society actors in the global North; in short, localization but only for some, and only in a certain way. Even when WPS initiatives are happening in the global South by people in the global South, much of WPS still seems to be about legitimizing white people's desires as a result of existing power hierarchies that ultimately sanction the actions of global North countries. These desires may be to see the global South as always in need of repair, as fragile, as failing.

Note

[1] These include: Denmark, UK, Sweden, Norway, Switzerland, Spain, Austria, Netherlands, Iceland, Finland, Portugal, Belgium, Italy, France, Canada, Ireland, USA, Germany, New Zealand, Japan and Luxembourg.

References

Acharya, A. (2004) 'How ideas spread: whose norms matter? norm localization and institutional change in Asian Regionalism', *International Organization*, 58(2): 239–275.

Ahmed, S. (2012) *On Being Included: Racism and Diversity in Institutional Work*, Durham, NC: Duke University Press.

Allen, R.L. (2004) 'Whiteness and critical pedagogy', *Educational Philosophy and Theory*, 36(2): 121–136.

Anievas, A., Manchanda, N. and Shilliam, R. (2015) 'Confronting the global colour line: an introduction', in A. Anievas, N. Manchanda and Shilliam, R. (eds) *Race and Racism in International Relations: Confronting the Global Colour Line*, Abingdon: Routledge.

Björkdahl, A. and Höglund, K. (2013) 'Precarious peacebuilding: friction in global–local encounters', *Peacebuilding*, 1(3): 289–299.

Bleiker, R. (2018) 'Mapping visual global politics', in R. Bleiker (ed) *Visual Global Politics*, Abingdon: Routledge, pp 1–29.

Crenshaw, K. (1989) 'Demarginalizing the intersection of race and sex: a black feminist critique of antidiscrimination doctrine, feminist theory and antiracist politics', *University of Chicago Legal Forum*, 1(8): 139–187.

Duncanson, C. (2016) *Gender and Peacebuilding*, Cambridge: Polity Press.

Dados, N. and Connell, R. (2012) 'The global South', *Contexts*, 11(1): 12–13.

Donais, T. (2009) 'Empowerment or imposition? Dilemmas of local ownership in post-conflict peacebuilding processes', *Peace & Change*, 34(1): 3–26.

Grewal, I. (2017) *Saving the Security State*, Durham, NC: Duke University Press.

hooks, b. (1989) *Talking Back: Thinking Feminist, Thinking Black*, Boston, MA: South End Press.

Hudson, H. (2016) 'Decolonizing the mainstreaming of gender in peacebuilding: toward an agenda for Africa (New York: Social Science Research Council)', Available from: www.ssrc.org/publications/view/2DC474C6-B02A-E711-80C4-005056AB0BD9/.

Jauhola, M. (2016) 'Decolonizing branded peacebuilding: abjected women talk back to the Finnish Women, Peace and Security agenda', *International Affairs*, 92(2): 333–351.

Leonardo, Z. (2009) *Race, Whiteness and Education*, New York: Routledge.

Lipsitz, G. (2006) *The Possessive Investment in Whiteness: How White People Profit from Identity Politics*, revised and expanded edition, Philadelphia, PA: Temple University Press.

Markusoff, J. (2017) 'Why Justin Trudeau used the c-word – "colonialism" – in his apology', *Maclean's*, Available from: www.macleans.ca/politics/why-justin-trudeau-used-the-c-word-colonialism-in-his-apology/.

Martín de Almagro, M. (2018) 'Producing participants: gender, race, class, and Women, Peace and Security', *Global Society*, 32(4): 395–414.

Mohanty, C. (2003) *Feminism without Borders: Decolonizing Theory, Practicing Solidarity*, Durham, NC: Duke University Press.

Mills, C.W. (1998) *Whiteness Visible*, Ithaca, NY: Cornell University.

Mills, C.W. (2017) *Black Rights/White Wrongs: The Critique of Racial Liberalism*, New York: Oxford University Press.

Parashar, S. (2019) 'The WPS agenda: a postcolonial critique', in S.E. Davies and J. True (eds) *The Oxford Handbook of Women, Peace and Security*, Oxford Handbooks, doi: 10.1093/oxfordhb/9780190638276.013.4.

Parashar, S. and Tickner, J.A. and True, J. (eds) (2018) *Revisiting Gendered States: Feminist Imaginings of the State in International Relations*, New York: Oxford University Press.

PeaceWomen (no date) 'Member states: National Action Plans for the implementation of UNSCR 1325 on Women, Peace and Security', Available from: www.peacewomen.org/member-states.

Pratt, N. (2013) 'Reconceptualizing gender, reinscribing racial–sexual boundaries in international security: the case of UN Security Council Resolution 1325 on "Women, Peace and Security"', *International Studies Quarterly*, 57(4): 772–783.

Puar, J. (2007) *Terrorist Assemblages: Homonationalism in Queer Times*, Durham, NC: Duke University Press.

Shepherd, L.J. (2016) 'Making war safe for women? National Action Plans and the militarisation of the Women, Peace and Security agenda', *International Political Science Review*, 37(3): 324–335.

Sartori, A. (2018) 'Whiteness in development: a critical content analysis of Peace Corps marketing', *Understanding and Dismantling Privilege*, 8(2): 27–49.

Shilliam, R. (2016) 'Race in world politics', in J. Baylis, S. Smith and P. Owens (eds) *The Globalization of World Politics: An Introduction to International Relations*, 7th edition, New York: Oxford University Press, pp 285–300.

United Nations Security Council (2002) 'Statement by the President of the Security Council', (October 31) UN Doc S/PRST/2002/32.

UN Women (2015) *A Global Study on the Implementation of United Nations Security Council Resolution 1325*, Available from: http://wps.unwomen.org/pdf/en/GlobalStudy_EN_Web.pdf.

WILPF (Women's International League for Peace and Freedom) (2013) *Women, Peace and Security National Action Plan Development Toolkit*, Available from: www.peacewomen.org/assets/file/national_action_plan_development_toolkit.pdf.

Yancy, G. (ed) (2004) *What White Looks Like*, New York: Routledge.

Primary Documents: National Action Plans
Australian Government (2012) *Australian National Action Plan on Women, Peace and Security 2012–2018*, Available from: www.peacewomen.org/sites/default/files/aust_nap2012_2018.pdf.

Austrian Federal Ministry for European and International Affairs (2012) *Revised National Action Plan on Implementing UN Security Council Resolution 1325 (2000)*, Available from: www.peacewomen.org/sites/default/files/austriaupdatednap2012.pdf.

Dutch NAP Partnership (2016) *The Netherlands National Action Plan on Women, Peace and Security, 2016–2019*, Available from: www.peacewomen.org/sites/default/files/Dutch_NAP_2016-2019.pdf.

France's Second National Action Plan *Implementation of United National Security Council 'Women, Peace and Security Resolutions, 2015–2018*, Available from: www.peacewomen.org/sites/default/files/2014–2016%20WPS%20NAP%20France.pdf.

Government of Canada (2017) *Gender Equality: A Foundation for Peace – Canada's National Action Plan (2017–2022)*, Available from: www.peacewomen.org/sites/default/files/cnap-eng.pdf.

Government of the Federal Republic of Germany (2017) *Action Plan of the Government of the Federal Republic of Germany on the Implementation of United Nations Security Council Resolution 1325 on Women, Peace and Security for the Period 2017–2020*, Available from: www.peacewomen.org/sites/default/files/170111_Aktionsplan_1325.pdf.

Government of Ireland (2015) *Ireland's second National Action Plan on Women, Peace and Security 2015–2018*, Available from: www.peacewomen.org/sites/default/files/Revised%20NAP%20Ireland%20(2015–2018).pdf.

Government of Ireland (2019) *Women, Peace and Security, Ireland's third National Action Plan for the implementation of UNSCR 1325 and related resolutions 2019–2024*, Available from: www.dfa.ie/media/dfa/ourrolepolicies/womenpeaceandsecurity/Third-National-Action-Plan.pdf.

Government of Japan (2015) *National Action Plan on Women, Peace and Security – Provisional Translation*, Available from: www.peacewomen.org/sites/default/files/Japan%20National%20Action%20Plan.pdf.

Government Offices of Sweden (2016) *Women, Peace and Security, Sweden's National Action Plan for the Implementation of the UN Security Council Resolutions on Women, Peace and Security 2016–2020*, Available from: www.peacewomen.org/sites/default/files/Sweden%20NAP%202016–2020.pdf.

Government of Portugal (2014) *II National Action Plan for Implementation of United Nations Security Council Resolution 1325 (2000) on Women, Peace and Security*, Available from: www.peacewomen.org/sites/default/files/portugal_nap_2014.pdf.

Government of Spain (2007) *Action Plan of the Government of Spain for the Implementation of Resolution 1325 of the Security Council of the United Nations (2000) on Women, Peace and Security*, Available from: www.peacewomen.org/sites/default/files/spain_nap_2007_english.pdf.

Her Majesty's Government (2018) *UK National Action Plan on Women, Peace and Security 2018–2022*, Available from: www.peacewomen.org/sites/default/files/National-Action-Plan-Women-Peace-Security-2018–2022.pdf.

Inter-ministerial Committee on Human Rights (2016) *Italy's Third National Action Plan, in accordance with UN Security Council Resolution 1325(2000), 2016–2019*, Available from: www.peacewomen.org/sites/default/files/49123_f_PlanofAction132520162019%20(1).pdf.

Kingdom of Belgium (2013) *Second National Action Plan 'Women, Peace, Security' (2013–2016), Implementing UN Security Council Resolution 1325*, Available from: www.peacewomen.org/sites/default/files/Belgium%20NAP%201325%202013–2016%20EN.pdf.

Ministry for Foreign Affairs (2018) *Iceland's National Action Plan on Women, Peace and Security, 2018–2022*, Available from: www.peacewomen.org/sites/default/files/Icelands-National-Action-Plan-on-Women-Peace-and-Security-2018v2(1).pdf.

Ministry of Foreign Affairs, Denmark (2014) *Denmark's National Action Plan for Implementation of UN Security Council Resolution 1325 on Women, Peace and Security, 2014–2019*, Available from: http://peacewomen.org/sites/default/files/Denmark%20National%20Action%20Plan%202014–2019.pdf.

Ministry for Foreign Affairs of Finland (2018) *Women, Peace and Security – Finland's National Action Plan 2018–2021*, Available from: www.peacewomen.org/sites/default/files/03_18_Women_Peace_Security%20(1)%20(2).pdf.

Norwegian Ministries (2015) *National Action Plan, Women, Peace and Security, 2015–2018*, Available from: www.peacewomen.org/sites/default/files/Norway%20Revised%20NAP%20(2015–2018).pdf.

New Zealand Government (2015) *New Zealand National Action Plan for the Implementation of United Nations Security Council Resolutions, including 1325 on Women, Peace and Security 2015–2019*, Available from: www.peacewomen.org/sites/default/files/NZ%20National%20Action%20Plan%20on%20Women%20Peace%20and%20Security.pdf.

Switzerland (2018) *Switzerland's Fourth National Action Plan to Implement UN Security Council Resolution 1325 2018-2022*, Available from: www.peacewomen.org/sites/default/files/Swiss%204th%20NAP.pdf.

The White House (2016) *The United States National Action Plan on Women, Peace and Security*, Available from: www.peacewomen.org/sites/default/files/women-national-action-plan.pdf.

10

Towards a Postcolonial, Anti-Racist, Anti-Militarist Feminist Mode of Weapons Control

Anna Stavrianakis

The last decade has seen some notable feminist victories in one of the 'hardest' areas of international security – the international arms trade. The inclusion of gender-based violence (GBV) as a stand-alone article in the United Nations Arms Trade Treaty (UN ATT) that regulates international arms transfers is described by Cynthia Enloe as 'a transnational feminist success', 'buried in its thirteen pages of formal diplomatic language' (Enloe, 2014, p 23). States such as Canada and Sweden have articulated a feminist foreign policy that has implied tighter controls on weapons exports to repressive states. Nonetheless, these are not straightforward or obvious successes. In the ATT, GBV risks have to constitute serious violations of international humanitarian law (IHL) or international human rights law (IHRL) in order to require states to deny exports. While many GBV violations do meet such legal thresholds, arms transfers also play a less direct role in facilitating and sustaining GBV. And despite their commitments to a feminist foreign policy, Sweden and Canada have faced criticism for their ongoing commitments to arms sales to states such as Saudi Arabia.

Feminist critique tells us that violence exists on a 'gendered continuum' and that *all* violence (direct and structural) facilitated by the circulation of weapons is gendered (Cockburn, 2004, pp 24–44). By extension, *all* weapons transfers have the potential for GBV: an indication of the scale of the challenge facing feminist accounts of weapons control, which are often implicitly anti-militarist in orientation. It is also indicative of the ongoing obstacles facing 'the development of anti-militarist politics of peace' in the Women, Peace and Security (WPS) agenda more widely (Shepherd, 2016, p 332), which has itself demonstrated a 'tendency towards militarization' (Basu and Shepherd, 2017, p 10). Anti-racist and anti-imperialist scholars and activists, meanwhile, assert the importance of defending the use of force in self-defence or as resistance (Dirik, 2017), probing the boundaries between anti-militarism, non-violence and pacifism.

Against this backdrop, this chapter discusses the overlapping imperatives of postcolonial, anti-racist and anti-militarist politics for feminist modes of weapons control as a contribution to the next generation of WPS scholarship. The argument, in short, is that efforts to integrate gender into initiatives to regulate or abolish the arms trade are inadequate unless they also centre racial and postcolonial politics within and between states and unless they address more directly the question of when the use of force is justified. While there are always strategic gains to be made and trade-offs to be conceded in the struggle for change, it is a mistake to focus on gender first, then race and postcoloniality, as if these are successive issues to be tackled rather than cross-cutting and compounding ones to be addressed together. Gendered relations are always already racialized relations. And global systems of weapons production, circulation and use – from nuclear weapons to small arms and light weapons – are predicated on relations within and between states that are both gendered and racialized and an international system in which the legacies of colonialism and decolonization still resonate.

Without explicitly addressing the racial and postcolonial politics of efforts at change, then, feminist strategies and scholarship risk reproducing an imperial politics of war, militarism and violence. As Chowdry and Nair argue, while feminists have emphasized the 'gendered sources of security, war, [and] militarism', they have neglected 'the relationship of gender to (neo)imperialism and race' and seem 'more hesitant to confront directly the exclusion of race in [International Relations] and its implications for the exercise of power' (2003, pp 3, 9). Addressing these relationships as they play out in the arms trade as a key source of the means of violence is a pressing political and analytical task.

The argument proceeds in three steps. First, I address the relative absence of discussion of the arms trade in the prevention pillar of the WPS agenda, a casualty of the narrowing of prevention to mean the prevention of certain types of violence *in* conflict rather than prevention *of* violent conflict per se, and the simultaneous near-absence of gender in debate about the arms trade. These parallel paths indicate the need for debates about WPS and weapons control to come into deeper conversation. Second, I address the postcolonial and anti–racist imperatives that need to be incorporated alongside gender in discussion of weapons circulation and its control, illustrating with three examples from contemporary weapons control debates: gun control (or the lack thereof) in the US and its ambivalent relationship to multilateral efforts at weapons control; what constitutes an illegitimate arms transfer in the UN ATT; and the inclusion of GBV in the ATT. Finally, I sketch out the beginnings of what a postcolonial, anti–racist and anti–militarist feminist mode of weapons control would look like.

The uncertain status of the arms trade in feminist agendas and of gender in arms control initiatives

Over the past two decades, WPS has become an established component of the global policy agenda in support of gender equality and con-flict resolution. There is a growing and wide-ranging literature on its origins, applications, achievements and limitations. Two things are of note in this rise in attention. First is the narrowing of the definition of 'prevention' in much WPS work, such that prevention is mobilized in terms of 'short-term, conflict-focused work, such as policies to prevent outbreaks of sexual violence in refugee camps through gender-sensitive logistics', rather than 'in the sense of sustained social change to undo the conditions that produce violent conflict in the first place' (Kirby and Shepherd, 2016b, p 391) – a shift away from opposition *to* war, towards a more limited opposition to certain practices *in* war and, at times, an accommodation *with* war. This narrowing has significant ramifications for the capacity of feminists to make broad anti–militarist demands that refuse to accommodate the state and capital's logics of military production and circulation. As Acheson and Butler argue (2019, p 698), 'WPS must focus on conflict *prevention* above engage-ment in the systems that generate and sustain conflict' – as such, 'the ATT and WPS must oppose militarism'.

Second is the relative disappearance from the contemporary WPS agenda of historical feminist commitments to disarmament. The 1915 International Congress of Women held in The Hague included the principle of 'Complete disarmament and state control of the arms industry' to 'remove the economic interests fueling war' (Tickner and True, 2018, p 226). While the Women's International League for Peace and Freedom (WILPF) – established in 1915 and central to both the Hague Congress and today's WPS agenda – continues to pursue 'total and universal disarmament' (WILPF, 2014), there is no call for disarmament in UNSCR 1325 or subsequent WPS resolutions, the limited and partial exception of disarmament, demobilization and reintegration (DDR) aside. Tickner and True explain the disappearance of demands for disarmament as 'a feminist pragmatic choice of what issues can best be pursued through international institutions today', but hold nonetheless that 'the WPS agenda has allowed for greater critical scrutiny of this trade in weapons and the purpose for which weapons are used' (Tickner and True, 2018, pp 226, 229). As will become evident later in this chapter, I am more sceptical about the purchase of historical and contemporary feminist demands on weapons control issues, due to their marginalization of questions of racialized and postcolonial hierarchies.

In the arms trade literature, meanwhile, the end of the Cold War saw a growth in attention to small arms and light weapons, complete with the recognition that it was neither the weapons themselves nor the problems they cause that are new, but rather the international attention to them (Krause, 2002). A significant strand of this literature has a specific gender focus (see, for example, Farr et al, 2009). But this focus has not been replicated in the wider literature on the circulation and regulation of major conventional weaponry. In the policy world, there have been a plethora of regional and international initiatives to regulate small arms in particular, none of which have a central gender component. Regional initiatives such as the 2004 Nairobi Protocol for the Prevention, Control and Reduction of Small Arms and Light Weapons in the Great Lakes Region and the Horn of Africa make no mention of gender; and the 2001 UN Programme of Action to Prevent, Combat and Eradicate the Illicit Trade in Small Arms and Light Weapons in all its Aspects (UN PoA) notes that the UN is 'gravely concerned' about the negative impact of the illicit trade in small arms and light weapons on women in the Preamble, but does not commit states to any actual practical action in relation to gender. It is not until the early 2010s that gender is integrated into weapons control, with the 2012 UN PoA Review Conference, 2013 UNSCR 2122, and the 2014 entry into force of the UN ATT, with its legally binding provision that states must take into account the risk of GBV when authorizing arms transfers (Small Arms Survey, 2014a).

The WPS agenda and arms trade literatures and initiatives have thus grown largely in parallel, with WPS not addressing weapons issues, and arms transfer control not integrating gender until very recently. This indicates both the historically masculinized orientation to weapons control and the ambivalent status of disarmament as a feminist goal. Due in no small part to the activism of civil society platforms and organizations such as WILPF and the Control Arms NGO coalition, this sounds like a good news story – indeed, it is widely celebrated as one. For the most part the remaining challenges are seen as strategic and tactical ones. But I want to argue that there is more at stake: a disavowal of racial and postcolonial politics structures the debate and the demands in ways that even if the demands were met, they would be inadequate. And racial and postcolonial politics are rarely named openly because of international structures that assume state sovereignty and equality despite massive inequalities; because of the racial politics within liberal democracies, in particular the USA, which is also the world's largest weapons producer and exporter; and because of the predominantly white and Northern domination of civil society, even as these organizations are doing better than states in terms of gender equality in participation. We need to have a realistic, racially aware and postcolonial – as well as gendered – understanding of the dynamics of the arms trade if we are to challenge it without further entrenching racialized inequalities within and between states.

Postcolonial and anti–racist feminist imperatives for weapons control

Susan Wright makes the feminist argument that the ostensibly distinct practices of 'disarmament' and 'arms control' are actually 'expressions of the same discursive practice, that is, the practice and legitimation of "war by other means"' (Wright, 2009, p 195). Further, Carol Cohn showed us over 30 years ago the centrality of masculinity to weapons production (Cohn, 1987) – in ways that continue to haunt us today (Cohn, 2018). One of the advantages of feminist analyses is that they challenge the domestic/foreign and private/public binaries. As Cockburn succinctly puts it, 'gender links violence at different points on a scale reaching from the personal to the international, from the home and the back street to the maneuvers of the tank column and the sortie of the stealth bomber' (Cockburn, 2004, p 43). Such a perspective allows us to talk about gun violence within communities and countries as well as armed conflict within and between states. Feminist security studies more broadly has taught us that 'absolutely distinguishing between the personal, national and international level of war and militarism lacks conceptual and empirical rigor at best'. That is, paying feminist attention allows us to understand both the impact of war and militarism on people (especially, but not only, women) as well as the gendered construction of war and militarism (Sjoberg and Via, 2010, pp 231–4).

Research on small arms control and gender challenges the common assumptions of a clear distinction between war and peace, and between public and private violence. Analysis that integrates the individual, relationship, community and societal levels emphasizes the importance of militarized social norms that shape and are shaped by gender roles and perpetuate armed violence (see, for example, Small Arms Survey, 2014b). There is now growing national and cross-national research that compares levels of gun violence between states across the global North and South. But the policy orientation of most of this research pushes analysts to adopt a relatively short historical timeframe and nationally-based research designs: this precludes discussion of the violent and transnational legacies of colonial rule and decolonization. Yet postcolonial feminists remind us of the continuities between colonial and contemporary militarism and the fundamentally gendered characteristics of the physical and structural violence at stake (Mama and Okazawa-Rey, 2012).

We also know that feminist activism has long been awkwardly bound up with racial, imperial and postcolonial politics. The articulations between gender, sexuality, race and class were central to the growth of empire and industrialization (McClintock, 1995) and 'gender-based violence was both overtly and covertly a weapon of settler administration' (Bennett, 2001, p 89). More recently, the end of the Cold War and collapse of the Soviet Union were a facilitating condition of the turn to gender analysis in security policy and practice. As Harrington argues, trafficking, wartime rape and domestic violence became 'important to the women's sector of the UN under US global hegemony ... because of [their] framing within new wars discourse as a reason for international policing and surveillance' (Harrington, 2011, p 565). We should therefore be wary of an uncritically celebratory account of the rise of gender analysis. Rather, we need to centre a 'genealogy of the conditions which foster violence against women' that pays attention to the inextricable connections between women's lives across the global North and South and the historical conditions of inequality that shape them (Mama, 2012, pp 47–48).

The arms trade is an excellent case study of the gendered, racialized and postcolonial politics of militarism, and of the challenges for peace and security. Let me illustrate with three contemporary examples: the politics of gun control (or the absence of it) in the USA and its relationship to international small arms activism; the North–South politics of 'illegitimate' arms transfers; and the treatment of GBV in the UN ATT.

The racial and postcolonial dynamics of gun control

Since the end of the Cold War there has been increased international attention to the problems posed to security – whether state or human – by small arms, now frequently labelled as the 'real weapons of mass destruction'. But the key multilateral instrument regulating them, the UN Programme of Action produces a 'gendered space, as it excises from consideration the sphere in which women are particularly vulnerable as women: the use of legally held guns in domestic violence' (Mutimer, 2006, p 39). And one of the key reasons for this framing of the small arms issue was the deliberate attempt to keep US civilian gun possession off the agenda. This is how the personal and the international are inextricably entwined: the exclusion of US gun politics from multilateral small arms control is not a mistaken absence but a deliberate omission on which wider action is predicated. It is a constitutive absence: while there has been an exponential increase in attention to small arms in multilateral fora and in aid, development and security assistance, there has simultaneously been the ongoing ability of the USA to have civilian possession as a redline and have it excluded from multilateral negotiations. This happens even though, indeed *because*, the US domestic market is the source for many of the illicit weapons in Latin America and the Caribbean; and because states that have become extremely violent through their historic and contemporary relationship with the USA (from slavery through incorporation into a global capitalist economy to current arms trafficking) variously want to be able to either better control weapons circulation, or their state forces are complicit in weapons trafficking and armed violence. This complex layering of transnational relations of weapons circulation cannot be understood without attention to the historically violent and asymmetrical relations between the global North and South.

Moreover, the US itself has the highest levels of gun violence in the global North, with gun violence more on a par with the southern parts of the Americas than with the European countries with which it is more commonly associated. And this is violence that is not only gendered but also deeply racialized and whose contemporary manifestations bear the ongoing traces of settler colonialism and slavery (see, for example, Dunbar-Ortiz, 2018). In this context, black women in the US are turning to guns in significant numbers, which suggests, according to Kimberlé Crenshaw, that black women are 'under siege' not just as black people but as black women; 'the state and private violence converge to endanger … and take the lives of black people', but for black women, 'the private dimension of the violence is interpersonal violence' (Crenshaw, in Gowrinathan, 2018). And they are turning *to* weapons in response. So feminist histories of gun circulation and gun control must not ignore those who turn to weapons for self-defence and to exercise agency in asymmetrical, masculinized and racialized contexts.

A WPS agenda that is serious about participation and prevention must address this racialized, gendered asymmetry in access to and use of weapons. WPS concerns around participation have started to surface in relation to weapons control recently. In 2018, the UN Secretary-General called for greater efforts to achieve 'equal, full and effective participation of women in all decision-making processes related to disarmament' (UNODA, 2018, p xi). And in October 2018, UN General Assembly First Committee duly encouraged states parties and signatory states to the Arms Trade Treaty 'to ensure the full and equal participation of women and men, in pursuing the object and purpose of the Treaty and its implementation' (UN General Assembly, 2018). However welcome – and challenging – this long overdue effort to address gender inequality in disarmament is, it remains marked by a heteronormative and cisprivileged monolithic, undifferentiated category of 'women' (Hagen, 2016), as well as by a silence on the postcolonial politics and political economy of states' abilities to be represented at multilateral fora (for an innovative although not explicitly feminist response to this, see Joseph, 2013).

The postcolonial politics of 'illegitimate' arms transfers

The UN ATT brings together humanitarian and human rights standards to regulate weapons in armed conflict and non-conflict situations. The combination of prohibitions based on international law and national risk assessment processes are designed to protect against the commission or facilitation of serious violations of IHL or IHRL. This means that, for arms transfers to be legal, states parties have to have a national set of laws and policies in place through which to authorize them, but they must also authorize them in a manner that is consistent with international humanitarian and human rights standards. In short, authorized transfers can still be illegitimate if they do not conform to these standards. This brings a human security standard to bear on state sovereignty, in the eyes of proponents of the treaty. In practice, this applies most commonly to non-western arms exporters, who have traditionally relied on state sovereignty as a defence of arms exports. Western arms exporters have ostensibly incorporated commitments to IHL and IHLR but nonetheless have controversial arms export records, and their rhetoric around international law garners accusations of hypocrisy from non-western states (see Stavrianakis, 2019).

What gets lost in the clamour is a feminist postcolonial voice that challenges the compounding effects of patriarchy and militarization (Chenoy, 2004). The shared masculinist politics of wanting to transfer weapons is shaped by a postcolonial politics of North–South asymmetry that complicates any simple understanding of what constitutes a progressive position. This shows the importance of foregrounding the postcolonial dimensions of a feminist argument. Activists need to be alert to the risk of co-option by states who themselves have problematic transfer practices and seek to mobilize liberal commitments for reputational purposes. Northern feminists in the anti-militarist movement need to respond to postcolonial states' criticisms, amplify Southern feminists' voices, and be more critical of western state practices, in order to better mobilize a progressive anti-militarist position.

Feminist anti-imperialist resistance

The UN ATT was subject to feminist interventions during its drafting and activists won a significant victory with the inclusion of provisions around GBV. Members of the treaty regime are legally bound to take into account the risk of weapons being used to commit or facilitate serious acts of GBV or serious act of violence against women and children, and to deny exports if the risk assessment indicates an overriding risk of serious violations of IHL or IHRL. Given that many acts of GBV are indeed violations of international law, most commentators see the treaty as a win for anti-GBV activism, 'mak[ing] it harder for perpetrators to access weapons' (Green et al, 2013, p 558). A series of operational challenges are now in view: states don't know how to do a gender-sensitive risk assessment, seeing it as a subset of the general human rights risk assessment; they can't conceive of a situation in which GBV would be the reason for a denial; and they mostly conflate gender with women (ATT Monitor, 2019). This is where the purchase of a postcolonial and anti-racist analysis of war and militarism needs to be translated into policy to have purchase. If feminists are right that all violence facilitated by the use of weapons is gendered, then all weapons have the potential for GBV.

Consider, however, the case of the Kurdish resistance, in particular the Women's Protection Units (YPJ) that have been militarily active in defence of Kurdish national self-determination. WILPF argues that 'Allowing women equal opportunity to kill in war does not amount to genuine liberation. It is rather a militarization of women's liberation' (Acheson and Rees, nd). In contrast, Dirik argues that such a position 'fails to qualitatively distinguish between statist, colonialist, imperialist, interventionist militarism and necessary, legitimate self-defence' (Dirik, 2017). She draws a distinction between self-defence and militarism and points to a key North–South dynamic of analysis and advocacy: 'when feminists in relative safety accuse militant women in the Middle East facing sex slavery under ISIS of militarism, we must problematize the liberal notion of non-violence which disregards intersecting power systems and mechanisms of structural violence' (Dirik, 2017). Liberal arguments about women's right to fight not-withstanding, this is a good example of how postcolonial relations are gendered, and vice versa. An adequate feminist analysis has to put imperialism, colonialism and resistance front and centre, while also resisting the temptation to romanticize armed struggle and recognizing the ambivalent, contradictory but always gendered causes and effects of armed violence (White, 2007). This is where the anti-racist and postcolonial imperatives of a feminist anti-militarist position kick in: how and where to draw the lines?

Towards an anti-racist, postcolonial, anti-militarist feminist mode of weapons control

With these lessons and examples in mind, what would a feminist, anti-militarist account of arms control that centred racial and postcolonial relations look like? First, it would pay reflexive attention to the racial and postcolonial dynamics of national and transnational movements for control, and how gender can compound these asymmetries. In the US, for example, young black activists have been organizing and fighting for gun reform for years without the same level of attention received by their white peers (Blades, 2018), while there is a 'particular white suburban praxis' to mothers' movements against guns, in which 'the theoretically race-neutral title of "mother" works to mobilize women around the deaths of white children' (Caelin, 2018). Transnationally, the majority membership of weapons control movements is often based in the global North; even when movements are majority southern-based, they remain dominated by a small number of western actors, with 'an overwhelming belief … that participants in the movement should do much more to include southern, non-western actors in the movement network' (Grillot et al, 2006, p 75). Changes in the social relations of who can speak, and be heard, about war, violence and the need for weapons control are a key part of the steps towards the sub-stantive goals of weapons control itself.

Second, efforts at weapons control need to simultaneously mobilize feminist and postcolonial analyses of the fundamentally gendered but also racialized character of war and violence. This would acknowledge that all weapons have the capacity for gendered forms of violence, and hence any mode of control needs to be anti-militarist. But it would also recognize that some forms of violence are legitimate attempts at self-defence and resistance, and so any effort at violence reduction must not disarm the weak without first disarming the powerful. These are necessarily political judgements: and we can make them by starting from the perspective of the most marginalized. That is why it is possible to defend black women in the US or Kurdish female fighters having access to weapons while also arguing against white supremacist men and institutions or states such as Assad's Syria having access to them. This is why campaigns for an end to police violence and racialized killings in the US also have demilitarization as a core goal (see, for example, Campaign Zero, nd).

Third, it would queer the feminist insight of the gendered harms of war and apply it to more than just women. The term 'GBV' often operates as a synonym for violence against women in conventional arms control, but it has a much more productive potential than this. We know that there is a spectrum of risk that crosses the public/private divide in generating harms for women – from the use of handguns by security forces to facilitate sexual violence to the increased risk of intimate partner violence that women face in the home when there is a gun present. Overcoming the obstacles to change posed by the public/private divide must, however, be accompanied by wider recognition of the diverse harms and forms of violence facilitated by weapons. Lethal violence against lesbian, gay, bisexual, transgender and queer (LGBTQ) individuals and communities because of their sexuality and/or gender non-conformity is a form of GBV that is sorely under-addressed in public policy, and policymakers often have little idea how to approach it or even recognize it. And if a feminist critique is serious about delegitimizing war, then it needs to address the masculinized harms of war. We often see civilian casualty figures that go on to specify the number of women and children harmed; but men are the greatest users and victims of weapons (whether handguns or major conventional weaponry), even if women are subject to disproportionate and gender-specific forms of harm. While there has been some discussion in arms control and anti-militarist circles of the targeting of military-age males by drones as a gendered human rights violation, for example, this logic is generally not extended further to argue that war is bad for men: is the targeting of predominantly male military forces in war itself a form of gender-based violence (see, for example, Segal, 2008)? Does a feminist analysis of war need, therefore, to be pacifist, and how does this rub up against the postcolonial imperative to keep the door open to the use of force in self-defence or resistance?

Fourth, an adequate mode of weapons control would operationalize the feminist and postcolonial critique of the domestic/foreign and war/peace binaries. This would mean that weapons control would have to focus on domestic military production and its contribution to militarization as much as it does on international transfers. To take an example, the UN ATT is a trade regulation treaty, not a disarmament treaty; this means that domestic production – whether of major conventional weaponry or handguns – is excluded from regulation. Relatedly, how are states and civil society to design weapons control policies that recognize that 'it is meaningless to make a sharp distinction between peace and war, prewar, and postwar' (Cockburn, 2004, p 43) and that '[l]ong before a man uses physical violence against a woman, she may experience "structural violence" in a marriage in which her husband or a constraining patriarchal community holds power over her' (Cockburn, 2004, p 30)? The distinctions between the recommendations by an anti-militarist movement such as WILPF and a regulatory campaign such as Control Arms are instructive here: WILPF want indicators such as girls' literacy rates, access to safe abortion and early marriage reports to be part of the analysis (WILPF, 2016), while Control Arms stick to indicators that can be directly linked to a weapons transfer, such as reports of sexual abuse by security officers, or vetting systems for the acquisition of firearms (Control Arms, 2018). These differences speak to the hard practicalities of designing policy with feminist goals in mind.

Conclusion

Kirby and Shepherd seek to recover the memory of WPS as 'a platform from which it was possible to imagine radical reform of peace and security governance' (2016a, p 249). My argument in this chapter is that any adequate feminist account of control of the means of violence has to place anti-racist and postcolonial politics within and between states at the forefront of its analysis and its demands. While we see in the UN ATT some of the putative wins of a 'femocrat' strategy (Kirby and Shepherd, 2016b, p 390), they must be subject to critical scrutiny. What is excluded, and whose voices, harms and agency are *not* heard, when campaign wins are celebrated? Which issues, and whose long histories of analysis and organizing are left out of our histories of feminist anti-militarist activism? Kirby and Shepherd are right that the paradoxically compromised character of transformation is 'constitutive and cannot be overcome. It can only be navigated, imperfectly' (Kirby and Shepherd 2016b, p 393). That navigation must be guided by an anti-racist and postcolonial politics if it is to steer us in the right direction.

Bibliography

Acheson, R. and Butler, M. (2019) 'WPS and Arms Trade Treaty', in S.E. Davies and J. True (eds) *The Oxford Handbook of Women, Peace and Security*, Oxford: Oxford University Press, pp 690–703.

Acheson, R. and Rees, M. (no date) 'Feminism and firearms: a response to calls to arm women', Available from: www.reachingcriticalwill.org/news/latest-news/10748-feminism-and-firearms-a-response-to-calls-to-arm-women.

ATT Monitor (2019) *Arms Trade Treaty Monitor 2019*, Available from: https://attmonitor.org/en/wp-content/uploads/2019/07/EN_ATT_Monitor-Report-2019_Online.pdf.

Basu, S. and Shepherd, L.J. (2017) 'Prevention in pieces: representing conflict in the Women, Peace and Security agenda', *Global Affairs*, 3(4–5): 441–453.

Bennett, J. (2001) 'Enough lip service! Hearing post-colonial experience of GBV', *Agenda: Empowering Women for Gender Equity*, 16(50): 88–96.

Blades, L.A. (2018) 'Black teens have been fighting for gun reform for years', *Teen Vogue*, 23 February, Available from: www.teenvogue.com/story/black-teens-have-been-fighting-for-gun-reform-for-years.

Caelin, M. (2018) 'Whose children? Mom activism and race in the gun control movement', *The Activist History Review*, April, Available from: https://activisthistory.com/2018/04/06/whose-children-mom-activism-and-race-in-the-gun-control-movement/.

Campaign Zero (no date) 'Campaign Zero', Available from: www.joincampaignzero.org/#vision.

Chenoy, A.M. (2004) 'Gender and international politics: the intersections of patriarchy and militarisation', *Indian Journal of Gender Studies*, 11(1): 27–42.

Chowdry, G. and Nair, S. (2003) 'Power in a postcolonial world: race, gender, and class in international relations', in G. Chowdry and S. Nair (eds) *Power, Postcolonialism and International Relations: Reading Race, Gender and Class*, New York: Routledge, pp 1–32.

Cockburn, C. (2004) 'The continuum of violence: a gender perspective on war and peace', in W. Giles and J. Hyndman (eds) *Sites of Violence: Gender and Conflict Zones*, Berkeley, CA: University of California Press, pp 24–44.

Cohn, C. (1987) 'Sex and death in the rational world of defense intellectuals', *Signs*, 12(4): 687–718.

Cohn, C. (2018) 'The perils of mixing masculinity and missiles', *The New York Times*, 5 January, Available from: www.nytimes.com/2018/01/05/opinion/security-masculinity-nuclear-weapons.html.

Control Arms (2018) *How to Use the Arms Trade Treaty to Address Gender-Based Violence*, New York: Control Arms.

Dirik, D. (2017) 'Feminist pacifism or passive-ism?', *Open Democracy*, 7 March, Available from: www.opendemocracy.net/5050/dilar-dirik/feminist-pacifism-or-passive-ism.

Dunbar–Ortiz, R. (2018) *Loaded: A Disarming History of the Second Amendment*, San Francisco, CA: City Light Books.

Enloe, C. (2014) *Bananas, Beaches and Bases: Making Feminist Sense of International Politics*, 2nd edition, Berkeley, CA: University of California Press.

Farr, V., Myrttinen, H. and Schnabel, A. (2009) *Sexed Pistols: The Gendered Impacts of Small Arms and Light Weapons*, Tokyo: United Nations University Press.

Gowrinathan, N. (2018) 'Kimberlé Crenshaw: up in arms, a conversation about women and weapons', *Guernica*, 28 March, Available from: www.guernicamag.com/kimberle-crenshaw-up-in-arms-a-conversation-about-women-and-weapons/.

Green, C., Basu Ray, D., Mortimer, C. and Stone K. (2013) 'Gender-based violence and the Arms Trade Treaty: reflections from a campaigning and legal perspective', *Gender and Development*, 21(3): 551–562.

Grillot, S.R., Stapley, C.S. and Hanna, M.E. (2006) 'Assessing the small arms movement: the trials and tribulations of a transnational network', *Contemporary Security Policy*, 27(1): 60–84.

Hagen, J.J. (2016) 'Queering women, peace and security', *International Affairs*, 92(2): 313–332.

Joseph, C. (2013) 'Reflections from the Arms Trade Treaty Negotiations: CARICOM punching and succeeding above its weight', *Caribbean Journal of International Relations and Diplomacy*, 1(1): 93–109.

Kirby, P. and Shepherd, L.J. (2016a) 'Reintroducing women, peace and security', *International Affairs*, 92(2): 249–254.

Kirby, P. and Shepherd, L.J. (2016b) 'The futures past of the Women, Peace and Security agenda', *International Affairs*, 92(2): 373–392.

Krause, K. (2002) 'Multilateral diplomacy, norm–building, and UN Conferences: the case of small arms and light weapons', *Global Governance*, 8(2): 247–263.

Mama, A. (2012) 'Sheroes and Villains: conceptualizing colonial and contemporary violence against women in Africa', in M.J. Alexander and C.T. Mohanty (eds) *Feminist Genealogies, Colonial Violences, Democratic Futures*, New York: Routledge, pp 46–62.

Mama, A. and Okazawa-Rey, M. (2012) 'Militarism, conflict and women's activism in the global era', *Feminist Review*, 101(1): 97–123

McClintock, A. (1995) *Imperial Leather: Race, Gender and Sexuality in the Colonial Contest*, New York: Routledge.

Mutimer, D. (2006) ' "A serious threat to peace, reconciliation, safety, security": an effective reading of the United Nations Programme of Action', *Contemporary Security Policy*, 27(1): 29–44.

Segal, L. (2008) 'Gender, war and militarism: making and questioning the links', *Feminist Review*, 88(1): 21–35.

Shepherd, L. J. (2016) 'Making war safe for women? National Action Plans and the militarisation of the Women, Peace and Security agenda', *International Political Science Review*, 37(3): 324–335.

Sjoberg, L. and Via, S. (2010) 'Conclusion: the interrelationship between gender, war, and militarism', in L. Sjoberg and S. Via (eds) *Gender, War and Militarism: Feminist perspectives*, Santa Barbara: Praeger, pp 231–234.

Small Arms Survey (2014a) 'Converging agendas: women, peace, security and small arms', *Small Arms Survey 2014*, Geneva: Small Arms Survey, pp 34–63.

Small Arms Survey (2014b) 'In war and peace: violence against women and girls', *Small Arms Survey 2014*, Geneva: Small Arms Survey, pp 8–33.

Stavrianakis, A. (2019) 'Controlling weapons circulation in a post-colonial, militarised world', *Review of International Studies*, 45(1): 57–76

Tickner, J.A. and True, J. (2018) 'A century of international relations feminism: from World War I women's peace pragmatism to the Women, Peace and Security Agenda', *International Studies Quarterly*, 62(2): 221–233.

UN General Assembly (2018) 'General and complete disarmament: the Arms Trade Treaty', 29 October, A/C.1/73/L.8/Rev.1. 2018, Available from: http://reachingcriticalwill.org/images/documents/Disarmament-fora/1com/1com18/resolutions/L8Rev1.pdf.

UNODA (UN Office for Disarmament Affairs) (2018) 'Securing our common future: an agenda for disarmament', UNODA: New York, Available from: www.un.org/disarmament/sg-agenda/en/.

White, A.M. (2007) 'All the men are fighting for freedom, all the women are mourning their men, but some of us carried guns: a raced-gendered analysis of Fanon's psychological perspectives of war', *Signs*, 32(4): 857–884.

WILPF (Women's International League for Peace and Freedom) (2014) 'Disarmament programme', Available from: https://wilpf. org/what-we-do/disarmament/.

WILPF (Women's International League for Peace and Freedom) (2016) *Preventing Gender-Based Violence through Arms Control*, Geneva/ New York: WILPF.

Wright, S. (2009) 'Feminist theory and arms control', in L. Sjoberg (ed) *Gender and International Security: Feminist Perspectives*, Abingdon: Routledge, pp 191–213.

11

The Privatization of War: A New Challenge for the Women, Peace and Security Agenda

Marta Bautista Forcada and Cristina Hernández Lázaro

Between 1995 and 2002, the demand for sex services in Bosnia and Herzegovina grew to provide for 'the influx of peacekeepers and contractors affiliated with the UN Mission in Bosnia-Herzegovina (UNMIBH)' (Sperling, 2015, p 170). Roughly a quarter of the women and girls working to supply that demand were forcibly brought from outside their local area, and thus trafficked; in 2002 it was believed that over 200 bars and nightclubs in Bosnia were engaged in human trafficking activities (Sperling, 2015, p 170). Contractors from the US company DynCorp Aerospace Technology UK Ltd were accused of frequenting the brothels where women were imprisoned and sexually enslaved (Schulz and Yeung, 2008, p 5). Although a former DynCorp employee acted as a whistleblower and revealed the abuses, the accused contractors enjoyed immunity as they served a UN mission; they were sent back to their countries of origin, where they were not prosecuted (Sperling, 2015, p 171).

The Women, Peace and Security (WPS) agenda does not include any provisions related to the escalating threat that private contractors hired to provide military and security services in conflict settings pose to international peace and security and human rights. The WPS agenda has focused on states, multilateral institutions, women's organizations and national and non-state militaries, but not on private military contractors. In the context of the changing nature of conflict, these private companies have taken on important roles and must be brought into focus within the WPS agenda, and by the WPS community.

Private military and security companies (PMSCs) have rapidly increased in size and rate of deployment since the 1991 Gulf War, notably during the Afghanistan and Iraq wars of 2001 and 2003 respectively. This growth of PMSCs in the last two decades has not been accompanied by an effective legal regulatory framework. The legal regulation of these companies remains insufficient and has been implemented in a slow and fragmented manner. This has made it very challenging to hold private contractors accountable for the gendered human rights violations they might commit, including the use of sex services of trafficked women, rape, the torture of prisoners with a gendered character, or the complicity or involvement in sex trafficking of both adults and children. Hence, growth in the PMSC sector goes hand in hand with a widening accountability gap.

This chapter argues that UN institutions, scholars, advocates and practitioners should incorporate the privatization of war as a new challenge within the WPS agenda. With this chapter, we intend to plant a seed. It is organized as follows: first, we briefly introduce the phenomenon of PMSCs and its origins, specifically exploring the impact of private military contractors on people in conflict zones or unstable contexts. We then focus on the legal regulatory frameworks created to regulate PMSCs and/or their activities, arguing that their growth has not been accompanied by sufficient binding legal mechanisms that can hold them accountable for their crimes, including gendered human rights abuses and crimes. The final section depicts the involvement of PMSCs in conflicts around the world as a new issue that the WPS agenda should embrace. The chapter ends by touching upon different ways in which the privatization of war can be addressed while acknowledging the existing limitations.

The appearance and growth of PMSCs: a contextualization

At the beginning of the 1990s, the externalization of military and security companies, and thus the privatization of war, shifted from being the exception to the rule (Daza, 2017, p 32). PMSCs emerged due to an increase in both demand for and supply of private contractors, and a shift in the economic paradigm to neoliberalism (Singer, 2001/02, p 193). The supposedly peaceful 'New World Order' of the post-Cold War world saw an increase in demand for people to fight in a wide range of conflicts, from sub-state civil wars to regional conflagrations, across Africa, the Middle East, Southeast Europe and the Asia–Pacific. At the same time, there was a surplus of trained military personnel, with many armies shrinking, as countries looked to cash in on their 'peace dividend' following the collapse of the Soviet Union (Andreopoulos and Brandle, 2012, p 144). In this new context, several interdependent factors combined: a shift in the nature of conflicts and military technology; an increase of armed forces' expeditionary operations; and a loss of military knowledge after military experts' layoffs (Perlo–Freeman and Sköns, 2008, p 1). Furthermore, the emergence and growth of private military and security actors was due to the contracting out and privatization of services that governments had been providing, as part of general neoliberal economic policies aimed at shrinking state expenditure (Palou and Armendáriz, 2011, p 23). The market-based policies affected every sector of the government, including the military. Through externalization, governments wanted to reduce the costs of the military, improve the quality of the services, have access to new knowledge, expertise and skills, and risk management (Perlo–Freeman and Sköns, 2008, p 4); the services offered by PMSCs range from fighting, to training, intelligence support, logistics and planning, among others. Currently, the estimated global worth of PMSCs is US \$200 billion (Transparency International, 2016).

The growing presence of these actors in the international arena is in part due to the incentives that they offer to the states that hire them. First, PMSCs sometimes represent a chance for militaries to 'buy in' advanced capabilities that they may be lacking. PMSCs allow them to buy these skills on an as-needed basis, rather than undertaking lengthy development and training processes. Second, just as PMSCs can be hired quickly, they can likewise be let go rapidly after their services are no longer required, meaning that regime leaders do not have to worry about domestic soldiers with combat experience and specialist knowledge lingering in barracks, potentially posing the risk of a coup d'état. Third, PMSCs position under international law is ambiguous because, although there are some soft law instruments aiming at regulating their actions, there are no hard laws that explicitly refer to the firms (Crowe and John, 2017, p 18). Consequently, states are not incentivized to create accountability mechanisms, which results in impunity for international law violations. Moreover, through the use of PMSCs, states do not need as much public support in order to engage in war as they do when they deploy national armies, as there is notably less public scrutiny regarding PMSCs' activities and impact. Lastly, states can use PMSCs in order to avoid popular opposition to war, as contractor deaths are not considered as politically resonant as soldiers' deaths (Gaston, 2008, p 235). In these senses, PMSCs represent 'good value for money' when there is fighting to be done.

The impact of PMSC's human rights violations: the case of gender-based violence

As the privatization of war is a 'gendered phenomenon' (Stachowitsch, 2015, p 364) that is rapidly growing, more and more scholars are paying attention to it. Scholars often examine this phenomenon using 'masculinities' as the analytical framework, often even 'militarised masculinities', which involves 'toughness, violence, aggression, courage, control, and domination' (Eichler, 2014, p 82) as well as gendered power relations in a male-dominated industry (Higate, 2007, p 101). As military masculinity is produced at and shaped through various institutions in and outside the military, scholars have recognized the existence of various militarized masculinities (Eichler, 2014, p 84). In fact, in recognizing these nuances, Paul Higate (2007, p 7) suggests the concept of 'privatised military masculinities', thus acknowledging the potential differences between the public and private sphere in which armed forces and PMSCs are respectively 'shaping preparations for and the carrying out of instrumental violence'.

As highly gendered institutions, PMSCs create gender hierarchies in which both women and some men are subordinated (Higate, 2007, p 11). Scholars have contended that the subordination of some men has a neocolonial nature, when it is 'third-world men' working as PMSCs personnel in supportive roles (Higate, 2007, p 11) with less pay and worse work conditions than western contractors (Eichler, 2014, p 86). For instance, in Iraq, there are many Fijian personnel employed by western PMSCs. A British firm paid its Fiji employees almost nine times less than western employees, and in some cases, they have also been slow in paying them (Higate, 2007, p 11). Thus, while invigorating subordinate masculinities, PMSCs reinforce hegemonic masculinities (WILPF, 2019, p 8).

PMSCs, as armed forces, are male-dominated institutions that privilege values associated with masculinity while marginalizing and excluding those associated with femininity, or incorporating them 'in highly specific ways' (Eichler, 2015a, pp 7–8). As Cockburn puts it, 'the military takes this "rough cast" of masculinity and gives it a shape that fulfills its own purpose' (2013, p 439). On top of that, many private contractors are former military forces personnel (Schulz and Yeung, 2008, p 9), thus coming from traditionally male-dominated institutions that reinforce masculinity values. This brings PMSCs to 'claim that their employees are the world's best security experts recruited from the elite units of Western militaries' (Joachim and Schneiker, 2015, p 119). According to Joachim and Schneiker (2012, p 501), PMSCs have reconstructed the concept of masculinity when they sell 'highly trained professionals' who are also 'ethical hero warriors', thus creating a dual image for PMSCs' personnel.

Research shows that wherever military forces are deployed, levels of prostitution and sex trafficking increase (Schulz and Yeung, 2008, p 5). Examples of US military bases with commercial sex zones include Baumholder in Germany, Fort Bragg in North Carolina and Songtan in South Korea (Vine, 2015b). In South Korea, for instance, prostitution in US military bases flourished after the end of the Second World War, despite efforts of both Korean and US governments to end the practice (Vine, 2015a). In 2007, a study found that 'the U.S. military bases in South Korea were found to form a hub for the transnational trafficking of women from the Asia Pacific and Eurasia to South Korea and the United States' (Hughes et al, 2007). As Cynthia Enloe argues, there is a purposeful relationship between military bases and sexual violence which is assumed to be 'natural' (2014, p 157). Over time, decisions by mostly male military and government officials have institutionalized sex around military bases, creating a male-dominated military environment in which women have been essentially reduced to the role of sex (Vine, 2015a, pp 182–183) and increasing the demand for prostitution, which often leads to the traffic of vulnerable women and children into the sex industry (Human Rights Advocates, 2006, pp 3–4).

Specific to PMSCs and 'private militarised masculinities', the lack of regulation of PMSCs interacts specifically with gendered abuse or violence. This has been pointed out by Maya Eichler (2015b, p 164), who observes that 'existing regulatory regimes covering PMSCs have serious limitations in regards to gender-based violence and discrimination, and [that] the privatization of war allows for a de-politicization of gender equality issues'.

The 'secretive nature' of these companies that shield themselves with proprietary information protections makes the collection of data of their activities and their consequences a challenging task (Singer, 2001/02, p 203; Andreopoulos and Brandle, 2012, p 149). To make things more complicated in terms of collecting data around crimes committed by contractors, the sensitivity of human trafficking, rape or sexual abuse leads to the fact that it is often underreported due to social and structural barriers (UNSC, 2014, p 2).

Despite the challenges mentioned earlier, and although limited, cases of gender-based abuses perpetrated by PMSCs in conflict-affected countries have been documented in Djibouti, Somalia, Iraq, Afghanistan, and, as illustrated at the beginning of this chapter, in Bosnia, where PMSCs personnel were accused of being complicit or involved in cases of human trafficking, and participating in prostitution resulting from coercion or sexual slavery. These examples show different types of gendered human rights violations that some PMSCs personnel have perpetrated. In Djibouti, investigative journalist Sanne Terlingen uncovered the use of prostitution with trafficked undocumented migrants, including children, by US PMSCs' personnel; she states that the existing demand levels for sex services were allowed to flourish (2015). As she spent a night at some nightclubs with some US contractors, she witnessed PMSCs and armed forces personnel taking 'sex workers' from the nightclub for their services; a contractor even asked how much it would cost to buy Terlingen's services (Terlingen, 2015). Terlingen quotes a report by Humanium, an international NGO focused on children's rights, which states that in 2009 alone, 2,430 prostitutes were arrested, about 17% of whom were minors aged between 10 and 17 years old. While 'purchasing sex or engaging in behavior that could facilitate human trafficking is forbidden for US military personnel and contractors', the levels of impunity in Djibouti are high (Acheson, 2017, p 31). In Somalia, survivors of sexual violence (mostly of rape crimes) identified armed actors including private actors as their perpetrators (UN Security Council, 2014, p 13). In Iraq, local prisoners at various detention centres including Abu Ghraib were submitted to torture practices by US PSMSCs (Center for Constitutional Rights, 2017). Male and female prisoners were subjected to various forms of torture, including gender-based violence such as rape, sexual assault, being forced to strip and stay naked, 'sensory deprivation, mock executions, stress positions, broken bones', or, as one victim reported, being 'forced to witness the rape of a female prisoner' (Center for Constitutional Rights, 2017). In Afghanistan, reports uncovered the emergence of brothels triggered by the deployment of private contractors in the country and showed that these contractors had been involved in sex trafficking (Schulz and Yeung, 2008, p 5; US District Court for the District of Columbia, 2009, p 3). An investigation in 2007 by the US State Department found that the ArmorGroup North America (AGNA), which was hired to provide security services at the US Embassy in Kabul, Afghanistan (US Senate Homeland Security and Governmental Affairs Committee, 2009, p i), had committed illegalities which included frequent visits by AGNA's project manager and employees to brothels in Kabul well-known for housing trafficked women, including young girls (US District Court for the District of Columbia, 2009, p 29).

PMSCs and the existing legal regulatory frameworks

When PMSCs exponentially grew in the late 1990s and early 2000s, the existing legal frameworks were not prepared to regulate their activities or hold them accountable for their crimes. As of today, there is still no specific legal obligation under international law that regulates the activity of PMSCs (Barrios and Hernández, 2018). Nonetheless, over the last two decades, there have been some 'catch up' initiatives to regulate these companies and their activities at the international and national levels. From a gender perspective, scholars (see, for example, Vrdoljak, 2009; Schulz and Yeung, 2008; Perrin, 2012) and international organizations such as the Women's International League for Peace and Freedom (WILPF) (2013), have pointed out both the lack of accountability of PMSCs and the gendered impacts. They have also highlighted the lack of harmonized and binding PMSCs' regulatory mechanisms and their limitations regarding gender-based violence and discrimination, adding that 'security privatization allows for a de-politicization of gender equality issues' (Eichler, 2015b, p 164). Furthermore, the WPS agenda, which aims at mainstreaming the gender perspective in peacekeeping and post-conflict reconstruction operations, does not mention the private sector specifically. This section presents and discusses these recent developments, highlighting the existing gaps regarding PMSCs' regulation and accountability, both at the international and national levels.

Due to these existing gaps – and due to the fact that the WPS agenda does not provide specific mechanisms directed at monitoring and regulating this sector – PMSCs remain unaccountable for the gender-based crimes perpetrated by their personnel; bringing attention to this phenomenon should therefore constitute an urgent and relevant task for the WPS. However, as explained by Vrdoljak (2015, p 188), 'PMSCs do not operate in a legal lacuna'. Existing regulatory frameworks such as international humanitarian law (IHL) can be applied to regulate PMSCs' activities in certain situations. Moreover, self-regulation instruments have also been put forward, as well as efforts to adopt an international legally binding instrument.

PMSC employees are obliged to comply with IHL when operating in armed conflict scenarios, and they can be criminally prosecuted by any state or by the International Criminal Court (ICC) if they are considered to be taking direct part in hostilities. According to IHL,

PMSC contractors are considered civilians, not combatants, as long as they are not part of a state army (Schulz and Yeung, 2008, p 11). Nonetheless, they can still be prosecuted for committing war crimes or crimes against humanity, such as rape and other forms of sexual violence (Vrdjolak, 2009, p 9). In addition, PMSC personnel must respect the principle of proportionality as well as other humanitarian rules concerning the use of certain means of warfare. The prosecution of these crimes often requires the involvement of a state in order to ensure crime accountability by searching for and prosecuting PMSC personnel, regardless of their nationality. In most cases, however, states within which PMSCs operate lack either political will or capacity to protect their population from these companies, especially in failed states. It is difficult to ask PMSCs for responsibility when operating in a third country, and few national legal systems contemplate this possibility, such as in the case of the USA and the UK (Schulz and Yeung, 2008, p 12).

There have also been international self-regulation initiatives for PMSCs. In 2008, with the support of the International Committee of the Red Cross (ICRC) and the Swiss government, the Montreux document was created with 18 signatory states including Afghanistan, France, China, Canada, Germany, Iraq, the UK and the USA. Though not legally binding, this document represents the first international instrument that aims to guide and assist states in the application of IHL and international human rights law (IHRL) when PMSCs operate in conflict. The document stipulates that states should consider the record of sexual offences committed by PMSCs and its employees when hiring military and security contractors. In 2010, Switzerland launched another self-regulation initiative, the International Code of Conduct for Private Security Service Providers (ICoC), a non-state mechanism that sets out principles of conduct for PMSCs based on existing IHL and IHRL principles. Paragraph 38 of ICoC addresses the prohibition of sexual or gender-based violence, and paragraph 39 addresses the prohibition of human trafficking and specifically the trafficking for sexual purposes. Both documents aim to promote the respect of IHL and IHRL by PMSCs. However, given that they are non-binding, the capacity of both the Montreux Document and the ICoC to render accountability is limited.

Acknowledging the limitations of the existing regulatory measures, efforts have been made by the international community to address the problem of PMSCs' lack of accountability and regulation. In 2005, the UN Commission on Human Rights established a Working Group, which aimed to ensure accountability for human rights violations committed by PMSCs in any context, including in conflict settings. One of the tasks mandated to the Working Group was to prepare proposals for standards, guidelines and principles to achieve further human rights protection. In July 2009, the Working Group presented the Draft International Convention on the Regulation, Oversight, and Monitoring of Private Military and Security Companies. This draft did not have the goal to prohibit PMSCs, but 'to establish minimum international standards for State parties to regulate the activities of the companies and their personnel and to set up an international oversight mechanism' (United Nations General Assembly, 2010, para. 39). This proposed convention would apply to both conflict and non-conflict situations; that is, to any situation where PMSCs are deployed, as well as to states and intergovernmental organizations in their relations with PMSCs (Palou-Loverdos and Amendáriz, 2011, p 71). This draft has not yet been approved, however, which shows the difficulty the international community is experiencing in deciding how to regulate (and to cooperate to regulate) PMSCs.

In April 2019, the Working Group organized an expert consultation to address the human rights impacts of PMSCs through a gender lens, and in July 2019, it published a report with the outcomes of the meeting. The Working Group concluded that there are enough reasons for all stakeholders 'to push forward a gender-transformative agenda within the industry', in a report that identifies 'gaps in awareness and understanding about the gender dimensions and gendered human rights impacts of those companies' (United Nations General Assembly, 2019, pp 2–3). This report is intended to be the first step for a longer conversation about the gendered impacts of PMSCs.

Additionally, the UN has also created the Guiding Principles on Business and Human Rights (United Nations Human Rights Office of the High Commissioner, 2011) and the Guidelines on the Use by the United Nations of Armed Security Services from Private Security Companies (UN Security Management System, 2012). The former underlines the states' obligations to 'respect, protect and fulfill human rights and fundamental freedoms' and requests businesses to 'comply with all applicable laws and respect human rights', while the latter (United Nations Human Rights Office of the High Commissioner, 2011, p 6) states that the contractor's proposal should include evidence on the personnel having successfully completed training on, among other fields, sexual abuse and exploitation, as well as evidence that they have not been involved in criminal offences or human rights violations (United Nations Department of Safety and Security, 2012, pp 3–4).

At the national level, governments have developed laws, policies, standards, guidelines and other measures to regulate private military companies and their activities, especially in those countries that are major exporters of private military and security services such as the United States or the United Kingdom (Schulz and Yeung, 2008, p 12). These national laws are not harmonized among different countries, and they should enforce IHL and IHRL norms until an international legally binding instrument that regulates PMSCs is adopted. Domestic laws among countries differ in that some countries put more emphasis on regulating the activity of PMSCs within their own borders, according to the principle of 'territoriality' (Quirico, 2009, p 8). These countries are rather permissive with the activities of PMSCs outside their territory, or do not regulate their services abroad at all (Quirico, 2009, p 8). In these cases, in order to regulate PMSCs' activities abroad, additional mechanisms can be established through contractual clauses. Others are more concerned with the regulation of PMSCs' activities abroad under the principle of 'nationality' (Quirico, 2009, p 8). There are situations in which none of the principles apply, leading to 'serious protection gaps' (Schulz and Yeung, 2008, p 12), given that there are states that have no capacity to control the actions of PMSCs in their own territory (for instance, failing or failed states). In these cases, the lack of enforcement in the home country of these companies can lead to the lack of protection of the citizens where PMSCs are being deployed, as is the case where many PMSCs operate (Schulz and Yeung, 2008). Therefore, as Singer (2004, p 535) assesses, 'the real risk of gross misbehavior by [PMSCs] is not during their operations in sound states like the U.S., but rather the contracts they have in weak or failing states'. In sum, 'the imposition of obligations on private persons or entities by human rights law remains exceptional and PMSCs may only be directly bound by human rights through national law' (Palou-Loverdos and Armendáriz, 2011, p 67).

PMSCs are mostly not regulated by binding laws and obligations. Prosecuting gender-based abuses perpetrated by PMSCs largely depends on whether the state where these crimes are committed has the will and resources to pursue such a process. Moreover, in the case of violations of IHL, 'to prosecute employees of PMSCs for international crimes, the substantive definition of these crimes includes onerous elements that are likely to be met only in the most egregious cases of gross misconduct' (Perrin, 2012, p 217).

The privatization of war as a new challenge for the Women, Peace and Security agenda

Nineteen years after the adoption of UNSCR 1325, there has there been slow and unsatisfactory progress on key elements of the WPS agenda including women's participation in peace agreements and the number of women in peacekeeping operations (Kirby and Shepherd, 2016, p 374). Further, new security and gendered challenges have arisen during this time. Among these new issues, the privatization of security and warfare is a critical matter that requires attention. Not one of the resolutions that make up the WPS agenda mentions private contractors, thus rendering them as non-state actors whose role and actions are not specifically monitored and reported by the provisions of the agenda. Because of its gendered impact – particularly in relation to women's security – WPS scholars, advocates and activists should address the privatization of war as a new challenge that represents a crucial aspect of women's security in conflict and thus use the agenda to address it.

The concerns presented in this chapter are only the tip of the iceberg. As already discussed, there are reasons to believe that there are many cases of gendered violence crimes that have not come to light, leaving the perpetrators with de facto impunity and the victims with no justice. The severe gendered impact that the privatization of war has on people's security in conflict and unstable contexts, the lack of transparency in how PMSCs operate, the lack of harmonization in their regulation, and the consequent lack of accountability for the crimes that they commit, make the privatization of warfare an issue that the WPS agenda urgently needs to take forward.

Nine UN Security Council resolutions have followed the passage of UNSCR 1325, constituting the WPS agenda and assigning responsibility to several actors: the UN Secretary-General, the UN member states, the parties to conflict, and the UN Security Council. Here, we seek to understand how the agenda can tackle the phenomenon of the privatization of warfare and security. With regard to the action that can be taken in order to protect women's, men's, boys' and girls' rights, the main areas of concern to which the resolutions refer are reports and indicators; guidelines and training; and accountability and respect for IHL.

The three UN Secretary-Generals at the helm since the passage of UNSCR 1325 have maintained (in theory) a policy of 'zero tolerance of sexual exploitation and abuse' (UNSCR 1820, para. 7; UNSCR 2106, para. 15), and a substantial institutional apparatus now exists to ensure monitoring and reporting to raise alerts of any case of miscon-duct and the non-implementation of commitments by parties in con-flict (UNSCR 1888, para. 26; UNSCR 1960, para.6; UNSCR 1960, para. 8; UNSCR 2242 para. 10). WPS resolutions also request member states 'to put an end to impunity and to prosecute those responsible for genocide, crimes against humanity, and war crimes including those relating to sexual and other violence against women and girls' (UNSCR 1325, para. 11). In sum, member states are called upon to ensure accountability and to comply with their obligations for prosecuting those responsible for gender-based crimes (UNSCR 1325, para. 11; UNSCR 1820, para. 4; UNSCR 1888, para. 6; UNSCR 2106, para. 2; UNSCR 2106 para. 15; UNSCR 2122 para. 12; UNSCR 2242 para. 14). The resolutions call for all parties in conflict to cease sexual violence (UNSCR 1820, para. 2; UNSCR 1889 para. 3; UNSCR 2106 para. 10), to take measures in order to protect women and girls from sexual violence (UNSCR 1325 para. 10; UNSCR 1820 para. 3; 1888 para. 3), and 'to respect fully international law applicable to the rights and protection of women and girls' (UNSCR 1325 para. 9; 1889 para. 1). Lastly, the UN Security Council expresses its willingness to, 'where necessary, adopt appropriate steps to address widespread or systematic sexual violence' (UNSCR 1820; para. 1).

The mechanisms provided by the WPS agenda can be divided into those referring to guidelines and training, accountability and respect for IHL, and reports and indicators. All of them do provide useful tools that, if applied to PMSCs, could contribute to addressing the existing regulatory gap in which these companies operate. With regards to the reports and indicators mechanisms, given the lack of transparency of the sector, a special focus should be put on PMSCs, if willing, to obtain data about their activities. As for the guidelines and training mechanisms, which are mainly directed at member states, the lack of recognition of the existence of other parties, and particularly of PMSCs, leaves a vacuum in terms of whether these companies are expected to participate in the stated trainings and receive the stated guidelines. Lastly, as for the mechanisms directed at ensuring compliance with IHL, they do not make reference to actors other than member states. Thus, given that not mentioning PMSCs in the WPS agenda as participants of conflict leaves the existing regulatory gap unresolved, it is necessary that the agenda does put a focus on private actors and particularly on PMSCs.

Given the availability of only a few cases of gender-based crimes committed by private contractors, strong efforts should be made to collect further data and cases by scholars. Feminist scholars are well placed to work closely with grassroots organizations to document cases of gender-based crimes, as well as to conduct in–depth research on the impact of private contractors on women's security. Substantive data is needed to help advocate for gender-sensitive reporting mechanisms for crimes committed by private personnel as well as gender-sensitive regulatory mechanisms to report these crimes. Research should also be expanded to explore the participation of private contractors in human rights violations in different contexts where they are working, including fragile contexts.

Monitoring and reporting mechanisms should be developed to facilitate the reporting of gendered crimes associated with PMSCs personnel (GAAV, 2015, p 23). Only through the implementation of monitoring and reporting mechanisms that specifically focus on PMSCs can accountability be ensured in cases of misconduct. International organizations such as the Office for the Coordination of Humanitarian Affairs (OCHA) should incorporate these mechanisms through regular contacts with research centres such as Shock Monitor and local organizations. OCHA reports should differentiate between impacts on human rights committed by public and security forces. As a result, the effective implementation of these mechanisms would also increase the availability of data.

Furthermore, WPS scholars and advocates should argue for reinforcing the regulation of PMSCs, by fortifying existing instruments from IHL and IHRL conventions as well as developing new international instruments and national legislation to regulate PMSCs, all the while including a gender perspective. As for the existence of international instruments to regulate PMSCs, as mentioned earlier, the possibility of a Convention on Private Military and Security Companies had been suggested as an international legally binding instrument to regulate PMSCs; this discussion should be re-visited.

Finally, advocates should lobby for other gender-specific preventive measures to be applied before private personnel are deployed (for those companies who don't do it already), including the provision of gender-sensitive training sessions, and for the prohibition of deployment of all private personnel with criminal records that include gender-based violence such as human trafficking, sexual abuse and rape. In this regard, states should be responsible for providing licensing activities of PMSCs. Without proper registration and licence, PMSCs are not able to operate. During this licensing process, the relevant state should define specific criteria and requirements to be met by the company and its personnel, such as no criminal record, specific gender-sensitive training, psychological checks of their personnel, due diligence mechanisms.

To acknowledge and address the privatization of war on the WPS agenda, there are various actions that need to be taken by the UN and its member states. First, the Report of the Secretary-General on Conflict-Related Sexual Violence mandated to the Special Representative on Sexual Violence in Conflict should be used as a tool to document cases of sexual violence committed by contractors where they occur. To a limited extent, it has done so; in 2013 and 2014 it reported that survivors of sexual violence had identified private security actors, among others, as perpetrators (UN Security Council, 2013; 2014). Furthermore, member states should ensure that National Action Plans (NAPs) on the implementation of the WPS agenda include provisions referring to private contractors. There are only a few examples of NAPs that refer to PMSCs: Switzerland's NAP 2013–2016 recognizes that PMSCs can be perpetrators of gender-based violence, as well as sexual exploitation, abuse and human trafficking, and upholds the ICoC as a means to protect the rights of women and girls, and prevent gender-based violence (Federal Department of Foreign Affairs, 2013, p 15). While this NAP can be taken as an example, provisions should include the creation of an ethical code, the creation of a gender-sensitive training session before departure, and the creation of reporting and monitoring mechanisms for the country where these contractors are sent. These measures should apply to home states of PMSCs, territorial states and client states (ICRC, 2008, p 9).

Efforts should focus on integrating this new mode of warcraft as a WPS agenda issue in order to increase PMSCs accountability for their human rights abuses, and in particular for gender-based crimes. While there is no need to adopt more resolutions within the WPS agenda to incorporate a focus on privatized war, greater effort should be expended in order to improve the current situation and increase the accountability of PMSCs at a local and international level, in particular for the violation of the physical integrity of civilian victims of gender-based violence. In recent history, there have been outstanding advances under IHL and IHRL to prosecute rape and sexual abuse, categorizing offences for the first time in history as crimes of war and crimes against humanity. International law should keep up with the reshaping of the world order and the resulting emergence of new, third party actors in sectors such as military and security provision, extending the framework of UNSCR 1325 to include specific clauses addressing PMSCs and their personnel; this would be an exceptional first step.

Conclusion

PMSCs have grown rapidly since the end of the Cold War, when states increased the externalization of services, including those concerning military and security issues. The growth of these companies was not accompanied by the development of adequate regulations, which has led to high levels of impunity in many of the cases of human rights violations registered by the UN and grassroots organizations. At present, there is an insufficient regulatory framework for holding PMSCs and contractors accountable for the crimes they might commit.

The growing presence of PMSCs in conflict scenarios around the globe is an issue that concerns the WPS agenda. The gendered nature of some of the crimes committed by private military contractors increases the vulnerability of civilians in scenarios where PMSCs operate such as in Bosnia or in Afghanistan, as illustrated earlier. As the nature of armed conflicts changes and the externalization of military and security services becomes the rule among governments and other entities such as the UN or humanitarian organizations, the WPS agenda must make efforts to specifically address this issue within the mechanisms that the Security Council has put forward, which do not address the issue of PMSCs. Hence, it is necessary to ensure that the privatization of war gains more attention and that the next steps taken by the international community, as well as states, are gender-sensitive. Practitioners, scholars, local activists and decision makers should take action in their own capacity with the goal to embrace all the concerns posed in this chapter, and work to address them through research and advocacy for prevention and accountability purposes.

References

Acheson, R. (2017) 'Remote warfare and sexual violence in Djibouti', *Reaching Critical Will of the Women's International League for Peace and Freedom*, Available from: https://wilpf.org/wp-content/uploads/2017/09/2017_RemoteWarfareAndSexualViolenceInDjibouti.pdf.

Andreopoulos, G. and Brandle, S. (2012) 'Revisiting the role of private military and security companies', *Criminal Justice Ethics*, 31(3): 138–157.

Barrios Trullols, L. and Hernández Lázaro, C. (2018) 'The neglected victims: PMSC, sexual abuse and physical violence against girls and women', *Shock Monitor*, Available from: http://shockmonitor.org/neglected-victims-pmsc-sexual-abuse-physical-violence-girls-women/.

Center for Constitutional Rights (2017) 'Accountability for torture by private military contractors', 22 September, Available from: https://ccrjustice.org/home/get-involved/tools-resources/fact-sheets-and-faqs/accountability-torture-private-military.

Cockburn, C. (2013) 'War and security, women and gender: an overview of the issues', *Gender & Development*, 21(3): 433–452.

Crowe, J. and John, A. (2017) 'The status of private military security companies in United Nations Peacekeeping Operations under the international law of armed conflict', *Melbourne Journal of International Law*, 18: 16–44.

Daza, F. (2017) 'Delimitation and presence of PMSCs: impact on human rights', in H. Torroja, H. (ed) *Public International Law and Human Rights Violations by Private Military and Security Companies*, New York: Springer, pp 31–57.

Eicher, M. (2014) 'Militarized masculinities in international relations', *Brown Journal of World Affairs*, 21(1).

Eichler, M. (2015a) 'Gender and the privatization of military security', in M. Eichler (ed) *Gender and Private Security in Global Politics*, Oxford: Oxford University Press, pp 1–16.

Eichler, M. (2015b) 'Private security and gender', in R. Abrahamsen and A. Leander (eds) *Routledge Handbook of Private Security Studies*, London and New York: Routledge, pp 158–167.

Enloe, C. (2014) *Bananas, Beaches and Bases. Making Feminist Sense of International Politics*, 2nd edition, Berkeley, CA: University of California Press.

Federal Department of Foreign Affairs (2013) 'Women, Peace and Security: National Action Plan to implement UN Security Council Resolution 1325 (2000)', Available from: www.peacewomen.org/sites/default/files/Revised%20NAP%20(2013–2016)%20Switzerland.pdf.

GAAV (Global Alliance on Armed Violence) (2015) 'Implementing the Women, Peace & Security agenda & reducing armed conflict', Global Alliance on Armed Violence & Armed Violence Working Group, submission for the 2015 High Level Review of the Women Peace and Security (WPS) agenda, April, Available from: www.allianceonarmedviolence.org/uploads/default/files534d7edd5834e025b1c9a76244979f53.pdf.

Gaston, E.L. (2008) 'Mercenarism 2.0? The rise of the modern private security industry and its implications for international humanitarian law enforcement', *Harvard International Law Journal*, 49(1): 221–248.

Higate, P. (2007) 'Peacekeepers, masculinities, and sexual exploitation', *Men and Masculinities*, 10(1): 99–119.

Hughes, D.M., Chon, K.Y. and Ellerman, D.P. (2007) 'Modern-day comfort women: The U.S. military, transnational crime, and the trafficking of women', *Violence Against Women*, 13(9): 901–922.

Human Rights Advocates (2006) 'Integration of the human rights of women and the gender perspective: written statement', 28 February, UN Doc E/CN4/2006/NGO/85, Available from: https://digitallibrary.un.org/record/569517.

Humanium (no date) 'Children of Djibouti: realizing children's rights in Djibouti', Available from: www.humanium.org/en/djibouti/.

ICRC (2008) 'The Montreux Document', Available from: www.icrc. org/en/doc/assets/files/other/icrc_002_0996.pdf.

Joachim, J. and Schneiker, A. (2012) 'Of 'true professionals' and 'ethical hero warriors': A gender-discourse analysis of private military and security companies', *Security Dialogue*, 43(6): 495–512.

Joachim, J.M. and Schneiker, A. (2015) 'The license to exploit: PMSCs, masculinities and third country nationals', in M. Eichler (ed) *Gender and Private Security in Global Politics*, Oxford: Oxford University Press, pp 114–130.

Kirby, P. and Shepherd, L. (2016) 'The futures past of the Women, Peace and Security agenda', *International Affairs*, 92(2): 373–392.

Palou-Loverdos, J. and Armendáriz, L. (2011) 'The privatisation of warfare, violence and private military & security companies: a factual and legal approach to human rights abuses by PMSC in Iraq', *Nova-Institute for Active Non-violence*, Available from: www.consciousbeingalliance. com/Informe_PMSC_Iraq_Nova.pdf.

Perrin, B. (2012) 'Mind the gap: lacunae in the international legal framework governing private military and security companies', *Criminal Justice Ethics*, 31(3): 213–232.

Perlo-Freeman, S. and Sköns, E. (2008) 'The private military services industry: SIPRI insights on peace and security', No. 2008/1, September, Available from: www.files.ethz.ch/isn/93157/2008_01_SIPRIInsight.pdf.

Quirico, O. (2009) 'National regulatory models for PMSCs and implications for future international regulation', EUI MWP; 2009/25.

Schulz, S. and Yeung, C. (2008) Gender and SSR Toolkit, 'Tool 10: private military and security companies and gender', Geneva Centre for the Democratic Control of Armed Forces (DCAF), Office for Democratic Institutions and Human Rights (OSCE/ODIHR), The United Nations International Research and Training Institute for the Advancement of Women (UN-INSTRAW), Available from: www. dcaf.ch/Publications/GenderSecurity-Sector-Reform-Toolkit.

Singer, P.W. (2001) 'Corporate warriors: the rise of the privatized military industry and its ramifications for international security', *International Security*, 26(3): 186–220.

Singer, P.W. (2004) 'War, profits, and the vacuum of law', *Columbia Journal of Transitional Law*, 42(2): 521–549.

Snell, A. (2011) 'The absence of justice: private military contractors, sexual assault, and the U.S. government's policy of indifference', *University of Illinois Law Review*, 2011(3): 1125–1164.

Sperling, V. (2015) 'Engendering accountability in private security and public peacekeeping', in M. Eichler (ed) *Gender and Private Security in Global Politics*, Oxford: Oxford University Press.

Stachowitsch, S. (2015) 'The reconstruction of masculinities in global politics: gendering strategies in the field of private security', *Men and Masculinities*, 18(3): 363–386.

Terlingen, S. (2015) 'Fear and loathing in Djibouti', *One World*, Available from: www.oneworld.nl/achtergrond/djibouti_trafficking/#h7.

Transparency International (2016) 'Private military and security companies: a call for better regulation', Available from: www.transparency.org/news/pressrelease/private_military_and_security_companies_a_call_for_better_regulation.

United Nations Department of Safety and Security (2012) 'United Nations Security Management System. Security Management Operations Manual', Available from: https://www.ohchr.org/Documents/Issues/Mercenaries/WG/StudyPMSC/GuidelinesAnnexAStatementOfWork.pdf.

United Nations General Assembly (2010) 'Report of the Working Group on the use of mercenaries as a means of violating human rights and impeding the exercise of the right of peoples to self-determination', A/HRC/15/25, 5 July, Available from: https://undocs.org/A/HRC/15/25.

United Nations General Assembly (2019) 'Report of the Working Group on the use of mercenaries as a means of violating human rights and impeding the exercise of the right of peoples to self-determination: the gendered human rights impact of private military and security companies', A/74/244, 29 July, Available from: https://undocs.org/A/74/244.

United Nations Security Council (2000) Resolution 1325: Women, Peace, and Security (31 October), S/RES/1325 (2000), Available from: https://undocs.org/S/RES/1325(2000).

United Nations Security Council (2008) Resolution 1820: Women, Peace, and Security (19 June), S/RES/1820 (2008), Available from: https://undocs.org/S/RES/1820(2008).

United Nations Security Council (2009) Resolution 1888: Women, Peace, and Security (30 September), S/RES/1888 (2009), Available from: https://undocs.org/S/RES/1888(2009).

United Nations Security Council (2009) Resolution 1889: Women, Peace, and Security (5 October), S/RES/1889 (2009), Available from: https://undocs.org/S/RES/1889(2009).

United Nations Security Council (2010) Resolution 1960: Women, Peace, and Security (16 December), S/RES/1960 (2010), Available from: https://undocs.org/S/RES/1960(2010).

United Nations Security Council (2013) Resolution 2122: Women, Peace, and Security (18 October), S/RES/2122 (2013), Available from: https://undocs.org/S/RES/2122(2013).

United Nations Security Council (2013) *Sexual Violence in Conflict*, Available from: www.un.org › wp-content › uploads › report › SG-Report-2013.

UN Security Council (2014) *Conflict-Related Sexual Violence: Report of the Secretary General* (S/2014/181), Available from: https://reliefweb.int/report/world/conflict-related-sexual-violence-report-secretary-general-s2014181.

United Nations Security Council (2015) Resolution 2242: Women, Peace, and Security (13 October), S/RES/2242 (2015), Available from: https://undocs.org/S/RES/2242(2015).

United Nations Human Rights Office of the High Commissioner (2011) 'Guiding principles on business and human rights', HR/PUB/11/04, New York and Geneva, 2011, Available from: www.ohchr.org/Documents/Publications/GuidingPrinciplesBusinessHR_EN.pdf.

United Nations Human Rights Special Procedures (2018) 'Mercenarism and private military and security companies', HRC/NONE/2018/40, Available from: www.ohchr.org/Documents/Issues/Mercenaries/WG/MercenarismandPrivateMilitarySecurityCompanies.pdf.

UN Security Management System (2012) 'Guidelines on the use by the United Nations of armed security services from private security companies. Annex A. Statement of Works', Available from: www.ohchr.org/Documents/Issues/Mercenaries/WG/StudyPMSC/GuidelinesAnnexAStatementOfWork.pdf.

United States District Court for the District of Columbia (2009) 'Gordon v. ArmorGroup North America. Case 1:09-cv-01717', Available from: www.kmblegal.com/wp-content/uploads/Gordon-v.-ArmorGroup-North-America.pdf.

US Senate Homeland Security and Governmental Affairs Committee (2009) 'New information about the Guard Force contract at the U.S. Embassy in Kabul', Subcommittee on Contracting Oversight, Staff Analysis, Available from: www.mccaskill.senate.gov/pdf/061009/StaffAnalysis.pdf.

Vine, D. (2015a) *Base Nation: How U.S. Military Bases Abroad Harm America and the World*, New York: Metropolitan Books.

Vine, D. (2015b) ' "My body was not mine, but the US military's": inside the disturbing sex industry thriving around America's bases', *Politico*, 3 November, Available from: www.politico.eu/article/ my-body-was-not-mine-but-the-u-s-militarys/.

Vrdoljak, A.F. (2009) 'Women's rights: the possible impact of private military and security companies', *European University Institute Working Paper* AEL 2009/22, Available from: www.researchgate.net/publication/40904753_Women's_Rights_The_Possible_Impact_of_Private_Military_and_Security_Companies.

Vrdoljak, A.F. (2010) 'Women and private military and security companies', in F. Francioni and N. Ronzitti (eds) *War by Contract: Human Rights, International Humanitarian Law and the Regulation of Private Military and Security Companies*, Oxford: Oxford University Press, pp 280–298.

Vrdoljak, A.F. (2015) 'Women, PMSCs, and international law', in M. Eichler (ed) *Gender and Private Security in Global Politics*, Oxford: Oxford University Press, pp 187–205.

WILPF (Women's International League for Peace and Freedom) (2013) 'Statement by the Women's International League for Peace and Freedom on accountability of private military and security companies', Available from: https://wilpf.org/wp-content/uploads/2013/03/Written-statement-on-PMSCs.pdf.

WILPF (Women's International League for Peace and Freedom) (2019) 'Submission by the Women's International League for Peace and Freedom (WILPF) on gender and private military and security companies (PMSCs) and gender to the working group on mercenaries', Available from: www.ohchr.org/Documents/Issues/Mercenaries/WG/Gender/WILPF_PMSCs_Gender.pdf.

12

Human Trafficking, Human Rights and Women, Peace and Security: The Sound of Silence

Gema Fernández Rodríguez de Liévana and Christine Chinkin

The Women, Peace and Security (WPS) agenda is rooted in international law – notably international humanitarian law, human rights and international criminal law. UNSCR 1325 specifically calls upon states to respect fully the obligations within these laws, including the Convention on the Elimination of All Forms of Discrimination against Women (CEDAW). Subsequent WPS resolutions emphasize the need for commitment to women's human rights and implementation of human rights law, without again referencing CEDAW until Resolution 2467 in April 2019 (UNSCR 2467, para. 18). Despite the evident association of subject matter, the first seven WPS resolutions after 1325 are surprisingly silent about trafficking in women and girls, including in armed conflict. Resolution 2467 does refer to trafficking in persons but only to ask the Security Council Counter-Terrorism Committee Executive Directorate to include in its country reports information about states' efforts to address it (UNSCR 2467, para. 29). This does not comprehensively locate trafficking within the WPS agenda.

Since 2016, however, human trafficking has been addressed by the Council in UNSCR 2331 (2016) on trafficking in armed conflict, and UNSCR 2388 (2017) on the maintenance of international peace and security. Resolution 2331 marked the first time that the Council has addressed human trafficking and identified the existence of links between such trafficking – when committed under certain circumstances – and the maintenance of international peace and security, for which it has primary responsibility under Article 24 of the UN Charter. The resolution text indicates that this link emerges from the implication of terrorist groups in the trafficking of women and girls in conflict-related areas and from the fact that trafficking serves as an instrument to increase the finances and power of these organized criminal groups.

Resolutions 2331 and 2388 highlight the relationship between conflict and post-conflict situations and trafficking. They aim at tackling the use of trafficking as a terrorist and a war economy tactic by terrorist groups. They operate at the interface of three UN 'agendas': i) CEDAW and WPS (including the work of the Special Representative of the Secretary-General on Sexual Violence in Conflict established under UNSCR 1888 in 2009); ii) the fight against trafficking in human beings, the criminalization of traffickers and the protection of victims of trafficking;[1] and iii) the Security Council's broader agenda for the maintenance of international peace and security. In addition, these agendas have become suffused with the agenda for countering violent extremism and terrorism.

In this chapter, we discuss the tension that exists between these agendas and in particular how the securitization of WPS and human trafficking by the Security Council has diluted and fragmented the discourse of women's human rights. We welcome the recognition of human trafficking as a threat to international peace and security but regret that the anti-trafficking resolutions fail to draw upon the frameworks for the protection of women's human rights, which place legal obligations on states to combat violence against women, including trafficking. We argue that, as a form of gender-based violence, human trafficking is subject to the human rights regime that has evolved to combat such violence and that the human rights mechanisms should be engaged to hold states responsible for their failure to exercise due diligence to prevent, protect against and prosecute those responsible – in the widest sense – for human trafficking. Further, the incidence of human trafficking (as a form of gender-based violence) in armed conflict means that it comes naturally under the auspices of the WPS agenda. The Security Council's silence in this regard constitutes of itself a form of violence that weakens the potential of the WPS agenda to bring structural transformation in post-conflict contexts. In agreement with the Special Rapporteur on trafficking in persons, especially women and children (SR on Trafficking) and cognisant of some of the downsides, we argue that 'in order to ensure more efficient anti-trafficking responses, a human rights-based approach ... should be mainstreamed into all pillars of the women and peace and security agenda' (UN Secretary-General, 2018). In turn, this would provide a new direction for the WPS agenda.

The securitization of trafficking in women and girls in times of conflict

Although the Security Council recognizes that trafficking in persons entails human rights abuses and sexual and gender-based violence, neither UNSCR 2331 nor UNSCR 2388 refer to CEDAW, other international human rights treaties, or the international legal regime that has evolved around combating such violence. The preamble to Resolution 2388 recognizes that 'trafficking in persons entails the violation or abuse of human rights' and that victims of trafficking must receive 'appropriate care, assistance and services for their physical, psychological and social recovery, rehabilitation and reintegration, in full respect of their human rights' (UNSCR 2388, Preamble). This formulation does not affirm victims' existing right to such services under human rights law, but only the more limited requirement that any such provision must be in full respect of their human rights. In the resolution's operative part this is further weakened by the omission of the words 'human rights': 'to adopt gender and age sensitive assistance, including adequate psychosocial support and health services, regardless of their participation in criminal investigations and proceedings' (UNSCR 2388, para. 13). The resolution thus falls short of recognizing human trafficking as violating women's human rights per se which would entail giving effect to the entire canon of human rights. The question remains as to how the trafficking resolutions can help to prevent human trafficking and to protect those vulnerable to being trafficked in the aftermath of conflict when they fail to explicitly reinforce the standards and language of human rights and women's rights.

There is currently legal fragmentation, whereby human rights guarantees, provisions relating to combating gender-based and sexual violence and regulation of human trafficking are found across a range of instruments. These comprise, among others, treaties, the jurisprudence of the CEDAW Committee and other human rights bodies and the Security Council resolutions on WPS and now its resolutions on human trafficking (Chinkin, 2018). By failing to incorporate the standards and the language of existing instruments and by omitting states' commitment to ensure 'the promotion and protection of human rights for all' and that 'effective measures to respond to trafficking in persons are complementary and mutually reinforcing' (UN Global Plan of Action, 2010) the Council's anti-trafficking resolutions contribute to the fragmentation of the legal regimes and thus further fuel the tension between them. Fragmentation is problematic in that it obscures the complexities of human trafficking by placing it within the box of each particular legal regime without looking at it as a whole. It undermines the role of international human rights law in providing an effective response to the human rights violations of trafficking. Fragmentation also facilitates addressing trafficking through the criminal law, immigration and/or security lenses to the detriment of human rights guarantees.

Further, Resolutions 2331 and 2388 seem detached from the Council's own WPS agenda. They recognize that trafficking during and post-conflict can be associated with conflict-related sexual violence, thereby implicitly bringing trafficking into the prevention of sexual violence in conflict framework – the WPS agenda. The only mention of WPS, however, is a single reference in each Resolution to the then-most recent WPS resolution, UNSCR 2242 adopted in 2015, in the context of expressing 'concern that acts of sexual and gender-based violence are known to be part of the strategic objectives and ideology of certain terrorist groups' (UNSCR 2331, Preamble; UNSCR 2388, Preamble). This omission of WPS is particularly surprising because it has been acknowledged that such groups and 'hybrid criminal-terrorist networks' use 'the bodies of women and girls as a form of currency in the political economy of war' as well as a tactic of terror, recruitment and radicalization (UN Secretary-General, 2017b). The trafficking resolutions build upon the nexus between trafficking for sexual exploitation, conflict-related sexual violence and terrorism, issues which fall squarely within the WPS agenda but without such reference.

Resolutions 2331 and 2388 are clearly and narrowly focused on conflict-related trafficking – and more precisely on terrorism. They reflect the Security Council's impoverished understanding of peace as a security issue, as opposed to that envisioned by the coalition of NGOs that lobbied for the adoption of UNSCR 1325. The latter is rooted in the feminist conception of a positive peace that would create 'global conditions in which all lives are valued and are able to be lived in dignity and equality, emphatically rejecting the idea that peace is merely the absence of war' (Otto, 2016). Trafficking too is securitized, addressed in these two resolutions as a security issue rather than as one of development and human rights, including economic, social and cultural rights, unequal access to which is linked to the structural causes that heighten the vulnerability of women and girls to being trafficked, both within and outside of conflict.

The Security Council's agenda to counter terrorism and violent extremism in conflict-affected areas (within its overall responsibility for the maintenance of international peace and security) has had several different impacts on women's rights organizing, women's rights organizations and gender equality (Duke Law, 2017). Research undertaken in conflict and post-conflict areas, as well as in those considered to be 'at risk' of terrorism and/or violent extremism, shows that women's rights defenders across the globe are frequently 'squeezed between terrorism and violent extremism on the one hand, and counter-terrorism or preventing and countering violent extremism on the other' (Duke Law, 2017, p 8). This calls for a shift in the Security Council's understanding of the underlying causes of violent extremism, terrorism and human trafficking. While these phenomena are tackled by looking solely at their ultimate manifestations without any deeper analysis of broader economic and social inequalities (including gender inequalities), the measures designed for their elimination will prove inadequate for structural transformation (Fernández, 2019).

The Council has securitized both WPS and anti-trafficking, bringing them within its agenda for preventing and countering violent extremism, including combating financing of terrorism, money laundering and corruption. By so doing, the Security Council inhibits any broader understanding relating to human rights, in particular economic and social rights, although these are deeply implicated in both gender-based violence against women and trafficking. Resolution 2331 creates a hierarchy of victims by affirming 'that victims of trafficking in persons ... and of sexual violence, committed by terrorist groups should be classified as victims of terrorism ... rendering them eligible for official support, recognition and redress available to victims of terrorism, have access to national relief and reparations programmes' (UNSCR 2331, para. 10).

Such support should be available for all trafficked persons, not just those trafficked by terrorist groups. The Security Council thus positions 'some victims as the authentic victim subject, silencing other less conventional narratives' (Henry, 2014, p 99).

Trafficking as a form of gender-based violence against women

The human rights law regime relating to gender-based violence that has evolved since the early 1990s is especially applicable to human trafficking. Trafficking in women and girls is a form of gender-based violence: 'violence that is directed against a woman because she is a woman or that affects women disproportionately' (CEDAW, 1992, para. 6). It includes psychological as well as physical and sexual harms and deprivations of liberty, which are all especially pertinent to trafficking (CEDAW, 1992, para. 6). The CEDAW Committee has observed that poverty and unemployment increase opportunities for trafficking in women, the impact of armed conflict on prostitution, trafficking in women and sexual assault of women and the need for specific protective and punitive measures (CEDAW, 1992, paras 13–16). The UN General Assembly has explicitly affirmed that violence against women encompasses trafficking in women and forced prostitution (UN General Assembly, 1993). Despite the inclusion of trafficking in the CEDAW Convention (by way of Article 6 and its recognition of trafficking as a form of gender-based violence), understanding of trafficking in human beings as a gendered phenomenon has only been slowly accepted (ICAT, 2017).

Human trafficking affects women disproportionately in numerical terms: an estimated 79% of all detected trafficking victims are women and children, although an increasing number of men have been detected as trafficking victims and traffickers are 'overwhelmingly male' (UNODC, 2016). Some forms, such as trafficking for sexual exploitation, for labour exploitation in domestic service and forced marriage, are especially disproportionately experienced by women and girls and give rise to further gendered harms such as pregnancy, forced abortion and sexually transmitted diseases (Fernández and Yoshida, 2018).

Gender-based violence such as trafficking may be a cause of, or perpetuate, conflict, when it reaches a dimension and gravity amounting to gross human rights violations, serious crimes, crimes against humanity, or, when it has the appropriate nexus with conflict, war crimes. Trafficking perpetrated by criminal or armed groups undermines the rule of law, disrupts communities and causes mass displacement, thereby empowering criminal groups and facilitating their control of territory. This is also linked with the closing of safe migration routes that allows trafficking to reoccur in transit countries, fostering instability and increasing the power of groups such as Boko Haram in Nigeria, or ISIS.

Understanding trafficking in women and girls through a gender lens as a form of gender-based violence entails its recognition as discrimination within Article 1 of CEDAW: 'Gender-based violence is a form of discrimination that seriously inhibits women's ability to enjoy rights and freedoms on a basis of equality with men' (CEDAW, 1992, para. 1). Trafficking is rooted in gender inequalities and asymmetric power relationships and simultaneously causes further gender-based discrimination, stereotyping, violence and sexual abuse. It was one of the four key areas of focus for the mandate identified by the Special Rapporteur on Violence against Women (SR VAW, 2009). Thus, trafficking of women and girls is not only itself a form of gender-based violence but also makes its victims vulnerable to other human rights violations, including gender-based and sexual violence such as rape, sexual abuse, forms of slavery, sexual slavery and gendered forms of persecution under refugee law. It can also amount to torture.

A state is responsible under human rights law 'for acts and omissions of its organs and agents that constitute gender-based violence against women', including those of officials in its executive, legislative and judicial branches (CEDAW, 2017, para. 22). CEDAW continues to be applicable in time of conflict requiring states to have 'an effective and accessible legal and legal services framework in place to address all forms of gender-based violence against women committed by state agents' whether such acts are committed on their territory or extraterritorially (CEDAW, 2010, paras 11–12). There are many ways in which states are complicit in trafficking, including: allowing for or creating the conditions that enable traffickers to run a billionaire business, overlooking the links between trafficking and corruption, or leaving trafficking victims vulnerable to traffickers through restrictive immigration laws or by closing safe and legal migration routes. In addition, states must exercise due diligence to prevent, investigate, prosecute and punish violence against women and pay reparations to all victims. The duty of due diligence with respect to the acts of non-state actors has been reiterated in treaty law (Inter-American, 1994, Article 7; Council of Europe, 2011, Article 5); by CEDAW in its General Recommendations 19, 28 and 35 (CEDAW, 1992; CEDAW, 2010; CEDAW, 2017); by the General Assembly (UN General Assembly 1993, Article 4 (c)); in the Beijing Platform for Action (Fourth World Conference on Women, para. 124 (b)); by the regional human rights courts (Opuz v Turkey, 2009; *González et al ('Cotton Field') v Mexico*, 2009; CWPS, 2013); and by the Commission on the Status of Women (CSW57, 2013).

The CEDAW Committee has developed further the relationship between the CEDAW Convention, human trafficking and armed conflict. In General Recommendation 30, it recommends that states parties: 'Prevent, prosecute and punish trafficking and related human rights violations that occur under their jurisdiction … and adopt specific protection measures for women and girls' (CEDAW, 2013, para. 41 (a)). It also recommends the adoption of a zero-tolerance policy on trafficking which addresses national troops, peacekeeping forces, border police, immigration officials and humanitarian actors (CEDAW, 2013, para. 41 (b)). The Committee thus applies the zero-tolerance policy that the Security Council has incorporated into the WPS resolutions with respect to international peacekeepers to the full range of relevant actors and perpetrators, including state agents (see, for example, UNSCR 1820, para. 7).

Applying human rights law and standards relating to gender-based violence directly to human trafficking would mean that states' due diligence obligations towards the prevention of trafficking, the protection of victims and prosecution of perpetrators would be triggered as soon as the state authorities 'know or ought to have known' about trafficking events taking place within its territory or jurisdiction (including extraterritorial jurisdiction, refugee camps, or camps for internally displaced persons) whether committed by public authorities or private actors regardless of the state being party to any specific anti-trafficking convention (CEDAW, 2013, para. 8).

Human trafficking in the peacetime-to-conflict continuum

The risk and incidence of human trafficking is heightened in armed conflict and post-conflict situations. The CEDAW Committee has explained that trafficking is exacerbated during and after conflict and that conflict-affected areas constitute places of origin, transit and destination for trafficking (CEDAW, 2013, para. 39; Swaine and O'Rourke, 2015, p 12). The SR on Trafficking has identified the linkage between trafficking in persons and conflict as fitting within her mandate. She has highlighted the forms and nature of trafficking related to the complex situation of conflict and focused on the gender dimensions of trafficking in conflict and post-conflict settings. She has also identified its nexus with conflict-related sexual violence and the Security Council's WPS agenda (UN Human Rights Council, 2015; 2016; 2018). In light of this understanding that trafficking in persons is so closely associated with armed conflict, preventive measures should be put in place immediately from its outset.

A particular form of trafficking in armed conflict is forced recruitment. Although it is hardly ever considered as such – even when the elements of the definition are met (Palermo Protocol, 2000, Article 3) – some states have accepted that it is exploitative, and that it may amount to trafficking (Gallagher, 2015, p 7). Recruitment for military activities primarily affects men and boys. Girls are often recruited for sexual exploitation, including forced prostitution, forced marriage and sexual slavery but also as exploitative labour in unsafe mines, as porters, 'mules' and domestic servants, and on the frontlines (Bermúdez et al, 2011; UN Secretary-General, 2017a). The continuum of gender-based violence across peace, conflict and post-conflict (Cockburn, 2014) is echoed in the way trafficking occurs throughout the peace–conflict cycle, from pre- to post-conflict economies. Conflict often originates in, and is fundamentally related to, fights for territory, land and natural resources (Oslender, 2009; Weber, 2016; Symposium on Land in Colombia, 2009). There is a need to acknowledge the dynamics that flow between conflict-related violence, which provokes internal displacement allowing for land dispossession, and the violence that is exercised in regions that are rich in natural resources as a means to prevent populations displaced by conflict from ever returning to their territories.

Conflict-related violence is used to strip natural resources, forcibly seize land and generate displacement, due also to violence linked to economic interests related to mining and the political economy of war. Gold and other mines located in remote areas where the government lacks the capability to monitor conditions and enforce laws, give rise to illegal mining. When these mines and other extraction zones are directly controlled by criminal groups, or are in areas controlled by organized crime, there is an increased risk of trafficking of women and girls for sexual exploitation and forced labour, which further fuels the predatory war economy. These zones are witness to different forms of gender-based and sexual violence by non-state actors, including private security services hired by companies and other armed groups. For instance, research has uncovered numerous instances of trafficking for labour, sex and child labour in Colombia and Peru (Global Initiative against Transnational Organized Crime, 2016). The same research found that women employed for sexual exploitation in illegal mining areas in Colombia are routinely forced to work long hours and are unable to refuse clients or insist that clients use a condom, resulting in high rates of sexually transmitted diseases. In some cases, they are forced to consume drugs or to have abortions (Wilches Gutiérrez, 2018). There are also multiple reports of torture at the hands of clients and traffickers.

The situation of young girls who are sexually exploited and forced into sexual slavery to 'provide for the needs' of the miners (including those mining illegally) has been documented in many regions of Colombia (Lima, 2013). The effects of mining, including the impact on local inhabitants and the gendered violence it creates against men and women, have also been analysed, yet not institutionally tackled (Ulloa, 2016). Illegal mining networks in Latin America have led to increased violence against women and communities that specifically affect indigenous, Afro-descendant and rural women (Bermúdez, 2012;

Ulloa, 2016). In Colombia, there are examples of social movements led by women which have been formed in response to mining and its negative impacts. These movements are rooted in so-called 'territorial feminisms' which seek to highlight the linkages between the violence that is exercised towards nature and territory through large scale mineral extraction activities and the violence asserted over women's bodies.

Like other forms of gender-based violence, human trafficking does not stop when the conflict ceases. On the contrary, reports on different conflict and post-conflict settings have shown that trafficking in persons, especially in women and children, remains prevalent, facilitated by economic chaos and the destruction of social structures that provide for basic needs. Escalation of other forms of gender-based and sexual violence in post-conflict settings increases vulnerability to trafficking (CEDAW, 2013, para. 35). Gender inequalities exacerbate the exploitation of women and girls, including through exploitative marriages as a means of obtaining income for their families. The impoverished conditions in which displaced families find themselves, combined with the reduction of refugee protection and the closing of migration routes to safe countries, create the conditions for women and children being offered by their families to traffickers for a number of purposes, with a high incidence of sexual enslavement and exploitation, forced prostitution, forced marriages, 'temporary' marriages, enlistment in fighting and organ removal (Secours Catholique, 2016; Gallagher, 2015, p 16). 'Trafficking is a systemic outcome of conflict' (CSW61, 2017) and women and girls are seen as commodities who can be 'used' for whatever is needed in a given context. Where there is economic activity that involves a concentration of male workers, such as mining and other extractive industries, sexual exploitation of women and girls is profitable.

The design and implementation of post-conflict measures should protect against the risks of further forms of violence and exploitation when a 'traditional armed force' withdraws from a territory and the 'status quo' changes, leaving a vacuum for other armed groups to take control over the territory. In these situations, vulnerability to trafficking is exacerbated (Secours Catholique, 2016). For instance, experience in Central America has shown how urban violence worsened after the peace agreements, allowing organized criminal groups to expand their power and influence, contributing to an increase of trafficking (UNODC, 2015). As a consequence of trafficking in women usually being overlooked as a form of conflict-related sexual violence, prevention and protection measures are often absent or insufficiently addressed or included in peace processes and agreements. As an example, human trafficking is mentioned only once in Colombia's Agreement to End Conflict and Build Peace, under the section on Tax Authority, together with other forms of illegal economic activity. This emphasizes that the participation of women in the design and implementation of post-conflict social and economic reordering, as spelled out in multiple WPS resolutions (see, for example, UNSCR 1889 para. 1; UNSCR 2122, para. 7), should be understood as including those with direct experience in the relevant issues, for instance trafficked persons, thereby supporting the linkage between trafficking and WPS.

Peacekeeping operations and humanitarian actions too can have negative effects, including an increase in trafficking in human beings, especially in women for sexual exploitation, as in the Balkans, when peacekeepers became implicated in trafficking (WILPF, 2012; Mendelson, 2005). Consequently, prevention of trafficking measures and a gender analysis should be mainstreamed into all policies and practices of humanitarian and peacekeeping operations.

Conflict can shape the way in which a country understands, experiences and responds to trafficking, sometimes for many years after hostilities have ceased. The extreme and often gender-based violence that takes place during conflict can set the scene for greater toleration of trafficking-related exploitation in so-called post-conflict peacetime (Gallagher, 2015, p 21). Trafficking is rarely included under the forms of conflict-related sexual violence to be addressed in planning for post-conflict reconstruction. As a consequence, trafficking victims are under-identified and the links between gender inequalities, conflict, displacement and trafficking are overlooked, including in peace processes. This leads to a missed opportunity for understanding how these dynamics work and introducing measures to combat them.

WPS and trafficking: the meanings of silence

The silence on trafficking in women and girls in the WPS resolutions remains a significant lacuna in protecting women's fundamental rights and weakens the potential of WPS to bring structural transformation in conflict and post-conflict contexts. The question arises as to whether there is any value in recognizing that, as a form of gender-based violence occurring in armed conflict, trafficking in women and girls falls within the WPS agenda. What is the 'value-added' of placing trafficking of women and girls within the framework of WPS? On the other hand, what does the silence mean? Is this resounding silence a violent one? Does the silence itself constitute violence?

There are evidently some downsides to explicitly bringing trafficking within the remit of WPS. There is the risk that this will strengthen the trend towards securitization and reduce still further the visibility of gender-based harms experienced during and post-conflict by women that are neither sexual violence committed as a tactic of war nor caused through being trafficked by terrorist or extremist groups. Another risk is overloading the WPS agenda, making implementation and allocation of adequate resources even less likely to be secured.

Nevertheless, there are a number of responses to the questions posed earlier that we consider to be significant for the future direction of WPS. One is that bringing trafficking into WPS provides for joined-up thinking across a number of different international agendas, grounded in international law and a rights-based approach, that centre on the need for prevention of gender-based violence and protection of women and girls against such violence in situations of armed conflict, displacement and post-conflict. As a form of conflict-related gender-based violence, an imminent risk of trafficking should be recognized from the outset of conflict and preventive measures automatically put in place from that time and maintained throughout the duration of the conflict and its aftermath. Further, UNSCR 2331 and UNSCR 2388 emphasize trafficking in the context of violent extremism and terrorism – notably the actions of Islamic State of Iraq and the Levant (ISIL, also known as Da'esh), and Al-Nusra Front (ANF) and associated groups and individuals (UNSCR 2331, Preamble, para. 11; UNSCR 2388, Preamble, para. 10). Understanding trafficking of women and girls in the WPS framework makes it more widely applicable to all armed conflict. The universality of human rights emphasizes state obligations towards all victims of gender-based violence in armed conflict not just those who have been trafficked in the framework of extremism or in armed conflicts that are on the agenda of the Security Council.

Another answer is that it brings trafficking of women and girls within the four pillars of WPS, which are centred on ameliorating the position of women in armed conflict and post-conflict, including as central actors as well as victims of crime, and emphasizing the importance of the empowerment of women and women's leadership. The SR on trafficking has provided practical examples and recommendations to states on how to better integrate a human rights-based approach to trafficking into the four WPS pillars and to UN bodies, civil society organizations and other stakeholders on how to mainstream trafficking into all their areas of work relating to conflict and post-conflict settings (UN Secretary-General, 2018).

Finally, there is a need to unpack what the silence of the WPS agenda about trafficking means for women and girls who are trafficked at any time in the peace–conflict–post-conflict continuum. This silence is telling, as it sends the message that trafficking is to be dealt with as a security issue, separated from other forms of gendered violence happening during conflict, including sexual violence. This works against legal and moral coherence. As feminist scholars have argued, there is a hierarchy of crimes and hence of harms and the silencing of certain victims is of itself a form of violence (Henry, 2014, p 99). This is because the silence involves complicity in the power dynamics which uphold systems of oppression including sexism, racism, imperialism and neo-colonialism. This is why women's participation is key to breaking the cycles of violence and silence (hooks, 1995).

It further raises a concern that women's rights are used as an excuse for further military intervention, the application of sanctions or other coercive measures to punish those committing acts of trafficking in conflict-related areas. In this logic, women's rights protection, including protection of trafficking victims, receives greater attention when it happens in conflict and in post-conflict areas because it can serve states' security and countering violent extremism (CVE) agendas (Fernández, 2019). This silence is to the detriment of those who are trafficked in other contexts such as for forced labour and domestic exploitation. States' action to fight trafficking needs to be coherent to be effective. This means it needs to reconcile and integrate the different approaches and agendas that deal with trafficking. And human rights law is the glue that can help in this task.

Acknowledgement

The authors gratefully acknowledge that this chapter has been written under the auspices of the European Research Council Advanced Grant project *A Gendered Peace*, part of the European Union's Horizon 2020 research and innovation programme (Grant agreement No. 786494).

Note

[1] The crime control agenda is represented by the Protocol to Prevent, Suppress and Punish Trafficking in Persons Especially Women and Children, supplementing the United Nations Convention against Transnational Organized Crime (Palermo Protocol). Criticized for its failure to adequately address victims' rights and to fully explore the causes and consequences of human trafficking, it also fails to incorporate a gendered approach despite its title. Notwithstanding its prevalence within human trafficking debates, we do not address the crime control angle.

References

Bermúdez, R.C., Rodríguez, T. and Roa, T. (2011) 'Mujer y Minería. Ámbitos de análisis e impactos de la minería en la vida de las mujeres. Enfoque de derechos y perspectivas de género', *Encuentro Latinoamericano Mujer y Minería*, Available from: http://desterresminees.pasc.ca/wp-content/uploads/2015/11/Bermudez-Rico-et-al-2011-Mujer_y_Mineria.pdf.

Bermúdez, R.C. (2012) 'Impacto de los grandes proyectos mineros en Colombia sobre la vida de las mujeres', in: *Minería, Territorio y Conflicto en Colombia*, Bogotá: Universidad Nacional de Colombia, Facultad de Derecho, Ciencias Políticas y Sociales, Instituto Unidad de Investigaciones Jurídico-Sociales Gerardo Molina (UNIJUS), pp 355–370.

CEDAW (Committee on the Elimination of Discrimination Against Women) (1992) General Recommendation No. 19, Violence against women, Available from: https://tbinternet.ohchr.org/Treaties/CEDAW/Shared%20Documents/1_Global/INT_CEDAW_GEC_3731_E.pdf.

CEDAW (Committee on the Elimination of Discrimination Against Women) (2010) General Recommendation No. 28 on the core obligations of States parties under Article 2 of the Convention on the Elimination of All Forms of Discrimination against Women, CEDAW/C/GC/28-12, Available from: www.refworld.org/docid/4d467ea72.html.

CEDAW (Committee on the Elimination of Discrimination Against Women) (2013) General Recommendation No. 30 on women in conflict prevention, conflict and post-conflict situations, CEDAW/C/GC/30, Available from: www.ohchr.org/Documents/HRBodies/CEDAW/GComments/CEDAW.C.CG.30.pdf.

CEDAW (Committee on the Elimination of Discrimination Against Women) (2017) General Recommendation No. 35 on gender-based violence against women, updating General Recommendation No. 19, CEDAW/C/GC/35, Available from: https://tbinternet.ohchr.org/Treaties/CEDAW/Shared%20Documents/1_Global/CEDAW_C_GC_35_8267_E.pdf.

Chinkin, C. (2018) 'International human rights, criminal law and the Women, Peace and Security agenda', *LSE WPS Working Paper Series*, 12, Available from: http://blogs.lse.ac.uk/wps/2018/01/11/international-human-rights-criminal-law-and-the-women-peace-and-security-agenda-christine-chinkin-122018/.

Cockburn, C. (2014) 'The continuum of violence: a gender perspective on war and peace', in W. Giles and J. Hyndman (eds) *Sites of Violence: Gender and Conflict Zones*, Berkeley and Los Angeles, CA: University of California Press, pp 24–44.

CSW57 (2013) Commission on the Status of Women, 57th session, 4–15 March, Agreed Conclusions: Elimination and prevention of all forms of violence against women and girls, Available from: www.unwomen.org/-/media/headquarters/attachments/sections/csw/57/csw57-agreedconclusions-a4-en.pdf?la=en&vs=700.

CSW61 (2017) Commission on the Status of Women, 61st session, 13–24 March, Remarks of Maria Grazia Giammarinaro, UN SR Trafficking, Available from: www.ohchr.org/en/NewsEvents/Pages/DisplayNews.aspx?NewsID=21401&LangID=E.

Council of Europe (2011) 'Convention on preventing and combating violence against women and domestic violence', CETS No. 210 (Istanbul Convention).

Duke Law (2018) *Tightening the Purse Strings: What Countering Terrorism Financing Costs Gender Equality and Security*, International Human Rights Clinic and Women Peacemakers Program, Available from: https://law.duke.edu/sites/default/files/humanrights/tighteningpursestrings.pdf.

CWPS (Centre for Women, Peace and Security) (2013) *EIPR (Egyptian Initiative for Personal Rights) and Interights v. Egypt*, 14 March (African Commission on Human and Peoples' Rights), London: CWPS, LSE, Available from: https://blogs.lse.ac.uk/vaw/landmark-cases/a-z-of-cases/eipr-and-interights-v-egypt/.

Fernández, G. (2019) 'Performing anti-trafficking: human rights, the Security Council and the disconnect with the Women, Peace and Security agenda', *LSE WPS Working Paper Series*, 20, Available from: www.lse.ac.uk/women-peace-security/assets/documents/2019/WPS20RodriguezdeLievana.pdf

Fernández, G. and Yoshida, K. (2018) 'Human trafficking as a gendered phenomenon: CEDAW in perspective', *Immigration, Asylum and Nationality Law*, 32(1): 28–49.

Fourth World Conference on Women (1995) Beijing Declaration and Platform for Action, UN Doc. A/CONF/177/20 Beijing.

Gallagher, A.T. (2015) *Trafficking in Persons and Armed Conflict*, Background report prepared for the United Nations Special Rapporteur on Trafficking in persons, Available from: https://works.bepress.com/anne_gallagher/46/download/.

Global Initiative against Transnational Organized Crime (2016) *Organized Crime and Illegally Mined Gold in Latin America*, Available from: https://arcominero.infoamazonia.org/GIATOC-OC_Illegally-Mined-Gold-in-Latin-America-3c3f978eef80083bdd8780d7c5a21f1e.pdf.

González et al ('Cotton Field') v Mexico, 16 November 2009 (Inter-American Court of Human Rights, Series C, No. 205) (Preliminary Objection, Merits, Reparations, and Costs).

Henry, N. (2014) 'The fixation on wartime rape, feminist critique and international criminal law', *Social and Legal Studies*, 23(1): 93–111.

hooks, b. (1995) 'Feminism and militarism: a comment', *Women's Studies Quarterly*, 23(3/4): 58–64.

ICAT (Inter-Agency Coordination Group against Trafficking in Persons) (2017) 'The gender dimensions of human trafficking', *Issue Brief* 4, Available from: http://icat.network/sites/default/files/publications/documents/ICAT-IB-04-V.1.pdf.

Inter-American Convention on the Prevention, Punishment and Eradication of Violence against Women 'Convention of Belém do Pará' (1994), Available from: http://www.oas.org/juridico/english/treaties/a-61.html.

Lima, J.B. (2013) *Campamentos de explotación de niñas en zonas mineras. Alrededor de las minas hay redes organizadas de trata de mujeres*, Available from: www.eltiempo.com/archivo/documento/CMS-12824463.

Mendelson, S.E. (2005) *Barracks and Brothels: Peacekeepers and Human Trafficking in the Balkans*, Washington DC: Center for Strategic and International Studies.

Opuz v Turkey, 9 June 2009 (European Court of Human Rights, Application no. 33401/02).

Oslender, U. (2009) 'Colombia: old and new patterns of violence', *Socialist Register* 45: 181–198.

Otto, D. (2016) 'Women, peace and security: a critical analysis of the Security Council's vision', *LSE WPS Working Paper Series*, 1, Available from: http://blogs.lse.ac.uk/wps/2017/01/09/women-peace-and-security-a-critical-analysis-of-the-security-councils-vision/.

Palermo Protocol (2000) Protocol to Prevent, Suppress and Punish Trafficking in Persons Especially Women and Children, supplementing the United Nations Convention against Transnational Organized Crime.

Secours Catholique (2016) *Trafficking in Human Beings in Conflict and Post-Conflict Situations*, Available from: www.academia.edu/33968353/TRAFFICKING_IN_HUMAN_BEINGS_IN_CONFLICT_AND_POST-CONFLICT_SITUATIONS_TRAFFICKING_IN_HUMAN_BEINGS_IN_CONFLICT_AND_POST-CONFLICT_SITUATIONS?auto=download.

SR VAW (Special Rapporteur on Violence against Women) (2009) '15 years of the United Nations Special Rapporteur on violence against women, its causes and consequences (1994–2009): a critical review', Available from: www.ohchr.org/Documents/Issues/Women/15YearReviewofVAWMandate.pdf.

Swaine, A. and O'Rourke, C. (2015) *Guidebook on CEDAW General Recommendation No. 30 and the UN Security Council Resolutions on Women, Peace and Security*, New York: UN Women.

Symposium on Land in Colombia (2017) 'Land rights, restitution, politics, and war in Colombia', *Journal of Agrarian Change*, 17: 733–78.

UN General Assembly (1993) UN GA Resolution 48/104, 20 December 1993, Declaration of Elimination of Violence against Women.

UN Global Plan of Action (2010) UN GA Resolution 64/293, 12 August 2010, United Nations Global Plan of Action to Combat Trafficking in Person.

UN Human Rights Council (2015) Special Rapporteur on trafficking in persons, especially women and children, Maria Grazia Giammarinaro. Report to the Human Rights Council, UN Doc. A/HRC/29/38, 31 March.

UN Human Rights Council (2016) Special Rapporteur on trafficking in persons, especially women and children, Maria Grazia Giammarinaro. Report to the General Assembly UN Doc. A/71/303, 5 August.

UN Human Rights Council (2018) Special Rapporteur on trafficking in persons, especially women and children, Maria Grazia Giammarinaro, Report to the General Assembly, UN Doc. A/73/171, 17 July.

UNODC (United Nations Office on Drugs and Crime) (2015) 'Estudio descriptivo del delito de la trata de personas que victimiza a niñas y mujeres en Medellín', [Descriptive Study on the Crime of Trafficking in Women and Girls in Medellín], Available from: www.unodc.org/documents/colombia/2015/Diciembre/cartilla_estudiodescriptivo.pdf.

UNODC (United Nations Office on Drugs and Crime) (2016) *Global Report on Trafficking in Persons*, Available from: www.unodc.org/documents/data-and-analysis/glotip/2016_Global_Report_on_Trafficking_in_Persons.pdf.

UN Secretary-General (2017a) Remarks at Ministerial Open Debate on Trafficking in Persons in Conflict Situations: Forced labour, slavery and other similar practices, Available from: www.un.org/sg/en/content/sg/speeches/2017-03-15/trafficking-persons-conflict-situations-remarks.

UN Secretary-General (2017b) *Report of the UN Secretary-General on Conflict-Related Sexual Violence*, UN Doc. S/2017/249.

Ulloa, A. (2016) 'Territory feminism in Latin America: defense of life against extractivism', Available from: http://nomadas.ucentral.edu.co/nomadas/pdf/nomadas_45/45-8U-Feminismos-territoriales.pdf.

Weber, S. (2016) 'Land, conflict and transitional justice in Colombia', Available from: https://consentido.nl/land-conflict-and-transitional-justice-colombia/.

Wilches Gutiérrez, J.L. (2018) 'Sexual and reproductive health in local mining contexts in Colombia', PhD Dissertation, University of Pittsburgh, Graduate School of Public Health.

WILPF (Women's International League for Peace and Freedom) (2012) 'Human trafficking and related crimes in the context of peacekeeping: state, organization, and individual responsibilities and accountabilities', Available from: https://wilpf.org/wp-content/uploads/2014/07/Compiled.M.Rees_.Trafficking.Report.pdf.

13

Addressing Future Fragility: Women, Climate Change and Migration

Briana Mawby and Anna Applebaum

Climate change and its consequences are among the greatest challenges facing the global community, with the potential to radically alter the structures of communities, states and international cooperation. As weather patterns shift and natural resources diminish, climate change is likely to threaten geopolitical stability, particularly in politically fragile states and for impoverished communities and other vulnerable groups. Among the many approaching challenges is climate change-related migration. Climate change will fundamentally reshape migration patterns around the world; as people choose to migrate to find safety and economic opportunities, their movements will affect how states manage their borders and national security and will further strain the already burdened mechanisms that help guide migration flows locally and internationally. The pressure of climate-related migration in both origin and destination communities requires rethinking international initiatives and national frameworks governing migration and resettlement. Without engaging in the relevant research, analysis and policy-making now, we may soon face a serious challenge as states struggle to adjust their immigration and national security policies to respond to a cycle of climate change impacts and migration.

These challenges are not borne equally. Women and men are shaped by their communities and cultures. In many places, women lack access to political, economic and social decision making and have limited financial and material resources. When a shock occurs, such as those caused by climate change impacts, it leaves women especially vulnerable and makes migration particularly arduous. Yet women will also be critical to determining the response to such events. Particularly in developing countries and in rural communities, women are often household managers and family caregivers, and they will bear much of the responsibility for moving their families and communities between towns, countries and continents. In order to understand the potential impacts of climate change-related migration, it is critical to understand women's roles and experiences. As responsive new policies and approaches are being designed, it is equally critical for women's perspectives, needs and expertise to be centred.

Over the past two decades, the field of Women, Peace and Security (WPS) research has re-examined long-standing assumptions about security processes, conflict prevention and resolution, and governance. Climate change-related migration is one such impending challenge that will require a significant shift in humanitarian response as well as legal and institutional norms, particularly to avoid future security threats and conflict. Given the importance of women's roles and experiences to navigating this future, WPS research frameworks have a unique vantage point on how best to prepare and address it. Given that scholarship on the WPS agenda frequently upends conventional analysis about international peace and security, it is well-suited to address new issues that emerge in the conflict and security sphere, such as the arising national border management and security apparatus challenges of climate change-related migration and associated gendered consequences. These consequences should not be misconstrued as a statement that migrants are dangerous or inherently security threats; migration can boost economies and strengthen cultural exchange. However, understanding how to address greater or different migration flows will involve national security and immigration institutions, and it is critical to take a long-term perspective so that the relevant actors can take thoughtful actions to facilitate orderly and safe migration. The WPS agenda is both security-based and provides a gender perspective, creating the potential for a more focused examination of the global and often far-reaching consequences of climate change. This helps break down the sometimes-siloed action taken on these issues and allows for feminist analysis that extends beyond state-led initiatives. Formally housed in the United Nations Security Council, the WPS agenda is well placed to support and work alongside other frameworks, such as CEDAW (Committee on the Elimination of Discrimination Against Women), multilateral environmental agreements, and the Sustainable Development Goals, to address climate change holistically. As the

Security Council increasingly turns its attention to climate change as a matter of relevance to international peace and security, the WPS agenda can provide a needed and realistically nuanced framework for analysis.

This chapter provides a discussion of the gendered consequences of climate change, the legal and policy gaps that exist for understanding and addressing gendered climate change-related migration, and the role that future WPS research and analysis can play in highlighting and addressing these issues.

Climate change, environmental harms and migration through a gendered lens

Climate change and its consequences have already begun affecting livelihoods and shaping daily decision making around the world, particularly in the global South (World Bank, 2013). Climate change has many manifestations and can occur through both rapid-onset and slow-onset events; these include a rise in average global temperatures, flooding, droughts, desertification due to changes in rainfall patterns, and unpredictable weather patterns that lead to more common or more intense natural disasters (Eastin, 2018). Rising sea levels and coastal erosion also threaten many low-lying areas. These impacts disrupt daily life and diminish biodiversity and natural resources; many climate change-related events, particularly rapid-onset events, result in death, injury or illness (World Bank, 2013). All of these impacts affect individual and community livelihoods, security and welfare.

For women, pre-existing vulnerabilities can worsen climate change impacts. Women often lack access to and control over resources and livelihood opportunities, which reduces their resilience to shocks. Namrata Chindarkar argues, 'Given that women tend to be poorer, less educated, have a lower health status and have limited direct access to or ownership of natural resources, they will be disproportionately affected by climate change' (Chindarkar, 2012, p 1). Manifestations of climate change and their impacts on communities vary regionally. In some geographic areas, sea level rise and flooding increase the likelihood of water-borne diseases, food scarcity and displacement. For women, this disruption of normal life may make them more vulnerable to violence and destroy the resources that they collect for their families (Azad et al, 2013, pp 191–193). Elsewhere, deforestation and ocean acidification affect women's livelihoods. As a result of deforestation, the resources found in forests, like firewood, food, herbs and timber are scarcer, and often women must travel longer distances to gather these resources (Steady, 2014, p 3). It should be noted that these impacts will affect developing countries first and more severely than developed countries; the geography of climate change is uneven as well as gendered. It is critical to recognize these factors in order to facilitate just solutions, including safe migration.

In many communities, climate change impacts will affect food and water security severely. As natural resources become less readily available, women and girls, who are often in charge of unpaid household chores, must take more time for their domestic duties and for gathering the materials they and their families need (Skinner, 2011, p 2). Globally, women and girls are responsible for collecting water in eight out of ten households (World Health Organization and United Nations Children's Fund, 2017, p 11), and women and children collectively spend an estimated 200 million hours per day collecting water (Graham et al, 2016). Increasing resource scarcity results in less time for school, work or other activities, and it can also put women and girls in danger as they travel greater distances to collect resources (Dankelman, 2009). Water scarcity further compromises hygiene and health for women and girls, especially due to the sanitation needs particular to pregnancy and menstruation. Poor women are the most likely to be affected by resulting illnesses, as they have limited access to healthcare, limited knowledge of the risks, and are often considered the primary caregivers for family members.

Climate change also intensifies the frequency and severity of storms and other weather patterns. Given that women are more likely than men to die during or in the aftermath of disasters (Neumayer and Plümper, 2007), more severe or frequent extreme weather will likely exacerbate women's vulnerability, particularly for those in the global South. Further, women's lack of social and economic power intensifies the danger following disasters and during reconstruction efforts. As Britton noted, 'Disaster is a social product; vulnerability is contingent on social preconditions' (1986, p 254). In many communities, social conditions for women include a lack of rights to property or access to legal or financial assets (Neumayer and Plümper, 2007). With more limited access to credit, information and relief services, women have fewer resources upon which to rely when a shock or disaster occurs (Shah, 2006). Not all women are equally vulnerable; women with existing economic or social vulnerabilities may be less secure as the impacts of climate change threaten community stability. This may be particularly severe for indigenous, widowed and poor women (United Nations Environment Programme et al, 2013) and women of other marginalized groups.

In the next decades, as climate change jeopardizes the natural and social environments for communities around the world, many people will migrate as an adaptive strategy to preserve their health, wellbeing, employment and safety. Predictions of future climate change-related displacement vary greatly,[1] reaching up to 250 million displaced people by 2050 (Brown, 2007; Boano et al, 2008). One study found that people were twice as likely to be displaced in 2015 than in the 1970s due to natural disasters (Ginetti, 2015). Climate change seems likely to increase displacement risk by increasing the frequency and intensity of weather-related hazards while also increasing communities' vulnerability, reducing the threshold at which people choose or are forced to move.

The decision to migrate is usually multifaceted, a combination of economic, political, social, demographic and environmental challenges that individuals or families face. These issues are exacerbated by climate change impacts (Black et al, 2011). The decision to migrate is often based on the perceived duration of the direct and indirect effects of climate change impacts and on whether additional shocks are expected in the future; individuals and families weigh the risks and benefits of migrating as compared to staying in a particular place at a particular time (Coniglio and Pesce, 2015). This decision is also influenced by factors such as high population density, lack of economic opportunities, inequitable distribution of resources, lack of access to land and violent conflict (Tacoli, 2009). It is important to note that it can be difficult to distinguish these factors from the impacts of climate change when understanding the choice to migrate, as they are likely to be reinforcing rather than mutually exclusive causes. While any individual climate event, such as a drought or more intense storms, may not cause displacement on its own, migration may be the only viable adaptation strategy for vulnerable populations experiencing multiple changes at once (Martin, 2013). It is also possible that in some geographic areas, such as small island states, climate change impacts will render land completely uninhabitable, forcing all residents to migrate (Yamamoto and Esteban, 2011).

There are several key issues involved in women's decisions to migrate. Climate change impacts are generally more devastating for the most vulnerable, which includes women (Bhatta et al, 2015; Islam and Shamsuddoha, 2017), and women may experience increased vulnerability as a result of intersecting marginalized social identities (for example, indigenous women may face challenges related to their indigenous identity as well as their gender). Climate change makes resources scarce, and when individuals have a low ability to adapt, they make the choice – often out of desperation – to migrate (IPCC, 2001). When men migrate and women do not, women may struggle with additional household and community responsibilities exacerbated by fewer resources (Sugden et al, 2014; Tiwari and Joshi, 2015). The decision to migrate for women is often related to this scarcity of natural resources, as women are often the primary resource gatherers in their families (Massey et al, 2010).

The decision – and ability – to migrate is inherently gendered. As Medhanit A. Abebe argues, 'Migration as a coping strategy is gendered because it requires not only physical mobility, but also economic and physical capacities that are not equally available to women' (Abebe, 2014, p 126). Climate change impacts and the ability to migrate are mediated through cultural norms and socioeconomic status, and this often makes women more vulnerable and less able to adapt to impacts. Thus, '[c]limate change-induced migration, both voluntary and forced, is a gendered and socially embedded process' (Chindarkar, 2012, p 3).

With the impacts of climate change come mass humanitarian consequences. Climate change increases the likelihood and severity of destabilizing rapid-onset events, such as natural disasters, and places immense political, economic and social strain on communities due to slow-onset challenges. Because of these and other impacts, climate change is predicted to challenge state borders, threaten political stability, and lead to an increase in armed conflict around the world (Campbell et al, 2007). The United States Department of Defense has characterized climate change as a 'threat multiplier', stating that it will exploit existing vulnerabilities while creating new security risks (Light, 2014, p 1799). Of the 15 countries with the highest vulnerability to disasters, 14 are among the top 50 most fragile states (Harris et al, 2013, p 7). Correspondingly, those living in fragile and conflict-affected states have reduced ability to respond to climate-related impacts; from 2005 to 2009, more than 50 percent of people affected by disasters lived in fragile and conflict-affected settings (Kellett and Sparks, 2012, p 31).

On an individual level, climate change impacts – and associated migration – will lead to injuries, poor health outcomes and loss of life for many (McMichael et al, 2012). Additionally, there is evidence that men and women respond differently to these potential consequences, making the choice to migrate at different times or considering different factors when determining if migration will address those consequences. One study conducted in Ethiopia found that drought nearly doubled labour-related movements and migration for men, particularly for men from land-poor households, while women's short-distance and marriage-related mobility were reduced by half, due to their decreased ability to finance weddings and new households (Gray and Mueller, 2012). Another study, conducted in Ghana, found that while women prefer temporary migration as an adaptive strategy, men favour permanent migration (Kumasi et al, 2017). A study focusing on local and distant migration in Nepal found that additional time required to collect fodder increases the odds of migrating for women, but not for men, and additional time required to gather firewood increases the likelihood of men migrating, but not for women (Massey et al, 2010).

Further, there are specific security and humanitarian relief issues for women during the migration process that may change their decision calculus, such as sexual and gender-based violence, a lack of safe shelter and the disintegration of social networks for women's safety (Gururaja, 2000). It must be noted that these studies depend on generalizations about how gender operates within societies, including assumptions about sexuality, gender identity and family structure; these may not apply universally, but they provide a baseline for analysis. Additional study and analysis are needed to understand the full range of gendered climate migration outcomes and related humanitarian needs. While it is not possible to extrapolate global findings from these studies, they suggest that when seeking to address the humanitarian consequences of climate-related migration, a perspective that bridges gendered humanitarian and security concerns is necessary.

International legal issues

Climate change impacts and climate change-related migration are powerful global challenges, but the current legal and governance structures addressing migration are not prepared for the predicted population movement. They are even less well-equipped to address the experiences and needs of women migrants. Yet the gendered needs and motivations of climate migrants will affect both what migrants seek in destination communities as well as the countries' ability to respond to migrants. While there are many frameworks, conventions and norms related to migration that may have some relevance to climate migrants, there are significant gaps in international law on this issue (Kweku Assan and Rosenfeld, 2012).

Within the limited range of law that covers climate migrants, there is even less attention paid to women climate migrants specifically. This group of migrants falls through the gap that exists between international law and agreements related to gender,[2] those that address the environment and climate change, and those dealing with migration. Thus far, multilateral environmental agreements have been useful for integrating gender and environmental issues. The 1992 Earth Summit, 1992 Convention on Biodiversity (CBD), 1992 UN Framework

Convention on Climate Change (UNFCCC) and the Basel, Rotterdam and Stockholm Conventions (BRS) have all addressed or included gender in some way, though the depth of the discussion varies across platforms and convenings. However, there remains a significant gap in international governance over migration, gender and the environment.

Refugee law[3] requires proof of legal causation for asylum – meaning that the reason *why* a refugee left their home must be recognized by national legal frameworks – and the parameters are largely focused on conflict-related or political persecution. Legal causation is extremely difficult to establish for climate migrants, because they are unlikely to be able to link their migration decision to legally defined persecution. Many of these challenges are similar, if not overlapping, for women seeking asylum for gender-based harm. Indeed, refugee law may not even be a relevant body of frameworks for climate migration, because most climate migrants are predicted to move within their own borders rather than crossing into a different country. Refugee law that incorporates climate migrants will also necessarily be a reactive, rather than a proactive, response; individuals would therefore be required to suffer considerable harm before leaving. Only suitable for individuals in crisis, it cannot address the structural issues underpinning climate migration (Environmental Justice Foundation, 2014).

Frameworks guiding displacement appear more relevant to climate migrants. However, these frameworks lack mechanisms for enforcement or accountability. The 1998 Guiding Principles on Internal Displacement explicitly refer to migration from 'natural or human-made disasters', but the Principles are soft law and thus have limited ability to provide for enforcement or redress. Additionally, the Principles exclude migration for economic reasons – and the decision to migrate because of climate change impacts is nearly always connected to the scarcity of resources and economic needs. The 2009 Kampala Convention for the Protection and Assistance of Internally Displaced Persons and the Nansen Initiative on Disaster-Induced Cross Border Displacement provide guidance for rapid-onset disasters but are less relevant for slow-onset processes. The Platform on Disaster Displacement, a follow-up to the Nansen Initiative, provides guidance for states and regional organizations to incorporate disaster risk reduction into their existing frameworks.

Climate change threatens the very existence of some states, particularly Small Islands Developing States (SIDS). The possibility of the complete physical disappearance of sovereign states is unheard of in modern history and will require innovative legal and normative responses. The international frameworks governing statelessness, such as the 1954 Convention Relating to the Status of Stateless Persons and the 1961 Convention on the Reduction of Statelessness, may become relevant as states disappear, physically or normatively, in the case of dire climate change impacts (Environmental Justice Foundation, 2014, p 11). However, for disappeared states, 'it is unclear whether [their] citizens will become stateless persons under international law or landless citizens of a state that no longer exists' (Burkett, 2011, p 353). There have been some creative explorations of how and what kind of sovereignty might be feasible for states that become uninhabitable or that physically disappear, including *ex situ* nationhood, Permanent Observer status at the United States, or the merging with 'host' sovereign states (Yamamoto and Esteban, 2011; Burkett, 2011). However, this is a largely unexplored area of international law.

This gap in legal definitions has serious ramifications for when and where people displaced by climate change will be able to find safety; the current governance and legal structures that address migration are not prepared for climate migrants. The 2018 UN Global Compact for Migration, signed by 164 countries, made a start by including a section on climate change in its effort to define a common approach to migration. However, the agreement is nonbinding, and stricter and more clearly delineated policies will need to follow. As new frameworks are drafted, it is imperative to include women's perspectives and experiences. As discussed here, women's experiences and strategic choices often differ from men's, and these roles are further complicated by intersecting marginalities and perspectives, and new global frameworks must be gender-responsive or they will fail to address key aspects of future climate challenges. The WPS field has focused on making many aspects of international security gender-responsive, and emerging climate migration frameworks is a key issue for the field to address.

Possible WPS responses

Climate change-related migration is among the most significant future global governance challenges stemming from climate change. As reviewed earlier, it is also a deeply gendered phenomenon. In combining a security-based perspective and a woman-centred focus, a WPS analytical framework is a critical tool for conceptualizing future harms and future solutions.

Since the challenges caused by climate change impacts will disproportionately affect the world's poor – a majority of whom are women – we must conceptualize the particular challenges of climate-related migration through a gendered lens. As an inherently cross-sectional framework of analysis, WPS can bridge the gap between the work done previously by environmental scientists and advocates and that of security experts, bringing an inclusive focus to the issue of climate change. WPS, by recognizing the importance of a gendered perspective, opens up analyses and policy perspectives that centre women and other marginalized individuals in order to yield a more effective response. The existing literature shows the importance of gendered factors as women choose to migrate (Curran and Meijer-Irons, 2014; Ghosh et al, 2018). However, women's perspectives must be brought more fully into the security conversation at the local, national and international levels.

Research under the WPS umbrella has successfully deepened analysis of current security issues such as displacement, disaster response and the management of armed conflict. WPS research unveils and analyses lived experiences that form and are formed by these crises, creating a better understanding of root causes and yielding more effective policy outcomes. The same dynamics are at play in these 'traditional' crises as in climate-related migration. As with post-conflict settings, climate-related migration may result in the upheaval of social norms surrounding women's roles and social capital, creating opportunities for advancement as well as retrenchment of patriarchal structures and behaviours (Djoudi et al, 2013). Chindarkar argues, 'On one hand [migration outcomes] may seem to be empowering women, while on the other they may actually exacerbate their socio-economic status and make them worse off. Gender distinctions in vulnerabilities not only determine who migrates, but also, for whom it is easier to return and restore their lives' (Chindarkar, 2012, pp 5–6). Analysing patriarchal structures and gendered behaviours, both individually and institutionally, yields a richer political and economic context for addressing climate-related migration.

Other international frameworks – notably CEDAW, the Beijing Platform for Action, the multilateral environmental agreements, the Sendai Framework for Disaster Risk Reduction, and the Sustainable Development Goals – are also useful for addressing climate change impacts and climate change-related migration. Each of these frameworks can play an important role in highlighting and guiding action on climate change, whether from a gendered perspective, an environmental perspective, or a development perspective. However, WPS is uniquely placed to address climate change-related migration because it bridges and integrates two key dynamics: security and gender. Further, WPS is situated in the United Nations Security Council, a governance body with significant normative and policy power. International migration frameworks, national immigration policy and humanitarian resources are largely unprepared for climate change-related migration flows, creating the significant potential for future humanitarian challenges and requiring adjustments in national security apparatuses and border management processes. WPS' entrenchment in the Security Council provides an opportunity to integrate both a climate and gender-oriented response to these impending challenges.

The WPS agenda is imperfect, however, and its location within the Security Council creates obstacles for implementation even as it provides a strategic advantage. The agenda has been critiqued for being too state-centric, lacking accountability for implementation, and being heteronormative. The framework does not exist in a vacuum; it is not the only framework needed to address climate change and climate change-related migration. However, it is a key framework situated in the heart of security policy in the international community. This makes the WPS agenda a critical structure for addressing an issue as broad and complex as climate change, climate change-related migration, and associated gendered consequences.

Expanding the scope of the WPS agenda to include climate change and climate change-related migration means building upon the work the field has already done in gendered security analysis and advocating for women's leadership at the highest levels of decision making. Debate and discussion on these issues is inevitable given the rapid progression of climate change. WPS research and analysis must be at the forefront of the conversation to build in gender-responsive approaches from the beginning.

Notes

[1] Predictions of future climate-related migration are highly contested and subject to many methodological challenges. There is no universal or even common definition of climate-related migration; many of the displacements occur intra-nationally, which can be harder to track than international movements; and estimates often do not account well for future demographic changes or adaption and mitigation strategies (Gemenne, 2001). An estimate by Myers that climate change will cause up to an additional 200 million environmental refugees by 2050 has become a widely accepted figure, but its basis has been questioned (Myers, 2002).

[2] The global women's rights agenda has a foundation in the 1945 United Nations Charter, 1948 Universal Declaration of Human Rights, 1966 International Covenant on Civil and Political Rights, 1984 International Convention against Torture and Other Cruel, Inhuman, or Degrading Treatment or Punishment and took form explicitly with the 1979 Convention on the Elimination of All Forms of Discrimination against Women, 1995 Beijing Platform for Action, and the Women, Peace and Security suite of resolutions. In 2009, CEDAW (Committee

on the Elimination of Discrimination Against Women) released a statement about the importance of including gender in climate change frameworks, and the Beijing Platform for Action includes a focus on women and the environment, addressing how women are affected by climate change and how women's voices should be included in environmental planning and management. However, these frameworks are the exception rather than the rule.

3   In this article, refugee law is considered to comprise the 1951 Convention Relating to the Status of Refugees, 1967 Protocol Relating to the Status of Refugees, 1969 Organization of African Unity Convention Governing the Specific Aspects of Refugee Problems in Africa, and 1984 Cartagena Declaration on Refugees.

References

Abebe, M.A. (2014–2015) 'Climate change, gender inequality and migration in East Africa', *Washington Journal of Environmental Law and Policy*, 4(1): 104–140.

Azad, A.K. et al (2013) 'Flood-induced vulnerabilities and problems encountered by women in Northern Bangladesh', *Journal of Disaster Risk Science*, 4: 191–193.

Black, R. et al (2011) 'The effect of environmental change on human migration', *Global Environmental Change*, 21, Supplement I (0): 3–11.

Bhatta, G.D. et al (2015) 'Climate-induced migration in South Asia: migration decisions and the gender dimensions of adverse climatic events', *Journal of Rural and Community Development*, 10(4): 1–23.

Boano, C., Zetter, R. and Morris, T. (2008) *Forced Migration Policy Briefing 1. Environmentally Displaced People: Understanding the Linkages between Environmental Change, Livelihoods and Forced Migration*, Oxford: University of Oxford, Refugee Studies Centre.

Britton, N. (1986) 'Developing an understanding of disaster', *Journal of Sociology*, 22(2): 254–271.

Brown, O. (2007) *Climate Change and Forced Migration: Observations, Projections and Implications*, New York: United Nations Development Programme.

Burkett, M. (2011) 'The nation ex-situ: on climate change, deterritorialized nationhood and the post-climate era', *Climate Law*, 2: 345–374.

Campbell et al (2007) *The Age of Consequences: The Foreign Policy and National Security Implications of Global Climate Change*, Washington, DC: Center for Strategic and International Studies.

Chindarkar, N. (2012) 'Gender and climate change-induced migration: proposing a framework for analysis', *Environmental Research Letters*, 7(2): 1–7.

Coniglio, N. and Pesce, G. (2015) 'Climate variability and international migration: an empirical analysis', *Environmental and Development Economics*, 20(4): 434–468.

Curran, S.R. and Meijer-Irons, J. (2014) 'Climate variability, land ownership and migration: evidence from Thailand about gender impacts', *Washington Journal of Environmental Law and Policy*, 4(1): 37–74.

Dankelman, I. (2009) 'Human security, climate change and women', *UN Chronicle*, XLVI (3 and 4).

Djoudi, H., Brockhaus, M. and Locatelli, B. (2013) 'Once there was a lake: vulnerability to environmental changes to northern Mali', *Regional Environmental Change*, 13(3): 493–508.

Eastin, J. (2018) 'Climate change and gender equality in developing states', *World Development*, 107: 289–305.

Environmental Justice Foundation (2014) *Falling Through the Cracks: A Briefing on Climate Change, Displacement and International Governance Frameworks*, London: Environmental Justice Foundation.

Gemenne, F. (2001) 'Why the numbers don't add up: a review of estimates and predictions of people displaced by environmental change', *Global Environmental Change*, 21: 41–49.

Ghosh, A.K., Banerjee, S. and Naaz, F. (2018) 'Adapting to climate change-induced migration: women in Indian Bengal Delta', *Economic and Political Weekly*, 53(17): 63–69.

Ginetti, J. (2015) *Disaster-Related Displacement Risk: Measuring the Risk and Addressing its Drivers*, Geneva: Internal Displacement Monitoring Centre.

Graham, J.P., Hirai, M. and Kim, S.-S. (2016) 'An analysis of water collection labor among women and children in 24 sub-Saharan African countries', *PLoS One*, 11(6): 1–14.

Gray, C. and Mueller, V. (2012) 'Drought and population mobility in rural Ethiopia', *World Development*, 40(1): 134–145.

Gururaja, S. (2000) 'Gender dimensions of displacement', *Forced Migration Review*, 9: 13–6.

Harris, K., Keen, D. and Mitchell, T. (2013) *When Disasters and Conflicts Collide: Improving Links Between Disaster Resilience and Conflict Prevention*, London: Overseas Development Institute.

IPCC (Intergovernmental Panel on Climate Change) (2001) *Climate Change 2001: Impacts, Adaptation and Vulnerability, Contribution of Working Group II to the Third Assessment Report of the Intergovernmental Panel on Climate Change*, Cambridge: Cambridge University Press.

International Organization for Migration (2007) *Discussion Note: Migration and the Environment*, Geneva: International Organization for Migration.

Islam, M.R. and Shamsuddoha, M. (2017) 'Socioeconomic consequences of climate induced human displacement and migration in Bangladesh', *International Sociology*, 32(3): 277–298.

Kellett, J. and Sparks, D. (2012) *Disaster Risk Reduction: Spending Where It Should Count, Global Humanitarian Assistance*, Bristol: Development Initiatives.

Kumasi, T.C., Obiri-Danso, K. and Antwi-Agyei, P. (2017) 'Smallholder farmers' climate change adaptation practices in the region of Ghana', *Environment Development and Sustainability*, 1–27.

Kweku Assan, J. and Rosenfeld, T. (2012) 'Environmentally induced migration, vulnerability and human security: consensus, controversies and conceptual gaps for policy analysis', *Journal of International Development*, 24(8): 1046–1057.

Light, S. (2014) 'Valuing national security: climate change, the military, and society', *UCLA Law Review*, 61: 1772–1812.

Martin, S. (2013) *Environmental Change and Migration: What Do We Know?*, Washington, DC: Migration Policy Institute.

Massey, D.S., Axinn, W.G. and Ghimire, D.J. (2010) 'Environmental change and out-migration: evidence from Nepal', *Population and Environment*, 32(2): 109–136.

McMichael, C., Barnett, J. and McMichael, A.J. (2012) 'An ill wind? Climate change, migration, and health', *Environmental Health Perspectives*, 120(5): 646–654.

Myers, N. (2002) 'Environmental refugees: a growing phenomenon of the 21st century', *Philosophical Transactions of the Royal Society of London Series B, Biological Sciences*, 357(142): 609–613.

Neumayer, E. and Plümper, T. (2007) 'The gendered nature of natural disasters: the impact of catastrophic events on the gender gap in life expectancy, 1981–2002', *Annals of the Association of American Geographers*, 97(3): 551–566.

Shah, P.K. (2006) 'Assisting and empowering women facing natural disasters: drawing from Security Council Resolution 1325', *Columbia Journal of Gender and Law*, 15(3).

Skinner, E. (2011) *Gender and Climate Change Overview Report*, Brighton: BRIDGE, Institute of Development Studies.

Steady, F.C. (2014) 'Women, climate change and liberation in Africa', *Race, Gender and Class*, 21(1/2): 312–333.

Sugden, F. et al (2014) 'Agrarian stress and climate change in the Eastern Gangetic Plains: gendered vulnerability in a stratified social formation', *Global Environmental Change*, 29: 258–269.

Tacoli, C. (2009) 'Crisis or adaptation? Migration and climate change in a context of high mobility', *Environment and Urbanization*, 21(2): 513–525.

Tiwari, P.C. and Joshi, B. (2015) 'Climate change and rural out-migration in Himalaya', *Change Adaptation Socioecological Systems*, 2(1): 8–25.

United Nations and Canada (1992) *United Nations Framework Convention on Climate Change*, New York: United Nations General Assembly.

United Nations Environment Programme et al (2013) *Women and Natural Resources: Unlocking the Peacebuilding Potential*, Nairobi and New York: UNEP, United Nations Entity for Gender Equality and the Empowerment of Women, United Nations Peacebuilding Support Office, and United Nations Development Programme.

The World Bank (2013) *Turn Down the Heat: Climate Extremes, Regional Impacts, and the Case for Resilience*, Washington, DC: World Bank and Potsdam Institute for Climate Impact Research and Climate Analytics.

World Health Organization (2014) *Gender, Climate and Health*, Geneva: World Health Organization.

World Health Organization and United Nations Children's Fund (2017) *Progress on Drinking Water, Sanitation, and Hygiene: 2017 Update and SDG Baselines*, Geneva: World Health Organization and United Nations Children's Fund.

Yamamoto, L. and Esteban, M. (2011) *Atoll Island States and Climate Change: Sovereignty Implications*, Tokyo: United Nations University Institute for the Advanced Study of Sustainability.

14

Feminist Challenges to the Co-optation of WPS: A Conversation with Joy Onyesoh and Madeleine Rees

Joy Onyesoh, Madeleine Rees and Catia Cecilia Confortini

The Women's International League for Peace and Freedom (WILPF) spearheaded women's efforts leading to the passage of UNSCR 1325 in October 2000. Founded in 1915 initially as a women's committee to stop the First World War, WILPF is now the longest-operating international women's peace organization in the world. Its involvement with the WPS agenda was premised on its identity as a feminist peace organization. As such, its ultimate goal has always been the elimination of war itself or, short of that, at least the establishment of gender-attentive systems for the just and nonviolent management of conflicts.

Like the other women's organizations that together worked to make UNSCR 1325 happen – and that coordinated themselves into the NGO Working Group on WPS to lobby the Security Council – WILPF was under no illusion about women's innate peacefulness. Rather, the organization insisted that women's experiences and voices, as well as feminist analysis, be included when attempting to counter violent conflict – from prevention, to post-conflict transitions, to peace processes – and in all locations where violence created situations of insecurity. This inclusion represented, in WILPF's view, a necessary step to achieve lasting peace, an ideal that they refer to as feminist peace (WILPF, 2018).

Once the resolution passed, WILPF started to work towards implementation. In parallel to WILPF's and other organizations' efforts, feminist scholars have analysed and critiqued the WPS agenda. Based on analyses of the process leading to the passing of UNSCR 1325; the language of the different WPS resolutions; and experiences with the implementation of WPS agenda (for example, Cohn et al, 2004; Cohn, 2008; Basu, 2016; Hagen, 2016; Kirby and Shepherd, 2016; Duncanson, 2019), they have advanced three kinds of critiques: first, they have found fault in WPS' subordination of women's antimilitarist agenda to states' security agenda; second, they have criticized how WPS understands women and gender as synonyms; and, third, they have objected to a focus on liberal rights often adopted in its implementation.

In this chapter, Madeleine Rees and Joy Onyesoh – WILPF Secretary General and International President of WILPF respectively – reflect on their first-hand experience of feminist advocacy on WPS over almost two decades, drawing particularly on WILPF's work in Nigeria and transnationally. They agree that in the implementation of WPS feminist analysis as a whole has been side-stepped in favour of an agenda dominated and co-opted by states. Moreover, they see gender as a contested terrain for feminists as well: identity labels intertwined with notions of liberal rights are limited in their transnational utility, and political strategies in this regard need to be contextualized. The weakness of a state-centric framework is made apparent, for example, when dealing with cyber security issues. At the same time, Rees and Onyesoh recognize the necessity of engaging in their day-to-day work with the system as it is, while not letting go of the aspirational goal of feminist peace.

Catia C. Confortini (CCC):   Joy, you were the President of the Nigerian Section of WILPF for many years, before being elected International President at WILPF's 2018 Congress in Ghana. In this capacity, you have been at the forefront of WPS efforts in Nigeria. Could you describe the Nigerian process for the implementation of the WPS agenda?

Joy Onyesoh (JO):   In Nigeria, the structured framework for WPS implementation is primarily the National Action Plan (NAP), which is actually called the 'National Action Plan for UNSCR 1325 and Related Resolutions'. We also have women doing a lot on the ground, however. The Federal Ministry of Women Affairs and Social Development and Nigerian civil society organizations

(CSOs) decided to accept that name instead of 'NAP on WPS' because we were worried that the plan would get marginalized as a women's thing, and we wanted to be sure that other state institutions would see the NAP implementation as part of their responsibilities.

The focal institution responsible for the NAP is the Federal Ministry of Women Affairs and Social Development, in collaboration with civil society. The process of NAP design was started in 2010 with advocacy and engagement with the Ministry by key WPS-focused organizations. The process was eventually driven by the Ministry with support from the Nigeria Stability and Reconciliation Program, which is an initiative of the UK government and UN Women Nigeria, and it led to what in the country is referred to as the 'first generation' NAP. This was launched in 2013. The process to get there, however, was top-down, with few, small consultations with civil society organisations. The resultant document was a very good first attempt and formed the building block for future work; but the dissemination process was not robust, and it led to low awareness. Engagement with the NAP was therefore lukewarm: most of the stakeholders didn't understand why they had to engage with it.

The NAP had a lifespan of three years, so, in early 2017, we started the process for updating it. During the consultations for the review, we found that very few stakeholders knew about it. For instance, when we held the South East regional consultations in 2017, out of the 40 people in attendance, only three had seen the NAP or heard about it. We realized that if you had a document which existed in name and in principle, but no one knew about it in terms of engaging with it – well, you can imagine what the implementation looked like. Just having it sit at the Federal Ministry of Women Affairs made implementation very difficult. It was basically civil society organisations like WILPF, West Africa Network for Peacebuilding (WANEP), and a handful of others that had a grip on the resolution. For WILPF it was what I'll call our 'bible' in Nigeria. We used that to do a lot of programmes on the ground and that enhanced our background and experience for supporting the second

NAP. We realized, through our work with this first NAP, that community women couldn't really engage in the WPS framework because they didn't understand how to adapt it and felt that it didn't adequately capture the realities on the ground.

It is worth mentioning that at the time of the first NAP, we didn't have a lot of communal crises in Nigeria, only very few boundary issues. By 2014, 2015 and 2016, a number of security issues had emerged that were not there when the first NAP was being designed. These issues became a menace in society: in the case of Boko Haram, of course, the crisis spiralled out of control. The killer herdsmen in Plateau State became a national crisis, not only limited to the most central parts of Nigeria but across other regions as well. And there are a number of crises now that make our communities unsafe. So we felt that the NAP had to be updated to address these issues.

During the course of the consultative process, which happened in six geopolitical zones of the country, the different stakeholders – and these included government agencies, civil society and religious bodies – all agreed that it was important to have not just the national plan, but also to have zonal action plans, state action plans, and then local government action plans. The three different tiers of the government (federal, state and local) could adapt the action plan to suit the different contexts and realities of women and other stakeholders at that level. In this way the NAP would have more meaning, and it would be easier to engage with at that level. One of the key things about the different levels of localizing the plan is that each plan would link directly to government projects on that thematic area. That is how the current 'second generation' NAP is structured.

This new NAP was launched in May 2017 and it now has these different tiers corresponding to the Nigerian government structure. Basically, I think that awareness should have been built before starting the process of drafting even the first NAP, but instead the NAP process generated the awareness, and as a consequence we now have a more robust NAP. Having it work at these different levels means that we have a lot more government institutions informed about the NAP, and that a lot of people will get involved at different levels as well.

Madeleine Rees (MR):   Just listening to what you're saying now, it seems from an outside perspective that the whole NAP process, from the beginning, was really very helpful for civil society, to actually get to organize, to consult, to make their positions clear, and then to have an entry point into the various places within the state where you wanted to have an impact. But where was the buy-in from the state?

JO: The state facilitated the spaces for all this to happen. They got funding from UN Women, they went ahead and put together the document. They ran trainings. They put together the monitoring and evaluation team, and then a national team for coordinating the implementation at the different levels. They now receive reports from the different states which then go to the federal level. So all the reports from the local government, from the states, and from the different non–governmental organizations go to the Federal Ministry of Women Affairs. Civil society groups are also required to submit a yearly report of what we have done.

    The reports then inform the work plans of various ministries as well as civil society's work plans. Increasingly we have seen that many of the groups working on the WPS agenda actually use the NAP in designing their projects. For example, each year the Federal Ministry of Women Affairs comes up with projects they want to run on WPS on a number of thematic areas. The NAP has the responsibility apportioned to other ministries and civil society organisations as well as traditional leaders. So each stakeholder is looking at what the NAP is saying that they are supposed to be doing, and then thinking through how they can do it.

MR: All of this sounds good, but then the security situation all over Nigeria, as evidenced by the last elections, has clearly gone in the wrong direction, despite all this apparent commitment to a WPS agenda.

JO: Now the thing is, the Federal Ministry of Women Affairs is a government institution, as we know. Their funding comes from the government in power. So we have a beautiful process spelled out, people appointed into these positions, mechanisms for reporting and feedback. But then in real terms, it is not working the way it's supposed to, because the primary institution for driving this is a political entity, whose leadership is appointed from the ruling political party. So when the ruling political party or the government have no demonstrable commitment to women, it limits what the Federal Ministry of Women Affairs can do. If you look at the current appointments we have in Nigeria, we lost a lot of women's representation, not just in elected positions, but even in appointed positions. In terms of implementing what the broader government institutions are supposed to do, there is no political will to do that.

CCC: So, if I hear you correctly, Joy, it seems that the process for the first National Action Plan was faulty. It was not broadly consultative. Then the women's organizations stepped in. You had gained experience and collective power in the process of implementing the first NAP. You had coordinated with each other. You were able to influence the government into holding broader consultations and have a good process toward the second NAP. Now you have all those structures put in place, and all nominally works, but it's very superficial, there's no actual commitment on the part of the ruling party. And so this lack of political will is one of the contributing factors toward the degeneration of the political situation in the country.

MR: I was just going to say that this is very symptomatic, I think, of this idea of the co-optation of the agenda by the state. What we have in almost every context is exactly what Joy describes. Women's groups and women activists organizing, clutching onto this WPS agenda as a lifeline to try to make sure that we get that participation that we've been promised. We spend all our time organizing and talking to each other in order to get something into what is almost always the Ministry of Gender or the Ministry of Women, either equally marginalized. And the structures of government themselves do not enable us to break in and make the changes. So it's a very nice little bubble that they've created for us. All this activism, and then all this great enthusiasm for change, and we think it's going to crack it, and no, because the structure itself hasn't allowed us to break through that membrane and get in there with enough warm bodies and feminist thinking behind us to make the difference. And that's replicated not just in individual countries, but in the overall structures within the UN system, which gave us the resolutions in the first place.

CCC: But let me play the devil's advocate a little bit here. What if the problem is not government structures but just political will? What if we leave the structures like they are, we put a bunch of women in government, women committed to WPS even, and everything works well?

MR: I think Joy's already answered that one. Basically, all governmental structures are entirely patriarchal. They may have women within them, but they have to toe a particular line in order to be in power. You don't get to be in a political party and secure a feminist agenda. Even if you're the Foreign Minister of Sweden, you may try, but even then, it doesn't work as one might hope. So, basically, you've got women having to go into systems where structures of power are exactly the same and remain unchanged – or they can at best be mitigated. These structures are so inhospitable that they either force feminists out or they force them to moderate their politics. The impact is that we don't get that critical mass of feminists in there who could make a difference. Essentially if you look at situations within the political party system, within government systems, within the UN system, the women who've gone through them and are now in positions of power haven't necessarily done what we would need them to do, if we are going to make these fundamental changes in the political economies of those institutions.

We can see this in the way that the WPS agenda went off course from the very beginning when states refused to contemplate WILPF's advocacy around having dis-armament included in UNSCR 1325. Clearly, WILPF was pushing for moving away from a militarized concept of security to human security and real, sustainable peace. So taking out those essential elements left the option of co-optation available for states – they could use the parts in WPS that we *did* want in order to bring us into what *they* wanted. And I think the major issues you see over time are related: for example, the emphasis on counting the number of women in different fora, whether it be in parliament, whether it be in governance structures. We're going to count them just as warm bodies and not ask about substance. And then there is the really pernicious one, the big push to have women in the military, which is just basically militarizing women. We congratulate South Africa for having increased its percentage of women in its forces to more than 30 percent. I think that's the sort of thing that has happened; this focus has made us chase the wrong things and have the wrong conversations.

That is also related to the idea of having NAPs. There are good reasons to help us organize around NAPs, but then – as in the case of Nigeria and the United Kingdom, Ukraine, Bosnia – you do all that work on a NAP, and frequently it's only dealing with the security sector, like in Bosnia. Or the NAP starts at the border of your country so it's somebody else's problem. So, for example, Britain will only deal with you 'poor people over there' who have problems with conflict, instead of showing that there is a continuum that connects to the domestic policies of that country that need to be fixed from a WPS perspective. Because of the wording and language of the WPS agenda, that has not happened. And neither do most NAPs cite sufficiently international legal obligations, so that all the gains that have been won through feminists slogging away with human rights treaty bodies, and with international criminal tribunals, and human rights mechanisms more broadly, have not really been brought fully into the WPS agenda to get the sort of equality that we want. It's always at best a marginalized affair, as Joy rightly pointed out, located often in the ministry of women, and so WPS never gets into the mainstream. So with all of that in play, we have a WPS agenda which is a graft-on to an existing structure, and it's very difficult to make it make a difference.

CCC: What would be the right structure? What would be a different way to implement WPS, a more feminist way?

MR: For us, I think that the most obvious one I would want us to be advocating for is to restructure the WPS agenda so that it impacts properly on all aspects of the

United Nations system. We've been working very hard on that and trying to make WPS directly implicated, for example, in the work of the human rights treaty bodies and the Universal Periodic Review.[1] It's hardly the scariest accountability mechanism for states but at least it's a mechanism for actually monitoring state compliance with human rights, and where civil society can organize in order to make sure that what we need in WPS is included.

For example, when I referenced the domestic policy of states, I meant that we need to look at situations in countries to assess levels of violence against women, discrimination in the provision of services, ownership, employment and so on. Austerity has had appalling consequences, particularly for women. No western state is immune. Wherever you have neoliberal policies, they affect women in a hugely negative and disproportionate way. So if a WPS agenda started in a country, and we did a political economy analysis from a gender perspective and saw exactly what women are doing in terms of how much access to rights they have, how much power and influence they exert within the household, within the community, within the education system, within the governance system, within the economic system, and what are the obstacles they're facing in being able to do that, then we would understand what real security and insecurity look like. Because if you have food insecurity, job insecurity, health insecurity, a WPS agenda in its militarized form has no resonance for you whatsoever. And unless we address those things, those fundamental things, then we don't have the beginnings of a WPS discussion in a country, let alone our efforts to create a movement which needs much greater equality in real peace and security internationally.

CCC: What I think you're saying here, Madeleine, is that WPS has been understood as relating to countries 'in conflict', as defined by a system that is very patriarchal and imperialist — and the two are related — and the system doesn't think that countries like the UK or the US are 'in conflict' because there is not a 'war' or 'conflict' in the way that UN defines 'war' or 'conflict'. Whereas you are saying that a feminist view of war and conflict would take into consideration the experience of women trans-nationally. When Hillary Clinton was Secretary of State and was drafting the US NAP in 2011, the US Section of WILPF ran a number of consultations with people at the State Department. The civil society organisations that participated in the process asked for an approach to UNSCR 1325 implementation that would involve all levels of the executive and that would consider women's experiences of violence domestically as well as outside the US. They asked that the NAP consider in particular how militarism and militarization affect women migrants, asylum seekers, refugees; how environmental degradation is linked to violence, including community and family violence, and so on. In other words, they wanted a 'whole government' approach to WPS and a 'greater investment in peace at home and abroad'. But none of this was taken on in the US NAP.

MR: Yes, we need to reframe the discussion, and the WPS agenda at the Security Council as it exists now does not do that. You've got a million fault lines in your so-called democracies where there's violence. And if you extrapolate from violence at home, it morphs and spreads into public spaces and in our overall way of being. You're not talking about a peaceful society if you're not talking about secure communities. You're talking about massive insecurity, particularly for women, but not exclusively for women. And the insecurity is differently experienced by men and women. We need to reframe it so that we look at security differently, so that we understand where violence comes from, who uses it, in what circumstances they use it, against whom they use it, and why it is used. But we're not joining all the dots together and really making a decent job of explaining it and therefore addressing it.

And we need to better understand gender and how we do our analysis as to differential impact, which means identifying what harms are being perpetrated and therefore surfacing what needs to be done to address and redress those harms so as to ensure that everybody has the right to participate on the basis of equality. For instance, the whole issue of LGBTQI ultimately shouldn't be isolated as a category on its own. Such a separation reinforces the idea that heterosexuality is the norm and we don't capture the essence of gender and sexuality. That said, in the current legal and cultural climate we do need to surface such discrimination as an issue that must be dealt with. But I also think that gender has to be seen an integral part of everybody's lives; we all have multiple and changing, fluid identities. I have a woman as a partner therefore I have an identity as a lesbian, I also have one as a woman, mother, a white person and a Brit, and many more. But we tend to fix people with one category and respond to them in that category rather than understanding the fluidity of what makes us who we are. It is difficult to express and to recognize as a matter of law.

CCC: What would that mean in practice for the WPS agenda: the recognition of men and boys as part of peacebuilding, the integration of LGBTQI issues into the agenda?

MR: I think we have to just be very clear that the WPS agenda was there to try to bring women into an existing structure which is very definitely about patriarchy. So bringing men and boys into the WPS agenda would, at first, appear to undermine the purpose, which was almost like affirmative action – a temporary measure to get women into all processes concerned with war, security and peace and to make sure women remain in them. We still need the emphasis on *women*, peace and security. But we also have to be intelligent about how we understand the gender relations that are within that.

The exclusion of references to men is one of the big arguments against the WPS resolutions: that they have discriminated against men and boys in the recognition of their suffering of sexual violence and their rights to have support and appropriate care afterwards.[2] That is an untruth, because I think nobody who works on WPS is saying, 'we don't care if men are raped'. Nobody says that. Basically, we have to understand that within the WPS agenda, what we're looking for is gender-sensitive and appropriate investigation, prosecution frameworks and accountability mechanisms with full application, access to healthcare and reparation for men as well as for women. And that means that what we're talking about is legal systems, and recognizing that there is a gendered difference to what legal systems now do. Basically, all legal systems are based on patriarchal perspectives, they discriminate against women rather than against men.

The surfacing of sexual violence against men has shown that the aftercare may not be there for men and this has to be addressed. So too must the actual process of prosecution which in domestic jurisdictions is pretty hideous for most women to participate in and that domestic practice has influenced international tribunals on many occasions. If we look at the ad hoc tribunals for the former Yugoslavia and Rwanda, or what happened at the ICC, there is little protection for women going forward. Deeply embedded in patriarchal belief is the idea that rape is the woman's fault, that she is somehow a loose woman, that she provoked, she enticed, she was in a place she should not have been. The justifications and excuses are legion, and are all aimed at taking the focus off the male perpetrator. It's still in that mindset of those who are adjudicating, like it or not, because it's just there. It's part of the cultural upbringing we've all been subjected to. Men don't suffer from that during the course of their testimonies. They don't get asked if they consented, nor the details of penetration or insertion of bodily parts. It's never happened.

What we need to do is to recognize that sexual violence is a particular form of violence which is perpetrated in armed conflict to men, women, boys and girls. How it's done is biologically determined. Whatever is going to hurt the most. The consequences are gendered. For example, in areas and places where homosexuality is illegal, men can't come forward if they've been raped for fear of being prosecuted and persecuted for homosexuality. So it's all of those things we have to look at and that's the role within the WPS agenda that law can and must play. And there's language going around at the moment about ensuring that there is the appropriate law and the appropriate care for men and boys, but recognizing that sexual violence is used disproportionately against women in armed conflict. That's part of this continuum of violence we keep on talking about. You know, it's not just in armed conflict. It starts way before armed conflict. It manifests during armed conflict and it manifests increasingly in terms of domestic violence after conflict. So for women, even though the peace deal may be signed, the conflict, the insecurity and the violence continue.

CCC: What you're talking about here is really a gender-sensitive approach to peace and security. But don't you think that by calling it *women*, peace and security, we undercut that gender lens and made it possible for states to marginalize that agenda into the women's ministries, like you and Joy said before?

MR: Yes. I think that's exactly right. And I think the reason for that is because we don't get gender. We don't understand what it is. So it's been reduced to a binary of basically men and boys versus girls and women. So it's those two. It's according to supposed biological sex. And now we have the United States trying to say there's no such thing as gender anyway. We have to be way more subtle than the binary that's been created. I'd like to see what we have now, the WPS agenda, as affirmative action, as I said earlier. As a matter of law, you've got to have your quotas. You've got to get your women in there. But, as I said, I remain unconvinced that just putting women into existing structures is going to change things. That is not enough. We absolutely have to do better in getting women into the existing structures as a matter of basic equality, but we cannot assume that merely adding women will change the system. Women are as vulnerable to co-optation, we enjoy power as much as men. What we need to do is to really look at what gender is and how it works. This would lead to a reframing of the approach to security, bringing all of us into a different perspective on where we are in relation to the instrumentalization of gender roles and relations and enabling us to take on patriarchy and its inimical effect on all of us.

JO: I think that calling it 'gender' or 'women' depends on the context. Because in Nigeria, saying that we want to look at it from a gender perspective, it would still end up at the Federal Ministry of Women Affairs. So most things that involve a gender framework nationally are subsumed under the Federal Ministry of Women Affairs and Social Development. There is even an apathy for the word 'gender' right now. So it's safer to use the word 'women' than to use the word 'gender'. And that is part of the challenges we had when trying to find a name for the NAP. We couldn't use 'women'. We couldn't use 'gender'. So we ended up with National Action Plan on UNSCR 1325 and Related Resolutions. I think the nomenclature is important, but at the same time, I think that the substance is more important. So although we call it the 'WPS agenda', it is the substantive issues we are engaging with that make the difference. It's about engaging with the dynamic relationships and the power structures we have at the different levels of society to enact a transformative process.

MR: Yes. Because what we've gained through the WPS agenda – and there has been progress, despite the problems discussed above – is now under threat, not just from the very obvious failure to apply the Arms Trade Treaty effectively, the failure to regulate illicit arms trade, the failure to recognize the weaponization of technology more broadly. But another, more subtle, threat is now coming from technology and social media as means of control. For example, the Saudi Arabian government app *Absher* allows a man to track female family members (wives, daughters, any female 'dependent') so that, basically, he knows where she is at all times, and he gives permission for so many hours out, distance travelled, and so on. Christine Chinkin and I have concluded that it is a form of control and essentially a *de facto* weapon, designed to produce a constant state of fear. And for Google, who hosts it, to say that it doesn't violate the terms and conditions of the company is absolutely outrageous.

More to the point, it shows just how patriarchy works: Saudi Arabia has built an apartheid state based predominantly on gender, which it needs to sustain the rulers in power. The state violence and human rights violations perpetrated against LGBTQI people and women, as well as those who stand up for human rights, is recognized internationally as appalling. But the royal family sits on an oil lake which we in the global North want, so we arm them, so that we can keep the oil lake safe and keep trading with them, and allow them to be hegemonic in the region – and make a lot of money off it on the side – while pretending we care about human rights and make a few bleating comments now and then. And then the tech company, Google, is quite happy to sustain that system in place by supporting the gender apartheid. And they're making money off it. This shows exactly how the patriarchal system works, the system we have to crack: we need to start looking at the way in which so-called simple things like apps can be weaponized. We need as well to look at the role of social media in contributing to violent conflict. This is a whole new dimension of the security part of women, peace and security that we're just not paying sufficient attention to. We've really got to start looking at how virtual space can be regulated within the framework of WPS.

JO: In Nigeria it's more about the social media space. We've seen an increase in cyber violence in the last few years, and it's getting very horrific. We have young men, older men, men of all categories who will rape a woman and then post it on social media as a means of shaming her, and it will go viral. Women commit violence on other women and take to the media space to brag about it. Social media has become a space of fear for many people. Then the government is also using social media to track those who are very active in opposition to the government and those who are very active on women's rights issues. So it's very important that even when we talk about WPS, we expand it to include this kind of discussion. It brings up the need for us as women human rights defenders and peacebuilders to protect ourselves from these new threats. Because what we do is captured by the media in new ways and it's much easier to be tracked. We don't even know what could happen to us.

And it's not only the Nigerian context. I believe that it is now a global issue, that seems to be spreading rapidly. So we need to start looking at how the WPS agenda can be brought in to address this new source of insecurity. We should ask ourselves who we need to bring to the table. How can we start interacting and engaging with certain people who have this kind of expertise in the field, so that when we're talking about security, we're also looking at cyber security and communication security?

CCC: It seems to me that the question of apps and social media poses quite a challenge for the WPS agenda as it is formulated and implemented now. Because even if WPS, like you said, has been co-opted by the state, and embedded in these existing mechanisms of state security, social media is defying any state regulation and the state system. But at the same time, maybe that's the opportunity for designing something that is outside the state.

MR: Well I'm not a 'techy' person, as you well know. But if, for example, we had language in a Security Council resolution which recognized the abuse of social media and certain apps, in particular to create situations of insecurity for women – harass them, intimidate them, and so on – that would open the door for our WPS advocacy in human rights fora. Then every time we had, say, Nigeria coming up for review by the Treaty Bodies or under the Universal Periodic Review, we could document the ways in which social media are contributing to violations. When Nigeria is reporting, for example, Joy could draw attention to the way in which social media are being abused by the government, by political actors, by armed militias, in order to target, harass, intimidate, track and terrorize women human rights defenders. And then that's when you can kickstart a serious discussion around regulation of the space. We would hope that individual member states would come up with creative solutions.

CCC: But that's still an approach that is dominated by a state system – one that, by what you say, is complicit with tech giants to create women's insecurity.

MR: Well, unfortunately we still have to operate within it. But the state system isn't what it was 20 years ago, even, because now it's been hijacked by corporations, tech giants included. We know all of that. But at the moment, the way the international legal system works is that states still have the responsibility for human rights protection, and they are the ones responsible for regulating peace and security. While it's great to think we can organize outside, and we do, of course we do, at some point, there has to be a connection with the state so that we can actually get appropriate reaction and response to the sorts of demands that we're making.

CCC: So where do we see hope now? Perhaps we should go back to Nigeria. Have there been some lessons or positive and unintended consequences, that would lead you to be maybe optimistic about the future of WPS in Nigeria?

JO: I think, for one, the networking that has happened as a result of the process of the NAP is a very positive one, because it has brought a lot more women-focused organizations into the WPS agenda process, and it has actually strengthened the bond across so many civil society groups. We have a lot of strategic partnerships being built, and a lot of engagement at the civil society level. Yes, there is the challenge that Madeleine describes, and we also realized that there can be no meaningful participation in WPS if we don't have enough women in the political process itself. That goes into tackling violent extremism as well: there needs to be a lot of social, political and economic infrastructure and political will by the government to support the process. Because women cannot break the barriers to their substantive participation and exclusions without that infrastructure and support.

During the first NAP implementation process, we were not connecting mainstream political participation in the legislative and executive structures and peace processes as much. Without participation at all levels of government, power structures will prevent women's meaningful participation in peace processes. These are rigid power structures, which we inherited from the colonial administration and which excluded women: we are talking about peace processes when there is not even participation in political structures. The Women's Situation Room created by WILPF Nigeria in this context is not only a governance project, but a concrete implementation of the WPS agenda. We established the project first to monitor the 2015 general, Governorship, and State House of Assemblies elections, and we are continuing to operate in different elections. But we do more than monitoring and observing. In the WPS agenda we talk about promoting participation and harnessing women as change agents, and that's what we really do in the Women's Situation Room: we train people in early warning and early response mechanisms. And we put women in formal decision-making positions. The project is in effect a grooming ground for women who want to enter formal political structures. This is because our understanding of a peace process is very broad and it includes every activity in daily life that allows women to participate fully in all areas of political life. When you resolve conflicts that would otherwise escalate, you raise awareness about zero tolerance for violence, you raise awareness about discrimination, promote early responses to conflicts, and show that people can go about their lives without fear, that's a peace process.

CCC: So what are the lessons that you think we should take, or you should take, to move forward? Do you see anything, any hope for moving forward?

JO: One of the areas where I see new opportunities open up is in mediation. Research suggests that we have less than 2% of women among mediators globally. I see the NAP as an opportunity for us to formally raise that number by increasing civil society's influence on government agencies to intentionally have that as one of the primary objectives of the pillars of the NAP. Then we will have female mediators across different levels, and we can actually push female mediators to participate in some of the regional dialogues which are now happening within Nigeria, in community dialogues, and even in states' dialogues, national dialogues, in national peace processes. I see that as an opportunity that has opened up.

CCC: But aren't female mediators also supported by states? What would prevent states from influencing that process to achieve their own ends, like they've done with WPS more broadly? Because there is government funding now behind the search for female mediators, and the trainings and all of that.

JO: Yes, the thing is, you cannot totally shut that door, we need to keep pushing and engaging until we get what we want. And I still think that the positive opportunities that this presents are greater than the negative implications. But it's also about accountability and credibility on both sides. Those of us working in CSOs and who have been doing that for a while do know organizations that are credible, and we also know individuals who are credible. In that respect, when we talk about female mediators, we can actually say, 'We know this person. We know what she has done on the ground. We can trust her to push the agenda forward' – or not!

MR: What Joy's describing is one of the new pathways. I really do believe this is possible. Because when governments talk about mediation it's always been about the need to have a female mediator at the highest level. And when you think of it, by the time you get to the highest level, it's already late. And what Joy's talking about, and I think that this is the growing understanding among the Nordic mediators and by the Commonwealth Mediators' Network, is that it doesn't start and end with just a list of very good women whom you could nominate to go and be a mediator. Not that they are ever called upon, of course, but they've been in existence for a long time and they have not been used. The aim now is to make this chain of mediation. Because if you think of it, who's doing the mediation, for example in Syria, on the ground all the time? It's been the women. From the very beginning, they've been negotiating prisoner release, getting children out of the prisons and out of harm's way, negotiating how to get humanitarian aid.

It's the same in every single conflict. It's the women on the ground who are trying to bring communities into states of semi-peacefulness in the middle of conflict and holding it all together and actually doing that mediation work between the various parties. And that experience is so vital, so important, but when you try to bring that experience into some sort of peace process, it's never recorded. As Bernadette Devlin[3] said, 'You know, it's not that women were written out of history, we were never written in.'

And yet the need is absolutely obvious, so you find out what is happening at the local community level. Who are the actors? What are the issues? And then through that mediation network, bringing people together to find solutions, which then can be taken to the next level. And it goes from the smaller communities into the broader communities into the regional, then up to and including those high-level mediators who must be taking that information and then giving back to those women on the ground what it is that's being said in that formal peace process. Now if we could do that, if we could actually start making that work, then we've got a whole new way of organizing women's participation in peace processes. With the Syria process where Lakhdar Brahimi (the second of the UN mediators), when asked about why he wasn't bringing women into the conversations, he just said 'It's complicated'. And then he did absolutely nothing to try and fix it. It was the system itself which was so rigid about just talking to men with power that it forgot that there's a context in which these men with power actually exist, and that's the context of what the female mediators are doing in the local communities. So that's what the new thinking is, that is real participation. And let's get rid of tracks 1, 2, 3, because it looks as if there's a hierarchy of importance, and there's not. Actually, all three have to happen simultaneously in order to make anything work, and it has to be holistic and integrated.

CCC: It seems to me that you're talking about a continuum of peace, or peacebuilding, as well as a continuum of violence – which is one of the great insights of feminist thought in this field.

MR: Absolutely. Whenever there is violence happening, there is always a peaceful opposition to that violence. And we don't look at it, we look at the violence and we document the violence and we report on the violence, and we talk about violent men all the time. And yet, what are the women doing? It's the *Pray the Devil Back to Hell* (Disney et al, 2008) scenario when journalists were walking over, stepping over women who were peacefully protesting to get to what the men were doing. And in fact, what brought the ending of that conflict? The women who were peacefully demonstrating. We miss it at our peril. Same in Northern Ireland. What were the women doing? Trying to rebuild trust, trying to address domestic violence, which is one of the biggest things present throughout the Troubles. And that goes back to my obsession, really, with structures, because issues that affect women and absolutely have a fundamental impact on peace are not written in. They're not seen. They're not recognized. They're not surfaced. If we did that, then we would probably have a very different approach to security, which I think would then lead to sustainable peace. And I'm talking about what women are doing, but I think we really have to look at it from a gender perspective, because not all men are these violent creatures.

One example can be seen again in *Pray the Devil Back to Hell*. When we showed it in Geneva for the first time, after it was finished, a woman, a Swiss diplomat, said out loud — she couldn't help herself — 'God, I'm so proud to be a woman.' And then a guy from UNICEF said, 'And I am so ashamed to be a man.' Abigail Disney, the producer of the film, was there, and she said, 'That's always the first reaction we get, but if you watch it again, don't just look at what the bad guys are doing.' She urged us to look at the ordinary shots of what people were doing and when. In those shots it was the ordinary men carrying the grandmas, looking out for people. And then there were the taxi drivers who were raising money so that the women could go and protest for peace. There was a whole infrastructure of male support for what women were trying to do, which is undocumented save for Abigail Disney's film, because the only snapshot we got from the media was of the violent men. We do not look at what the vast majority of men are doing and what the vast majority of men want. And I think we miss this at our peril.

I firmly believe in common humanity and solidarity. Because we see both, even if our existing systems have created ways in which division and othering seem to take precedence. Much is based on fear, the sort of fear which then demands a militarized security, and that is highly gendered. Power is surrendered to the state in what is often believed to be a democratic process — that is where there are democracies. In reality there are far greater influences on our governance than the individual with a ballot. This is our great challenge. In Sudan, they have just toppled a vicious dictatorship through peaceful protest: men and women together. Solidarity came from other states and the people within them. Change is possible when we want it enough and are not afraid to demand it. The state is supposed to be the people who are within it. The United Nations is supposed to be about the people. It was not conceived only as a state-centric organization. The Charter refers to 'We the people of these United Nations', not, 'We, the member states of the Security Council'. Imperfect as it is, the WPS agenda gives us the opportunity to assert that, to reframe security, to demilitarize it, to ensure inclusivity and bring the word 'Peace' to the forefront of the work that is undertaken in the Security Council. It is not a panacea, but it can be one of many paths to reclaiming our common humanity and ending violent conflict.

Notes

[1] The Universal Periodic Review (UPR) is a UN mechanism, through which UN member states – in turns of 14 every 4.5 years – report to the Human Rights Council their domestic human rights situation and the actions they have undertaken to improve it. The Human Rights Council then reviews each record and issues recommendations through an outcome document. The UN-UPR was established by Resolution 60/251 of the UN General Assembly on 15 March 2006.

[2] For example, Sivakumaran, 2010; Féron 2017.

[3] Irish Republican civil rights leader and former member of the UK Parliament for Mid Ulster.

References

Basu, S. (2016) 'Gender as national interest at the UN Security Council', *International Affairs*, 92(2): 255–273.

Cohn, C., Kinsella, H. and Gibbings, S. (2004) 'Women, peace and security: Resolution 1325', *International Feminist Journal of Politics*, 6(1): 130–140.

Disney, A.E., Hogan, P. and Reticker, G. (2008) 'Pray the devil back to hell', an episode from *Women, War & Peace*, New York and San Francisco, CA: THIRTEEN and Fork Films in association with WNET and ITVS.

Duncanson, C. (2019) 'Beyond liberal vs liberating: women's economic empowerment in the United Nations' Women, Peace and Security agenda', *International Feminist Journal of Politics*, 21(1): 111–130.

Féron, É. (2017) 'Wartime sexual violence against men: why so oblivious?', *European Review of International Studies*, 4(1): 60–74.

Hagen, J.J. (2016) 'Queering women, peace and security', *International Affairs*, 92(2): 313–332.

Kirby, P. and Shepherd, L.J. (2016) 'The futures past of the Women, Peace and Security agenda', *International Affairs*, 92(2): 373–392.

Sivakumaran, S. (2010) 'Lost in translation: UN responses to sexual violence against men and boys in situations of armed conflict', *International Review of the Red Cross*, 92(877): 259–277.

WILPF (Women's International League for Peace and Freedom) (2018) 'Feminist peace in Africa: highlights from WILPF Forum Report, *Women's International League for Peace and Freedom Blog*, 8 April, Available from: https://wilpf.org/feminist-peace-in-africa-highlights-from-wilpf-forum-report/.

Index